FROM 'LUGAL.GAL' TO 'WANAX'

Sidestone Press

FROM 'LUGAL.GAL' TO 'WANAX'

KINGSHIP AND POLITICAL ORGANISATION IN THE LATE BRONZE AGE AEGEAN

edited by

Jorrit M. Kelder & Willemijn J. I. Waal

Published by Sidestone Press, Leiden
www.sidestone.com

Lay-out & cover design: Sidestone Press
Photograph cover:
Mask by Agamemnon © Antonio Gravante | stock.adobe.com
Ruins of a tomb in Mycenae © Siete_vidas1 | stock.adobe.com

ISBN 978-90-8890-798-2 (softcover)
ISBN 978-90-8890-800-2 (hardcover)
ISBN 978-90-8890-799-9 (PDF e-book)

Contents

Foreword

Jorrit Kelder and Willemijn Waal

In October 2016, a workshop with the title 'From LUGAL.GAL to *Wanax*' was held in Leiden. The aim of this workshop was to address the much-debated problem of the political organisation in Mycenaean Greece. From the early 14th century BCE onwards, Hittite texts refer to a land Aḫḫiya(wa). The exact geographic position of this land has been the focus of academic debate for almost a century, but most specialists nowadays agree that it must have been a Hittite designation for a land within the Mycenaean world. The Hittite king refers to the ruler of Aḫḫiyawa as 'Great King', a title which was reserved for a select group of kings of the great powers at that time (such as the kings of Egypt, Assyria, Mitanni, Babylon and Ḫatti itself). The fact that the king of Aḫḫiyawa is also called a 'Great King' by the Hittite king implies that there must have been a ruler of similar supra-regional importance in the Aegean. Such a concept, however, is at odds with the currently prevalent view of the Mycenaean world as a collection of culturally similar – yet politically independent – palatial states.

In recent years, various attempts have been made to explain this apparent dichotomy. Although there has been a growing acceptance that there was some sort of collaboration between various (often unspecified) palatial states, there is no consensus as to its specific nature: what this collaboration entailed, which palaces were involved, whether it had a permanent or *ad hoc* character, and whether or not there was a clear hierarchy of palaces and rulers.

For the workshop, experts from various disciplines came together to discuss the now available evidence for the organisation and political structure of the Mycenaean world, combining Near Eastern (especially Hittite) and Aegean textual and archaeological evidence. Participants included John Bennet, Konstantinos Kopanias, Sofia Voutsaki, Frans Wiggermann, Jorrit Kelder, Willemijn Waal and Bert van der Spek (chair). Unfortunately, Oliver Dickinson was unable to join us in Leiden, but his paper, which he had provided in advance, was read and discussed during the meeting.

The present volume includes three papers that were presented at the workshop: those of Dickinson, Kopanias and Waal. Regrettably, Bennet, Voutsaki and Wiggermann were not able to publish their papers in this volume, but we would like to thank them for their valuable input during the workshop. We are grateful that Fritz Blakolmer accepted our invitation to write an article about royal iconography (or the lack thereof) in the Aegean. We have further welcomed the contribution of Michael Bányai about the political organisation of the Mycenaean world and we are indebted to drs. Hielko van der Zee for proofreading this paper. The workshop and this publication would not have been possible without the support of the Leiden University Fund, the Royal Netherlands Academy of Sciences (KNAW), and Leiden University's knowledge valorisation department LURIS.

'My brother, a Great King, my peer'. Evidence for a Mycenaean kingdom from Hittite texts

Willemijn Waal

1. Introduction

With the decipherment of the Hittite language in 1915, an invaluable new source of information about Late Bronze Age Greece has become available to us. Among the thousands of cuneiform tablets discovered in the archives of Ḫattuša, the capital of the Hittite Empire (ca. 1650-1180 BCE), there are some 26 texts that mention 'Aḫḫiyawa', a term which has long been the object of much controversy.

In 1924 Emil Forrer suggested that the Aḫḫiyawa were to be identified with the Mycenaeans, a proposal that met with strong resistance, Ferdinand Sommer being his fiercest opponent. The history of the 'Aḫḫiyawa-controversy' has already been much discussed elsewhere (recently Beckman et al. 2011: 1-6, Latacz 2004: 121-8; Gander 2017: 275-8) and need not be repeated here, as it can now be considered as settled. New insights and evidence since 1924 have confirmed the identification suggested by Forrer. It is clear that Aḫḫiyawa refers to an (overseas) entity west of Anatolia, which for some time was present on the Anatolian west coast. The Hittite texts indicate that the city Millawanda (Milete) was under Aḫḫiyawan control or influence during the 14th/13th century. The information is corroborated by archaeological evidence, as there is demonstrable Mycenaean material presence in Milete at that time. As Beckman, Bryce and Cline (2011: 3) accurately put it:

> Ahhiyawa must, essentially by default be a reference to the Mycenaeans. Otherwise, we would have, on the one hand, an important Late Bronze Age Culture not mentioned in the Hittite texts (the Mycenaeans) and, on the other hand, an important textually attested Late Bronze Age "state" without archaeological remains (Ahhiyawa).

In the last decades, it has become more and more clear that contacts all across the Mediterranean existed in the Late Bronze Age, and long before (for a recent overview, see Broodbank 2013). In light of this high degree of interconnectivity it is unthinkable that

in: Kelder, J.M. and Waal, W.J.I. (eds) 2019: *From 'LUGAL.GAL' to 'Wanax'. Kingship and Political Organisation in the Late Bronze Age Aegean*, Sidestone Press (Leiden), pp. 9-13.

there would have been no contacts between the Aegean and Anatolia, considering the close vicinity of these regions. Needless to say, the modern dichotomy placing Greece in the 'West' and Anatolia in the 'East' did not exist in antiquity.

Though the identification with Aḫḫiyawa and the Mycenaean world is now generally accepted, there is still much debate about to which Mycenaeans exactly this term refers and whether or not this Aḫḫiyawa was a great kingdom – the very topic of this volume. In this paper, I would like to explore what the Hittite texts may tell us about the status of the Aḫḫiyawa, by comparing Hittite interactions with Aḫḫiyawa to those with contemporary great powers such as Egypt, Babylon, Assyria and Mitanni. In doing so, I will gratefully make use of the invaluable edition of the Hittite Aḫḫiyawa texts by Beckman et al. 2011.[1]

2. The reliability of the Aḫḫiyawa texts

Before embarking on the content of the Hittite Aḫḫiyawa texts, a brief discussion of their status and reliability seems in order. The texts are written on clay tablets in cuneiform and stem from the tablet collections of Ḫattuša, the capital of the Hittite Empire.[2] They are direct sources, which have been buried under the ground for millennia until their rediscovery at the beginning of the 20th century. The fact that they are direct sources makes them more reliable than, e.g., classical texts, which have been transmitted indirectly over many centuries, but this does of course not mean that they are unfailing. Political agendas can make them less trustworthy, and if they deal with evens in the past, or present later copies of earlier compositions, they may be inaccurate.[3]

With respect to the Aḫḫiyawa texts, we are in all cases dealing with contemporary documents and not with later copies. The texts can be dated from the early 14th to the late 12th century BCE (see Beckman et al. 2011: 268).[4] They include several letters, oracle reports, royal annals and some texts of other genres: two prayers, one treaty, one indictment, one edict, one list, one inventory, and some fragments of unknown nature.

As for the reliability of the texts discussed in this paper, the most subjective texts are probably the royal annals (AhT 1). We do not know for what precise purpose these texts were written – whether they are accounts represented to the gods or (also) had a more public propaganda function – but, though they may lack the boasting rhetoric of, e.g., Assyrian royal inscriptions, they are meant to justify and exalt the actions and deeds of the Hittite kings. In this particular case, the most important information from the annals of king Muršili II (ca. 1321-1295 BCE) relevant for this paper – namely that the Aḫḫiyawa were present in Western Anatolia – is confirmed by archaeological evidence.

The so-called Indictment of Madduwatta (AhT 3) also has a clear bias. This text recounts the misbehaviours of a Hittite vassal named Madduwatta. It is written from the perspective

1 All translations follow those of Beckman et al. 2011 unless indicated otherwise. The abbreviation AhT (Aḫḫiyawa Texts) refers to the text numbers in Beckman et al. 2011, who provide transliterations, translations, discussion and references to earlier literature.

2 This paper will only discuss the texts mentioning Aḫḫiyawa found in Ḫattuša. Note that Beckman et al. 2011 also include two texts that do not explicitly mention Aḫḫiyawa but that are clearly related to the 'Aḫḫiyawa-dossier', as well as two texts from Ugarit and an inscription from Adana mentioning (Aḫ)ḫiyawa.

3 It was quite common for certain text genres to be copied over time; not infrequently we have an Old Hittite composition that was written down in the Late Hittite period, see, e.g., Van den Hout 2002.

4 Note that the Hittites as a rule did not date their texts, so we mostly have to have to rely on palaeographic and linguistic features in order to establish in what period they were written down.

of the Hittite king, who presents the actions of Madduwatta as immoral, whereas he (and his father) are not to blame for anything. Undoubtedly, Madduwatta would have had a different account of the events described. This document should therefore be treated with some caution.

Letters are more reliable, as they are not directed to the gods and/or the population at large, but rather represent direct communication with a concrete addressee about affairs which were in principle known to both parties. Though distortion cannot be excluded and the sender could present events according to his own view, he did not have complete liberty to invent and twist facts. The same applies to treaty texts.

The most reliable documents discussed here are the oracle reports and the inventories. Here, there is no reason to misrepresent the truth, in case of the oracle reports this is even undesirable, since the very aim of these texts is to find out precisely what had happened and what sin or evil had brought on the anger of the gods (see below §5.4). The inventories are purely administrative records devoid of any political meaning. In sum, the documents essentially have no reason to lie and there is no reason to a *priori* distrust the Aḫḫiyawa texts (cf. Latacz 2004: 169).

There is, however, an important *caveat* when dealing with these texts. Durable as clay tablets may be, they can be damaged or broken. Often, the missing parts can be restored with quite some confidence, but sometimes restorations are more speculative. In this paper, it will be clearly indicated when the restorations are uncertain.

3. The Great King of Aḫḫiyawa

3.1. 'But now my brother, a Great King, has written to me'

During the Late Bronze Age, the ancient Near East was dominated by several large empires including Ḫatti, Egypt, Babylon, Mitanni and Assyria, which were ruled by 'Great Kings'. Between these Great Kings, who treated each other as equals, extensive diplomatic contacts existed in the form of correspondence and gift exchange. The most significant textual evidence for these international contacts are the letters found in the famous archive of Tell el'Amarna dating to reign of Akhenaten (ca. 1353-1335 BCE). Another important source are the tablet collections of Ḫattuša, in which Late Bronze Age correspondence between Hittite kings and the kings of Egypt, Babylon, Assyria, Mitanni, and the king of Aḫḫiyawa has been found.

The letter which has received most attention in the discussion about the status of Aḫḫiyawa is the so-called 'Tawagalawa letter' (AhT 4), a document composed by a Hittite king – probably Ḫattušili III (ca. 1267-1237) – addressed to a king of Aḫḫiyawa, whose name is unknown.[5] The preserved part of the document mostly deals with a certain Piyamaradu, a renegade subject

5 Unfortunately, the beginning of this long and intriguing document is not preserved. The colophon at the end of the tablet informs us that it is the third (and last) tablet in a series. Though the document is generally classified as a letter, this identification is not certain and not supported by, e.g., its physical features (Heinhold-Kramer 2002: 360; Hoffner 2009: 297; Waal 2016: 87). Possibly, we are dealing with a draft or briefing document for envoys (Heinhold-Kramer 2002: 360) or a document that had a function comparable to that of the Indictment of Madduwatta (AhT3, see Waal 2016: 238-9). The pXRF provenance study of Goren et al. 2011: 11 has shown that the document must have been composed in the region of Ephesus (Hittite Millawanda). Regardless of the exact status of the Tawagalawa letter, however, it is clear that the king of Aḫḫiyawa is being addressed here, and it contains references to previous correspondence with him. Note that a new edition of this document is currently being prepared by Hawkins et al.

of the Hittite king, whose rebellious actions in western Anatolia are a constant source of trouble for the Hittite Empire. This Piyamaradu appears to have enjoyed the support of the king of Aḫḫiyawa and to have used Aḫḫiyawa-controlled territory as a base for his anti-Hittite operations. In the letter, the Hittite king appeals to his colleague for help in this matter and asks him to use his influence and talk to Piyamaradu (see also below §5.6).

Throughout the letter, the Hittite king addresses the king of Aḫḫiyawan as his equal. No less than three times he explicitly addresses the king of Aḫḫiyawa as a 'Great King' (LUGAL.GAL):[6]

1. But now my Brother, **a Great King**, has written to me – should I not listen to the word of my [peer]? (KUB 14.3 obv. ii 13-4, Beckman et al. 2011: 106-7);
2. Did **the Great King, my peer**, [(KUB 14.3 obv. iii 44. Beckman et al. 2011: 113-4);
3. When Tawagalawa himself, **the Great King**, crossed over to Millawanda (KUB 14.3 obv. i 71-3, Beckman et al. 2011: 106-7).

Note that in no. 2 the king of Aḫḫiyawa is not only explicitly called 'Great King' by the Hittite king, but also his 'peer' or 'equal' (Hitt. '*annawali*'- 'of the same birth/rank', obv. iii 44). In all likelihood, this term *annawali* is also to be completed in text no. 1.

In no. 3, it is unclear whether Tawagalawa – possibly the Hittite rendering of the Greek name Eteocles, which is also attested as *e-te-wo-ke-le-we* in contemporary Linear B texts – was a former king of Aḫḫiyawa or a representative of the present king.[7] Regardless of the precise interpretation, he is referred to as a 'Great King'.

Further, the Hittite king often calls the king of Aḫḫiyawa 'my brother', which was the normal way of addressing a person of equal rank, with whom one was on good terms.[8] The significance of this appellative is aptly illustrated by the letter of a Hittite king to the king of the newly rising power Assyria. The Hittite king grudgingly acknowledges that the king of Assyria, after the conquest of most of the territory of the former kingdom of Mitanni, is entitled to call himself 'Great King', but he is displeased by the latter calling him his brother:

4. For what reason should I write to you about brotherhood? Who customarily writes to someone about brotherhood? Do those who are not on good terms customarily write to one another about brotherhood? On what account should I write to you about brotherhood? Were you and I born from one mother? (translation Beckman 1999: 146-7, no. 24).

---

6 Note that the fact that Aḫḫiyawa was a 'Great Power' did not necessarily mean that it was of the same might and size as Egypt – among the great powers there was a hierarchy, which Malamat (1998: 204) describes as a 'pyramid' of equal states with Ḫatti and Egypt on top.

7 The complete passage may be translated as: 'When Tawagalawa himself, the Great King, went to the side of Millawanda, Kurunta was [already?] here. The Great King drove to meet you / He drove to meet you, the Great King. Was he not a mighty king?'. The text, which refers to an incident in the past, could be taken either to mean that Tawagalawa, who is called the brother of the king of Aḫḫiyawa, was a predecessor of the present king of Aḫḫiyawa (thus Miller 2006), or that Tawagalawa here acted as representative of his brother, the Great King (thus Beckman et al. 2011:106; Hoffner 2009: 305).

8 See KUB 14.3 obv. i 27, 52, 53(?), 60, ii 9, 12, 13, 17, 19, 36, 56, 67, ii 1, 8, 11, 13, 42, 50, 57, 62, 63, iv 14, 17, 24, 25, 27, 32.

This sore reaction of the Hittite king shows that to him the appellative 'brother' was meaningful and not to be used lightly (Bryce 2003a: 74-8).

3.2. Further possible references to the king of Aḫḫiyawa as 'brother'

In a second – unfortunately poorly preserved – letter (AhT 6) which has been identified as a letter of the king of Aḫḫiyawa to a Hittite king, the former refers to his colleague as 'my brother', which means that he was corresponding with the latter on equal terms.

5. In the [p]revious years, **my brother** wro[te] to me…' (KUB 26.91, obv. 5', Beckman et al. 2011: 134-5).

Lastly, in the fragmentarily preserved letter AhT 10 there may be a possible further reference to the king of Aḫḫiyawa by the Hittite king as 'my brother'.

6. to **my brother, the king of Aḫ[ḫiyawa]** (KUB 23.98, obv. 8', Beckman et al. 2011: 153).

The restoration of the name A[ḫḫiyawa] in no. 6 is likely, but not completely certain, so this example should be treated with caution. Example no. 5 is more solid, as the name Aḫḫiyawa is preserved in the opening lines. This means that, apart from the Tawagalawa letter, there is at least one, possibly two, text(s) in which the king of Aḫḫiyawa and the Hittite king correspond with each other on equal terms.

3.3. 'And the kings wo are my equals in rank …'

The status of the king of Aḫḫiyawa as Great King is confirmed by another document, a treaty between Tudḫaliya IV and Šaušgamuwa of Amurru (AhT 2). This treaty is one of many examples of Hittite vassal treaties that have come down to us.[9] These treaties overall follow a similar pattern, and may include stipulations about foreign policy. Tudhaliya dictates to Šaušgamuwa that with respect to international affairs, the Hittite king's friend should be his friend and the Hittite king's enemy should be his enemy. Tudḫaliya then lists the Great Kings of those days:

7. And the Kings who are my equ[als] in rank are the King of Egypt, the King of Babylonia, the King of Assyria, ~~and the king of Aḫḫiyawa~~[10] (KUB 23.1+, rev. iv 1-3, Beckman et al. 2011: 60-1).

This sentence has been the cause of much debate, since the last entry, i.e. that of the king of Aḫḫiyawa has been erased. It is, however, still clearly visible and there is no doubt that the name was originally written there. This simultaneously raises two intriguing questions: why was this name erased and why was it written there in the first place?

It has been suggested that at the time the document was composed the power of Aḫḫiyawa was waning and had therefore lost its status as Great Kingdom (Beckman

---

9 For Hittite treaties, see Beckman 1999 and Kitchen and Lawrence 2014.

10 Note that the title 'Great King' is usually only employed in direct speech; in other contexts the kings of Egypt, Ḫatti etc. are simply referred to as 'king' (LUGAL). See also the epilogue of Kelder and Waal in this volume (§5).

et al. 2011: 67-8; Bryce 2005: 308-9; Kelder 2010: 32). This supposed decline in power has been linked to the loss of control over Millawanda mentioned in Hittite texts and the first destructions of Mycenaean palatial centres (Kelder 2010: 32). Possibly, the scribe copied the list from an earlier document when Aḫḫiyawa still enjoyed the status of a Great Kingdom, but since its power was disintegrating at the time the present document was written, it was deleted.[11] This explanation is attractive, but inevitably speculative.

Regardless of the exact reasons, however, the initial inclusion of Aḫḫiyawa is telling and implies that at least at some point Aḫḫiyawa was considered to have had the status of a great power, otherwise it would be an inexplicable mistake. The fact that the 'Great Kings' are so explicitly mentioned in this treaty – as well as in others – incidentally also illustrates the great importance that was attached to this rank and that it was considered to be something exclusive.

4. Aḫḫiyawa: A force to be reckoned with

4.1. The strong presence of Aḫḫiyawa in Anatolia

Apart from the explicit references to Aḫḫiyawa as a Great Kingdom and its king as 'Great King' discussed above, the overall picture that emerges from the Aḫḫiyawa texts confirms the idea that Aḫḫiyawa was a powerful entity. For a period of almost two centuries, Aḫḫiyawan presence at the west coast of Anatolia was a source of ongoing concern for the Hittites. Aḫḫiyawa had control over Millawanda for a while, which meant that they held a substantial and sizeable stronghold on the Anatolian west coast.

Further, Hittite texts mention Aḫḫiyawan support of western Anatolian vassal states rebelling against their Hittite overlord.[12] Although we do not know what precisely this support entailed, it is clear that Aḫḫiyawa played a significant role in West-Anatolia and the Hittites could not deal with them effectively. They did not succeed to subject them and make them a vassal state, as they did with so many (smaller) opponents. As an indication for the military might of Aḫḫiyawa, attention has been drawn to an early text in which the Aḫḫiyawa (spelled as Aḫḫiya) occur, the Indictment of Madduwatta (AhT 3). In this text, an individual named Attariššiya, the man from Aḫḫiya appears, who is chasing Madduwatta in Anatolia.

8. But [later] **Attariššiya, the ruler of Aḫḫiya,** came and was plotting to kill you, Madduwatta. But when the father of My Majesty heard, he dispatched Kišnapili, infantry, and chariotry in battle against Attariššiya. And you, Madduwatta, again did not resist Attariššiya, but yielded before him. Then Kišnapili proceeded to rush [...] to you from Ḫatti. Kišnapili went in battle against Attariššiya. **100 ch[ariots and ... thousand infantry] of Attariššya [drew up for battle].** And they fought. One officer of Attariššiya was killed, and one officer of ours, Zidanza, was killed (KUB 14.1+, ov. i 60-4, Beckman et al. 2011: 80-1).

11 Another explanation holds that Aḫḫiyawa was included by the scribe 'out of habit' but was later deemed irrelevant for a treaty so distant from Aḫḫiyawa (e.g., Bryce: 2003b: 71; Kelder 2010: 32 with references).

12 See, e.g., AhT 1 A and B, AhT 4, AhT 11 (Beckman et al. 2011).

If Beckman's restoration – which in light of other comparable texts seems plausible – is correct, Attariššiya of Aḫḫiya came with an army of 100 ch[ariots (1 ME ^{GIŠ}GIGIR, obv. i 63) and an additional unknown number of infantries. This would constitute a significant force, which, as has been pointed out by Kelder, would mean his military capacity would be three times as large as the capacity of, e.g., Pylos (Kelder 2005: 159, 2010: 34 see now also Beckman et al. 2011: 5).[13] However, as noted above, this document is biased. It presents the account of the Hittite king who may well have exaggerated the size of Attariššiya's army, to make the Hittite victory more glorious and to underline how grateful Madduwatta should be to his saviour.

In the above-discussed Tawagalawa letter the Hittite king is clearly anxious to gain support of the king of Aḫḫiyawa and needs his help in dealing with troublemaker Piyamaradu (see also below §5.6). This also implies that Aḫḫiyawa was no small kingdom that could be ignored, but rather was a power to be taken seriously (thus also Kelder 2010: 21-30).[14]

4.2. Requests for help to the king of Aḫḫiyawa by a former Hittite king?

Possibly, there is another example of a (former) Hittite king appealing for help to the king of Aḫḫiyawa, but the context here is less clear. After Urḫi-Teššub (whose throne name was Muršili III) had been deposed from the Hittite throne by his uncle Ḫattušili III, he was looking for ways to regain his former position. He appealed for support to several foreign kings, including the kings of Babylon, Egypt and Assyria, and potentially also the king of Aḫḫiyawa (Beckman et al. 2011: 166). The fragmentary letter AhT 14 seems to mention that the king of Aḫḫiyawa, and probably another king, will or will not come to the aid of Urḫi-Teššub:

9. The king of Aḫḫiyawa [and the king of ...] did [not?] come to [the aid] of [Urḫ]i-Teššub (KBo 16.22, obv. 3-4, Beckman et al. 2011: 164-5).

If one accepts Beckman's restoration, this fragment informs us that Urḫi-Teššub, a former king of Ḫatti, had asked for the help of the king of Aḫḫiyawa, which would be a further confirmation of the latter's importance. However, this interpretation is uncertain, since the text is quite damaged.

5. Diplomatic interactions between Aḫḫiyawa and Ḫatti

Though the interactions between Aḫḫiyawa and Ḫatti were often in the form of (indirect) military conflicts, as both powers had interests in western Anatolia, they also maintained more friendly relations. The nature of the diplomatic contacts between these two entities confirm their equal status.

---

13 The Madduwatta text further informs us that the 'man of Aḫḫiya' in the company of some other men was able to regularly raid the island of Cyprus (Alašiya), which was at that time (at least nominally) under Hittite control. However, it is unclear on what scale these raids were executed. On the status of Cyprus, see the contribution of Mantzourani et al. in this volume.

14 When discussing the importance of Aḫḫiyawa, an often-used argument is a passage in the above-discussed Šaušgamuwa treaty, which supposedly refers to an embargo preventing Aḫḫiyawan ships to go to Assyria. However, this passage is heavily damaged and its interpretation is uncertain, for a recent discussion see Devecchi 2010; Beckman et al. 2011 67-8.

5.1. *Et dona non ferentes*

As mentioned above, diplomatic contacts between the Great Kings did not only consist of exchanging letters, but also greeting gifts. This practice is well attested in the Amarna letters (including various amusing complaints about the amount and/or quality of these gifts by the receiving parties) as well as in the international correspondence found in Ḫattuša. The texts inform us that the Hittite kings exchanged gifts with the kings of Assyria, Babylon, Egypt, and also Aḫḫiyawa.[15]

In §5 of the already discussed Tawagalawa letter, the Hittite king complains that the messenger of the king of Aḫḫiyawa did not bring him any greeting gifts:

10. But when the messenger of my brother met me, he did not bring me [any greetings] or any gift. He just spoke as follows: (KUB 14.3 obv. i 53-5, Beckman et al. 2011: 105, see also no. 18 below).

The messenger of Aḫḫiyawa apparently did not bother with rules of etiquette, but merely delivered his message, which was clearly not appreciated by the Hittite king. The Hittite king reprimands the king of Aḫḫiyawa for this, which shows that he expected the latter to know that this was improper behaviour among kings of equal status. This rebuke also nicely illustrates the significance of such diplomatic customs.

5.2. *Gift swapping*

Of particular interest is text AhT 8, a letter sent by a Hittite official to the Hittite king. This official had apparently received orders to dispatch a diplomatic gift to Aḫḫiyawa. He is not sure what to do, as he does not know whether or not the king of Aḫḫiyawa had sent any greeting gifts to the Hittite king, and, if so, what kinds of gifts they entailed. He therefore decides to take some objects that were meant to be sent to Egypt and use these as gifts for the king of Aḫḫiyawa:

11. [Concerning the diplomatic gi]ft intended for the King of Aḫḫiyawa about which you wrote to me, because I don't know about it – whether h[is messenger] brought anything or not – I have now taken a silver rhyton and a [rhyton] of gold from the diplomatic gift for Egypt, and I have sent [these to him] (KBo 2.11 obv. 11'-4', Beckman et al. 2011: 146-7).[16]

This text passage shows that the greetings gifts for Aḫḫiyawa and Egypt were discussed and treated on the same level, which may be seen as another indirect confirmation of the status of Aḫḫiyawa as a great power. The concern of the Hittite official about what kind of gift to send also reveals how important it was that the greeting gifts to be sent were equal in value and quality to those received (see also Beckman et al. 2011: 149, Bryce 2003a: esp. 94-7).

---

15 Note that the practice of gift-exchange among equal kings is also attested in Mari in the 18th century, see recently Cline 2014: 18-9.

16 Previously, this passage was taken to mean that the sender had taken the objects from gifts received from Egypt, which would make this text an early example of 'regifting'. However, since he appears to ask the king to send him goods as a replacement in the following lines, it seems more likely that it concerns a gift that was still to be sent to Egypt, see Beckman et al. 2011: 276-7.

5.3. A vessel from Aḫḫiyawa?

Here, we may briefly mention the reference to an 'Aḫḫiyawa vessel' which is made in an inventory of goods (AhT 19).

12. 1 iron goblet for the cupbearer; [... 1(?)] copper ...-vessel from **Aḫḫiyawa**; 1 copper vessel for pouring out; 1 copper pot from Egypt (KBo 18.181 rev. 32'-4': Beckman et al. 2011: 181).

Unfortunately, it is unclear whether concerns a vessel 'from Aḫḫiyawa' or 'in the style of Aḫḫiyawa', or how it got to Ḫattuša – by means of regular trade or as a diplomatic gift.

5.4. A divine visit from Aḫḫiyawa?

Apart from letters, there are a number of oracle reports that mention Aḫḫiyawa.[17] The most fascinating is text AhT 20, a Hittite oracle report concerning the illness of the Hittite king – in all likelihood Muršili II. Like many ancient people, the Hittites saw bad events and disasters as manifestations of anger or displeasure of one or more of their gods. In order to find the cause of divine punishments, the Hittites had several divinatory techniques at their disposal, such as extispicy, augury and the intricate KIN oracle performed by Wise Women. By means of yes/no questions, they could determine which god(s) were angry and why, and what needed to be done to appease them. This long and elaborate elimination process – there were many gods and they could be annoyed for many reasons! – has been recorded on clay tablets. The reports usually include the question, and the 'result' given by the oracle investigations.

The following passage builds further on previous oracles inquiries in which it has been established that the deity of Aḫḫiyawa and the deity of Lazpa (Lesbos) and the personal deity of the king have to undergo a ritual of 'releasing'. It now needs to be established how and when precisely this ritual is to be performed:

13. Concerning the fact that the 'releasing' of the deity of Aḫḫiyawa and the deity of Lazpa and the personal deity have been determined (by oracle investigation) for his Majesty – when/how they bring the personal deity of the king, will they also bring those? And how/when [they perform] the ritual for them during three days, will they [do] it in the exact same manner as for the deity of Aḫḫiyawa and the deity of Lazpa during three days? (KUB 5.6+, obv. ii 57'-61', see also Beckman et al. 2011: 192-4).

Several things are of interest here. First, the fact that the deity of Aḫḫiyawa and Lazpa have been determined by the oracle means that these deities were included in the oracle inquiry. This implies that these deities were known at the Hittite court. Secondly, the two deities are to be brought to Ḫattuša to undergo the ritual of releasing and – though it is not entirely clear what this ritual entailed – this shows that Aḫḫiyawa and Ḫatti were apparently on such terms that their deities could be exchanged for ritual purposes. Unfortunately, we do not know why these particular gods were singled out and whether (the statues of) these deities actually travelled to Ḫattuša, but this report shows that this

17 See AhT nos. 20-4, Beckman et al. 2011: 183-243.

was not unthinkable, which confirms that good relations between Ḫatti and Aḫḫiyawa existed (see also Beckman et al. 2011: 209).

The travel of a deity to another country is also attested in a letter from the Amarna archives: in EA 23, a letter from Tušratta, the king of Mitanni, to the Egyptian pharaoh it is announced that the deity Šauška will be sent to Egypt, apparently upon her own request, and then to be returned to Mittani. This was not her first and only trip to Egypt; she had also visited this country in the time of Tušratta's predecessor:

14. Thus Šauška of Nineveh, mistress of all lands: 'I wish to go to Egypt, a country that I love, and then return.' Now I herewith send her, and she is on her way. Now, in the time, too, of my father .. went to this country, and just as earlier she dwelt there and they honoured her, may my brother now honour her 10 times more than before. May my brother honour her, (then) at (his) pleasure let her go so that she may come back (EA 23, translation Moran 1987: 61-2).

Considering the above, it seems safe to say that visits of (statues of) deities could be a normal part of diplomatic relations between befriended great powers.

5.5. Agreements about the extradition of refugees

In the Aḫḫiyawa texts, there are a number of references to hostages or fugitives. In a broken passage in the Tawagalawa letter, the Hittite king informs the king of Aḫḫiyawa that a fugitive is allowed to return to Aḫḫiyawa:

15. Let a fugitive come [back] to my brother. Whether he is a nobleman or [a slave] – it is allowed (KUB 14.3 rev. iii 42-4, Beckman et al. 2011: 113-4).

Vice versa, the Hittite king also expected fugitives to Aḫḫiyawa to be extradited to him (see below text no. 18). The fact that fugitives were allowed to return was by no means self-evident and only seems to occur between states which were of equal rank. In Hittite treaties with vassal kings it was explicitly stated that fugitives were *not* allowed to return – unless they did not perform their tasks properly – see, e.g., the following passage in the treaty of the Hittite king Muwatalli with king Alakšandu of Wiluša.[18]

16. I have established the matter of fugitives under oath as follows: If a fugitive comes [in flight] from your land to Ḫatti, [he will] not [be given] back. It **is not permitted [to give] a fugitive back from Ḫatti.** [But] if [some] craftsman flees, [. . .] , and he does not deliver his assigned work, [he will be arrested and] turned over to you. [If some fugitive] from the land of an enemy is captured, [and he flees from Ḫatti], and [goes] away through your lands, [and you do not seize him] and send him on to me, [but] give [him] back [to] the enemy, this too shall be placed under oath (KUB 21.1+ rev. iii 61-72, translation Beckman 1999: 91, no. 13).

18 For this treaty and the possible connections with Alakšandu of Wiluša and Alexandros/Paris of Troy, see, e.g., Latacz 2004.

By contrast, in the famous peace treaty between Ramses II of Egypt and Ḫattušili III of Ḫatti, it is stipulated that fugitives are to be returned (unharmed) to their country of origin:

17. [And if] a single man flees from [Ḫatti, or] two men, [or three men, and they come to] Ramses, Beloved [of Amon, Great King, King] of Egypt, his brother, [then Ramses], Beloved of Amon, Great King, [King of Egypt, must seize them and send them] to Ḫattušili, his brother [. . .] – for they are brothers. But [they shall not punish them for] their offenses. They shall [not] tear out [their tongues or their eyes]. And [they shall not mutilate(?)] their ears or [their] feet. [And they shall not destroy(?) their households, together with their wives] and their sons.

    And if][a single man flees from Egypt, or] two men, or three men, [and they come to Ḫattušili, Great King], King of Ḫatti, brother shall seize them and send [them to me, Ramses, Beloved of Amon, Great King, King] of Egypt – for Ramses, Great King, King [of Egypt and Ḫattušili are brothers. But they shall not punish them for their offenses. They shall] not [tear out [their tongues] or their eyes. And [they shall not mutilate(?)] their ears or their feet. And they shall not destroy(?) their households], together with their wives and their sons (KBo 1.7+, §18-9, translation Beckman 1999: 99, no.15).

The agreements the Hittite king made regarding mutual exchange of fugitives with the king of Aḫḫiyawa are the same as those with the king of Egypt and they can be seen as typical for the relations between great powers, which were based on parity.

5.6. Dealing with state enemies on the run

At times, Hittite kings explicitly called upon the existing arrangements about fugitives and asked their colleagues for the extradition of political opponents. From the already discussed Tawagalawa letter we learn that the Hittite king had in the past asked the king of Aḫḫiyawa for the extradition of troublemaker Piyamaradu. At that time Piyamaradu apparently resided in the territory of Atpa, the king of Millawanda (Milete), which was at the time under the control of Aḫḫiyawa. Upon this request the king of Aḫḫiaywa ordered his subject Atpa to hand over Piyamaradu to the Hittite king:

18. But when the messenger of my brother met me, he did not bring me [any greetings] or any gift. He just spoke as follows: 'He [i.e. the king of Aḫḫiyawa] has written to Atpa: "Turn Piy[amaradu] over to the King of Ḫatti!"' (KUB 14.3 obv. i 53-5, Beckman et al. 2011: 105)

Unfortunately for Ḫattušili, Piyamaradu manages to escape in time. The Hittite king then lowers his expectations and asks his colleague to at least help him by preventing Piyamaradu to make war against Ḫatti.[19] The king of Aḫḫiyawa is to give Piyamaradu the following two options: he can either return to Ḫatti to reconcile with the Hittite king, or he can remain in Aḫḫiyawa, but only on the condition that he will no longer attack Hittite territory:

19 See Beckman et al. 2011: 120-1.

19. My brother, write to him this one thing, if nothing (else): ‘Get up and go off to Ḫatti. Your lord has reconciled with you. If not, then come over to Aḫḫiyawa, and in whatever location I settle you, [...] Get up [and] resettle in [another] location. So long as you are hostile to the King of Ḫatti, be hostile from another land! Do not be hostile from my land. If you(!) would rather be in Karkiya or Maša, go there. The King of Ḫatti has persuaded me about the matter of the land of Wiluša concerning which he and I were hostile to one another, and we have made peace. Now(?) hostility is not appropriate between us.’ [Send that] to him (KUB 14.3, rev iii 63 – iv 10, Beckman et al. 2011: 115-116).[20]

These negotiations about Piyamaradu are very reminiscent of those between Ḫattušili III, who is in all likelihood also the author of the Tawagalawa letter, and Ramses II of Egypt with respect to his disposed nephew Urḫi-Teššub, whom we have already encountered above (§4.2). At a certain point, Urḫi-Teššub had managed to escape to Egypt. As we learn from a letter of Ḫattušili to the king of Babylon, Ḫattušili had asked Ramses for the extradition of Urḫi-Teššub, but Ramses did not comply:

20. My enemy who fled to another country went to the king of Egypt. When I wrote to him ‘Bring my enemy’, he did not bring my enemy. Then I and the king of Egypt became enemies of one another, and to your father (i.e. Kadašman-Turgu) I wrote: ‘The king of Egypt went to help my enemy’. So your father kept the messenger of the king of Egypt at bay (KBo 1. 10 + KUB iii 72 (CTH172) obv. 67-9, translation Wouters 1989: 230, see also Bryce 2005: 265).

Later, when Urḫi-Teššub has escaped from Egypt and is on the loose in Syria, Ḫattušili apparently asks Ramses to help find him and bring him back to Egypt and to prevent him from making war against Ḫatti.

21. ‘Let the Great King, the King of Egypt, have his infantry and [his chariotry] exert themselves, and let him expend his gold, his silver, his horses, his copper [and his garments] in order to take [Urḫi-Teššub to Egypt. He shall not allow him to become strong] and [to wage war against Ḫatti] (KBo 1.24+, obv. 15-19 (CTH 166), translation Beckman 1999: 130).[21]

The dealings of Ḫattušili regarding the wanted fugitive Urḫi-Teššub with the Egyptian pharaoh are very similar in tone and content to those with the king of Aḫḫiyawa about Piyamaradu.[22] First, he demands their extradition, and when this turns out to be impossible, he asks his colleagues to then at least make sure that his enemies will not wage war against Ḫatti.

20 This passage has received a lot of attention due to the reference of a conflict between Aḫḫiyawa and the Hittites over Wiluša, which has been identified as Troy, see, e.g., Latacz 2004.

21 This passage stems from a letter of Ḫattušili to Ramses quoted by Ramses in his letter to Kupanta-Kurunta of Mira (see also below n. 31).

22 Another possible example of extradition of refugees may be found in a (damaged) passage from the annals of Muršili II (AhT 1A, KBo 3.4+: obv. iii 3-8). If Beckman's restoration is correct, an Aḫḫiyawan king delivers refugees into Hittite custody, see Beckman et al. 2011: 22-4, 48.

5.7. Travel and banishment to Aḫḫiyawa?

To the examples of contacts between Aḫḫiyawa and Ḫatti, one may add two texts: one mentioning a possible banishment of a Hittite Queen to Aḫḫiyawa (AhT 12) and one possibly referring to a journey to Aḫḫiyawa (AhT 15). The contexts are very unclear and broken, but these attestations further support the idea that good contacts between the two countries existed. It has been proposed that the above discussed fragmentary letter (§3.2, example no. 5) from a king of Aḫḫiyawa to the Hittite king refers to a diplomatic marriage (Beckman et al. 2011: 138). This would be highly interesting, but the context is unfortunately quite opaque. The remainder of the texts in which Aḫḫiyawa is mentioned are too fragmentary to draw any conclusions about its political status.

6. Means of communication

In the above it has been shown that contacts between Aḫḫiyawa and Ḫatti existed on various levels. The possible modes in which this took place have been extensively discussed (e.g., Melchert [forthc.]; Beckman et al. 2011: 138-9; Hoffner 2009: 299; Surenhagen 2008: 260-5; Bryce 2003a: 199-200). The Late Bronze Age *lingua franca* in the ancient Near East was Akkadian. If we look at the preserved Ḫatti-Aḫḫiyawa correspondence, all documents have been written in Hittite, by a native speaker and in a typical Hittite *ductus*. This also applies to the letter that was probably written by the Aḫḫiyawan king to the Hittite king (AhT 6). This situation is not entirely unparalleled, as some of the Hittite-Egyptian correspondence unearthed in Ḫattuša is also written in Hittite.[23]

Various scenarios have been offered for the way(s) in which written interaction between Aḫḫiyawa and Ḫatti took place. Harry Hoffner (2009: 290-1) has suggested that the Hittite version of the letter from the king of Aḫḫiyawa represents a translation of a communication between bilingual messengers at the border, and that this document was brought home together with his oral recollections. Susanne Heinhold-Kramer (2007: 192) assumes that the Aḫḫiyawan king had scribes who were able to write in cuneiform. Beckman et al. 2011 argue that the letters may have been written by a Hittite or Luwian scribe residing at the Aḫḫiyawan court, who was fluent in Hittite and Greek. Melchert, taking up a suggestion made by Beckman, proposes that there were two messengers on such diplomatic missions, one from each side. This custom is, for instance, attested in the Deeds of King Šuppiluliuma II (ca. 1350-1322), where it is mentioned that an Egyptian messenger Ḫani came back from Egypt along with his own Hittite messenger. Likewise, one of the Amarna letters (EA 3) refers to a joint trip of messengers from Egypt and Alašiya.

23 These letters could be Hittite drafts for Akkadian letters to be sent to Egypt, and/or copies for the archives to be used as reference works for future correspondence. Alternatively, the letters may have been sent to Egypt in Hittite. In the Amarna archive, two letters that were written in Hittite (as well as some in Hurrian) have been discovered. These Hittite letters concern the correspondence of the Egyptian pharaoh Amenophis III to king Tarḫadaradu of Arzawa, at a time when the Hittite kingdom appeared to be over and done with and Arzawa arose as a new power, and this may imply that no knowledge of Akkadian was present in Arzawa. This would not be surprising since Arzawa was no great power, but only promised to become one in light of the (temporary) decline of the Hittite Empire. One of the letters in Hittite contains a post script in which the scribe asks his colleague to write to him in Hittite. This means that some knowledge of Hittite was present at the Egyptian court. As pointed out by Melchert [forthc.], however, it seems likely that as a rule the correspondence between the two great powers Ḫatti and Egypt was conducted in the *lingua franca* Akkadian.

Whatever the precise mode and language of communication may have been, it seems likely that the messengers were qualified to (orally) elaborate on the (written) message (cf. Hoffner 2009: 299). The reliability of messengers is a recurring topic in international letters (see also in the Tawagalawa letter §15, Beckman 2011 et al.: 118-9) – they are often blamed for being untrustworthy, though it is unclear to what extent they were indeed unreliable, or if they conveniently served as 'scapegoats' who had to take the blame for unpleasant messages or disappointments. These practical problems, however, did not impede extensive contacts between kings speaking different languages all over the Near East.

7. How representative are the Aḫḫiyawa texts?

7.1. The intensity of contacts

It has been pointed out that the corpus of texts (26) mentioning Aḫḫiyawa is quite meagre, and that one would expect more evidence if Aḫḫiyawa indeed was a great power. However, if we compare the attestations of Aḫḫiyawa in Hittite texts to those of other great powers, we see that this amount is certainly not alarmingly low.[24] Mitanni, the direct neighbour of Ḫatti in the south-east, has also been attested in some 26 texts, Assyria in some 40 texts, Babylon in ca. 55 and Egypt in some 75 texts (which for a substantial part consists of the elaborate correspondence between Ḫattušili and Ramses and their relatives).[25] The amount, as well as the type of texts mentioning Aḫḫiyawa within the Hittite corpus, seem to be in line with those of other contemporary foreign powers.

7.2. A case of ad hoc *diplomacy?*

With respect to the fact that the king of Aḫḫiyawa is called 'Great King' by the Hittite king in the Tawagalawa letter, it has been suggested that the Hittite king merely did this to flatter him because he needed his support. Beckman et al. 2011: 122 state that 'the Aḫḫiyawan king is accorded by Ḫattušili a status that must have far exceeded his actual importance in the Near Eastern World in general' in his attempts to 'win over a man whose cooperation he was so anxious to secure'. Likewise, Bryce (2003b: 66) suggests that if the 'genuine' Near Eastern counterparts would have heard about it, this may have provoked an incredulous, if not derisory reaction. Though such a scenario can theoretically not be excluded, it is strictly hypothetical and one may question its likelihood.

First of all, the term 'Great King' was by not used lightly, nor was the appellative 'brother' (see above §3 and Beckman 2011 et al.: 122). Secondly, it is not only in the correspondence to Aḫḫiyawa that it is referred to as a Great Kingdom. The initial inclusion of Aḫḫiyawa among the list of Great Kings in a treaty with Amurru in northern Syria can hardly be explained as flattery to the king of Aḫḫiyawa. Thirdly, it is telling that the king of Ḫatti feels the need to please the king of Aḫḫiyawa and is so eager to win him over. This implies that he was not some ruler of a small kingdom, but rather a force to be reckoned with, which is also apparent from the other dealings with Aḫḫiyawa (see above §4).

---

24 Reportedly, additional texts mentioning Aḫḫiyawa have been unearthed in Šapinuwa (modern Ortaköy) but they remain unpublished to this date.

25 See Del Monte and Tischler 1978, 1992.

Lastly, though the tone of the Hittite king in the Tawagalawa letter is indeed very conciliatory and pleasing, this does not exclude the fact that the king of Aḫḫiyawa also was his equal. There are various letters of king Ḫattušili III – who is, as said, the most likely author of the Tawagalawa letter – to this colleagues Ramses of Egypt, Adad-Nirari of Assyria and Kadašman-Enlil of Babylon that are equally flattering and appeasing. In a long letter to the latter Ḫattušili III tries to restore the good relations with between Ḫatti and Babylon that existed in the past, but that have now gone bad. The new king of Babylon, Kadašman-Enlil has discontinued the sending of messengers to Ḫatti. Ḫattušili III attempts to win his favour, among others by putting the blame for the distorted relations on Assyria and by addressing to the king of Babylon as a Great King:

22. Does Assyria hold back your messengers so that you, [my brother], cannot cross [to] my [land]? **My brother, you are a Great King,** and in a long life [may you be . . .]! Look, my brother, how I keep sending [my messengers] out of love for my brother, while my brother does not send his messenger. Does [my brother] not know [this]? Every word which my brother sent me I will retain (Beckman 1999: 140, no. 23).

The approach of Hittite kings was quite different when asking for the favour or assistance of vassal states. The following fragment stems from a letter of king Šuppiliuliuma II, in which he tries to convince Niqmaddu, a vassal king of Nuḫašše in northern Syria, to stand by his side and to not join neighbouring countries that have rebelled against the Hittites. Šuppiluliuma firstly appeals to the good relations between the two countries, but then the tone changes:

23. While the land of Nuḫašše and the land of Mukiš are hostile to me, you, Niqmaddu, shall not fear them. Trust in yourself! As previously your forefathers were at peace with Ḫatti and not hostile, now you, Niqmaddu, shall thus be hostile to my enemy and at peace with my friend. And if you, Niqmaddu, hear and observe these words of the Great King, your lord, then you shall surely experience the favor which the Great King, your lord, will show to you. In the future you will see how the Great King deals with the kings of the land of Nuḫašše and the king of the land of Mukiš, who renounced the peace treaty with Ḫatti and became hostile to the Great King, their lord (Beckman 1999: 125-6, no. 19).

Here, a diplomatic approach is combined with an implicit threat: if Niqmaddu does not obey, his fate will be the same as that of the rebellious kings of Nuhašše and Mukiš. This is quite a different tune compared to that of the letters to the kings of Aḫḫiyawa, Babylon and Egypt. In other words, though the Hittite king may indeed be trying to win over the king of Aḫḫiyawa and is flattering him, there is no reason to assume that the latter was *not* also a Great King.

7.3. The wider Near Eastern scene

7.3.1. The Amarna archive

Scholars who are sceptical of the evidence for a Great Kingdom of Aḫḫiyawa have pointed to the fact that Aḫḫiyawa is not mentioned in other archives in the ancient Near East, such as the Amarna archive (see, e.g., Bryce 2003b: 65). It is indeed conspicuous that Aḫḫiyawa is not mentioned in the Amarna archive. However, it is good to realise that this archive – valid as it may be to us – only shows a brief and selective glimpse of the correspondence between 'brothers', and, for example, Elam is also not represented.

The letters in the archive appear to be a quite arbitrary and unbalanced selection (Bryce 2003a: 226). The two most vexing questions are why only these letters have been preserved, and what has happened to the rest. Trevor Bryce (2003a: 226) has suggested that the office archives of Akhetaton (Tell el-Amarna) were officially ransacked and some documents, that were still considered to be relevant were taken to the new capital Memphis (and are thus lost to us), whilst others were left there since they no longer had any significance – ironically the ones which have survived to this day. Bryce himself acknowledges that this is a hypothetical reconstruction, but it offers an attractive scenario.

In any case, it seems safe to say that the Amarna archive is not a representative collection of all international diplomatic activity in the Late Bronze Age, but instead offers a rather random snapshot. All international correspondence of Egypt in preceding and following periods has not been preserved, though we know from the letters of Ramses II and his family found in Ḫattuša that such documents must have existed.[26]

7.3.2. The Mesopotamian silence

As for the fact that Aḫḫiyawa is not mentioned in Mesopotamian texts, this may not be as significant as it at first glance appears, if we look at the available sources. The Late Bronze Age archives discovered in Mesopotamia have mainly yielded administrative and private documents, as well as religious and literary texts, but no collections of international correspondence comparable to those found in Ḫattuša and el-Amarna have been unearthed.[27]

Aḫḫiyawa does occur in correspondence from Ugarit, a Hittite vassal state in present day Lebanon that was destroyed around the same time as Ḫattuša. In two letters written by the Hittite king to his vassal in Ugarit mention is made of Ḫiyawa-men in relation to a shipment of copper ingots and there is growing consensus among scholars that Ḫiyawa is an aphaeresised form of (Aḫ)ḫiyawa (Beckman et al. 2011: 261, for a different view, see Gander 2017: 275).

8. Archaeological evidence for (diplomatic) contacts

Archaeological records confirm that there were well-established relations between the Aegean and western Anatolia during the 15th – 13th century BCE (see recently Beckman et al. 2011: 267-8, Cline 2014: 70-2). By contrast, there is much less evidence for Aegean contacts with inland Anatolia. Very few Mycenaean objects have been found in Ḫattuša

26 Though Aḫḫiyawa may not be represented in the royal correspondence, we do have evidence for Mycenaean contacts in the Amarna period in Egypt. A substantial amount of Mycenaean pottery has been found, which has been interpreted as diplomatic gifts (Kelder 2010). Also in previous times, during the reign of Tuthmosis III contacts with the Aegean are well attested (Cline 2014: 23-5), and they also occur in the famous Aegean list dating to the reign of Amenhotep III (Cline 2014: 46). Likewise, in the Aegean, Egyptian objects have been found (Cline 2014: 48-51).

27 For archives in the Late Bronze Age, see Pedersén 1998. With respect to the earlier Old Babylonian period, we have the Mari archives including the correspondence of Zimri-Lim which demonstrates contacts with Crete (Cline 2014: 18-9).

and *vice versa* the possible Hittite objects in the Aegean constitute only 1% of all *orientalia* discovered there (Cline 1991: 140).

For this absence several solutions have been proposed. The paucity of the archaeological material has led Eric Cline (1991) to suggest that there may have been a trade embargo against the Hittites. Though this is of course possible, there is no urgent reason to assume this, since – as Cline himself also admits – other explanations are possible as well. The objects exchanged may have been perishable (e.g., olive oil, wine, wood, textile, metals) and as pottery was not suitable for overland transport the goods may have been placed into other, unbreakable containers, such as leather bags (most recently Beckman et al. 2011: 268-9 with references).[28]

As for gift exchange, we know from the international correspondence that these gifts often consisted of perishable goods such as textiles, horses, humans (slave and experts), and precious metals, which would leave no recognizable archaeological trace. One further has to bear in mind that the limited evidence for contacts in Hittite archaeology is a general problem: in Ḫattuša, there is a comparable dearth of objects from Egypt, Babylonia and Assyria.[29] To some extent this is unsurprising, since – apart from pottery – cultural material remains that have come down to us from Ḫatti are relatively limited. No graves containing rich gifts have been discovered and the capital appears to have been evacuated before it was destroyed (Seeher 2001). It is assumed that most valuable goods may have been taken along – and/or were melted down in later times.

The scarcity of Aegean objects in the Hittite heartland is thus not exceptional and should not be seen as evidence that contacts were limited. The same applies to the scarcity of Hittite objects in the Aegean: the number of Hittite objects in Syria, Egypt and Mesopotamia is equally low.[30] Based on the archaeological evidence, there is no reason to assume that Hittite contacts with the Aegean were less intense than with Babylonia or Egypt.

Though the evidence may seem meagre, Mycenaean presence in Ḫattuša is not completely absent. Probably the best-known example is the shard with the depiction of a Mycenaean warrior found in Ḫattuša (see fig. 1). Further, there are the painted plaster remains found in Temple 9 and Temple 5 in the Upper City of Ḫattuša and in the royal palace on Büyükkale, which appear to be of Mycenaean style (Brysbaert 2008; for photos see Neve 1996: 30, Müller-Karpe 2003: 292 and Özyar 2006: 131). These plasters are fragmentarily preserved, but their iconographic presentations, which include half-rosettes, hair or feathers from animal scenes and spirals, can be linked to Mycenaean and the Amarna-paintings (Brysbaert 2008: 102; Müller-Karpe 2003: 392-3). In her study of painted plaster in the Bronze Age Mediterranean Ann Brysbaert (2008) observes that the Ḫattuša plasters (and those of Tell el-Dab'a, Qatna and Tel Kabri) seem to fall in the same category as those at later Mycenaean mainland sites and she concludes that technological transfer of both knowledge and materials must have taken place.

On the Aegean site, some dozen objects that may be identified as Hittite have been excavated (Beckman et al. 2011: 268 with references). Further, there are various architectural parallels between Ḫattuša and Mycenae (Thaler 2007) and the Lion Gate of

28 Regrettably, the textual sources are not very helpful here, as we lack basically all types of documentation about trade. Possibly, this kind of records were written on wood (Waal 2011).

29 Genz 2011: 311f. For a somewhat different view, see Cline 2014: 70-1.

30 Genz 2011: 319f.

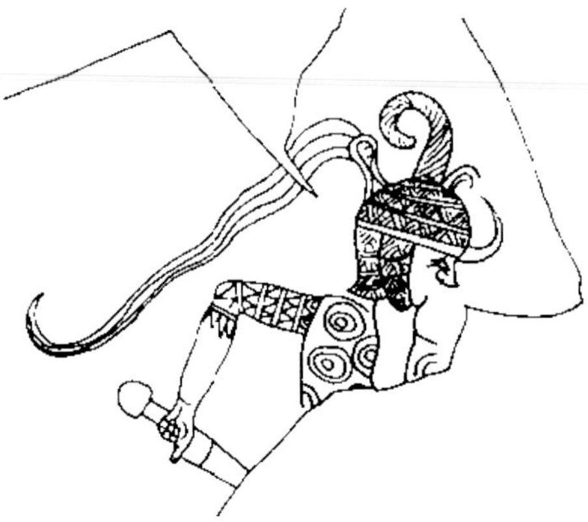

Fig.1: Sherd with the depiction of a Mycenaean warrior incised on a vessel from the Hittite capital Ḫattuša (after Kelder 2010: 41, fig. 1).

Mycenae appears to be made by Hittite tools and techniques (Blackwell 2014). This, like the frescoes found in Ḫattuša, implies exchange of knowledge and experts. The requests for doctors and sculptors from abroad in the international correspondence show that this kind of knowledge exchange was common practice (see, e.g., Bryce 2003a: 113-9).

9. Conclusions: The Iron Curtain has yet to fall?

The most important aspects of the above overview of the relations between Ḫatti and Aḫḫiyawa may be summarised as follows:

- The king of Aḫḫiyawa was considered to be an equal of the Hittite king. He was called 'Great King' and addressed as 'my brother' and 'my peer' on several occasions;
- The king of Aḫḫiyawa was at some point included in the list of great powers on a par with Babylon, Assyria and Egypt;
- Aḫḫiyawa had a substantial presence in the west coast of Anatolia for nearly two centuries and for some time had control over the stronghold Millawanda (Milete);
- The Hittites were not able to conquer or submit Aḫḫiyawa;
- The relations with Aḫḫiyawa appear to be similar to those with other Great Powers with respect to:
    - gift exchange;
    - extradition of fugitives;
    - contact frequency;
    - exchange of deities;
    - mode, manner and tone of communication.

The lack of archaeological evidence for contacts between Aḫḫiyawa and Ḫatti is in line with the general dearth of foreign objects in Ḫattuša and Hittite objects elsewhere in the ancient Near East.

From the above, it seems safe to conclude that Hittite dealings with Aḫḫiyawa were comparable to those with the great powers of Assyria, Babylon, Mitanni and Egypt.

However, there is an important *caveat* here. When discussing Hittite contacts with Aḫḫiyawa, the only point of comparison we have are either contacts with kings of equal status or vassal kings.[31] We do not have any evidence for contacts of Hittite kings with rulers of smaller, independent kingdoms. This is hardly surprising, as in the Late Bronze Age the Near East was dominated by a small group of Great Powers, who each controlled several smaller vassal states. Indeed, from an ancient Near Eastern perspective the existence of small, independent kingdoms in the Aegean would be an extraordinary situation. Though such a scenario can of course not be excluded – a possible exception may be Cyprus – the Hittite textual evidence forces us to re-examine the current paradigm and raises the question to what extent the present reconstruction of Late Bronze Age Greece is not the result of an (unconscious) *polis*-based Hellenocentric view of history.

With the growing awareness that the Aegean was part of the same cultural continuum as the ancient Near East, which is, e.g., also apparent from the many similarities in Greek and ancient Near Eastern literature (Burkert 1984; West 1996, recently Haubold 2015; Bachharova 2016), it may be time to also consider Greece with respect to its political structures as – in the words of Martin West – 'part of Asia'.[32]

Bibliography

Bachvarova, M.R. 2016. *From Hittite to Homer. The Anatolian Background of Ancient Greek Epic*, Cambridge.

Beckman, G.1999. *Hittite Diplomatic Texts* [2nd edition] (Writings from the Ancient World 7), Atlanta.

Beckman, G.H., T.R. Bryce and E.H. Cline. 2011. *The Ahhiyawa Texts* (Writings from the Ancient World 28), Atlanta.

Blackwell, N.G. 2014. 'Making the Lion Gate Relief at Mycenae: Tool Marks and Foreign Influence', *American Journal of Archaeology* 118.3: 451-488.

Broodbank, C. 2013. *The Making of the Middle Sea. A History of the Mediterranean from the Beginning to the Emergence of the Classical World*, London.

Bryce, T. 2003a. *Letters of the Great Kings of the Ancient Near East. The Royal Correspondence of the Late Bronze Age*, London – New York.

Bryce, T. 2003b. 'Relations between Ḫatti and Aḫḫiyawa in the Last Decades of the Bronze Age' in G. Beckman, R. Beal, and G. McMahon (eds.), *Hittite Studies in Honor of Harry A. Hoffner Jr.*, Winona Lake, Ind.: 59-72.

Brysbaert, A. 2008. *The Power of Technology in the Bronze Age Eastern Mediterranean: The Case of Painted Plaster*, London.

Burkert, W. 1984. *Die Orientalisierende Periode in der griechischen Religion und Literatur* (Sitzungsberichte der Heidelberger Akademie der Wissenschaften 1984.1), Heidelberg [second revised edition: 1992. *The Orientalizing Revolution. Near Eastern Influences on Greek Culture in the Early Archaic Age*, Cambridge MA – London].

Cline, E. H. 1991a. 'A Possible Hittite Embargo Against the Mycenaeans', *Historia* 40.1: 1-9.

Cline, E.H. 1994. *Sailing the Wine-Dark Sea: International Trade and the Late Bronze Age Aegean*, Oxford.

31 As a rule, there were no contacts between vassal kings and foreign Great Kings. An exceptional case is the letter of the Egyptian pharaoh Ramses II to the king of Mira, who was a Hittite vassal at that time (see text no. 21 above). The letter was found in Ḫattuša, which leads Beckman (1999: 130) to conclude that this letter was sent via the Hittite capital, since it was inappropriate for a vassal of one Great King to directly communicate with another.

32 West 1966.

Cline, E.H. 2014. *1177 B.C. The year civilisation collapsed,* Princeton.
Del Monte, G.F. and J. Tischler. 1978. *Die Orts- und Gewässernamen der hethitischen Texte* (Répertoire géographique des textes cunéiformes 6), Wiesbaden 1978.
Del Monte, G.F. and J. Tischler. 1992. *Die Orts- und Gewässernamen der hethitischen Texte. Supplement* (Répertoire géographique des textes cunéiformes 6/2), Wiesbaden.
Devecchi, E. 2010. 'The Aleppo Treaty Reconsidered', *Welt des Orients* 40.1: 1-27.
Gander, M. 2017. 'The West: Philology', in M. Weeden and L.Z. Ullmann (eds.), *Hittite Landscape and Geography,* Leiden – Boston: 262-280.
Genz H. 2011. Foreign Contacts of the Hittites, in H. Genz and D.P. Mielke (eds.), *Insights into Hittite History and Archaeology* (Colloquia Antiqua 2), Leuven – Paris – Walpole MA: 301-332.
Haubold, J. 2013. *Greece and Mesopotamia. Dialogues in Literature,* Cambridge.
Heinhold-Kramer, S. 2002. 'Zur Erwähnung Šaḫurunuwas im 'Tawagalawa-Brief', in S. de Martino and F. Pecchioli Daddi (eds.), *Anatolia Antica: Studi in memoria di Fiorella Imparati* (Eothen 11), Firenze: 359-375.
Heinhold-Kramer, S. 2007. 'Zu diplomatischen Kontakten zwischen dem Hethiterreich und dem Land "Aḫḫiyawa"', in E. Alram-Stern and G. Nightingale (eds.), *Keimelion. Elitenbildung und elitärer Konsum von der mykenischen Palastzeit bis zur homerischen Epoche. Akten des Internationalen Kongresses vom 3. bis 5. Februar 2005 in Salzburg* (Österreichische Akademie der Wissenschaften. Philosophisch-historische Klasse. Denkschriften 350), Wien: 191-207.
Goren Y., H. Mommsen and J. Klinger 2011. 'Non-destructive provenance study of cuneiform tablets using portable X-ray fluorescence (pXRF)', *Journal of Archaeological Science* 38: 684-696.
Hoffner, H.A. 2009. *Letters from the Hittite Kingdom* (Writings from the Ancient World 15), Atlanta.
Kelder, J. 2010. *The Kingdom of Mycenae. A Great Kingdom in the Late Bronze Age Aegean,* Bethesda.
Kitchen, K.A. and P. Lawrence. 2012. *Treaty, law and covenant in the Ancient Near East,* Wiesbaden.
Latacz, J. 2004. *Troy and Homer: Towards a Solution of an Old Mystery,* Oxford.
Niemeier, W.-D. 2008. 'Ḫattušas Beziehungen zum westlichen Kleinasien und dem mykenischen Griechenland nach den neuesten Forschungen', in G. Wilhelm (ed.), *Ḫattuša – Boğazköy – Das Hethiterreich im Spannungsfeld des Alten Orients* (Colloquium der Deutschen Orient-Gesellschaft 6), Wiesbaden: 291-349.
Malamat, A. 1998. *Mari and the Bible* (Studies in the History and Culture of the Ancient Near East 12), Leiden – Boston – Köln.
Melchert, H. C.[forthc.]. 'Mycenaean and Hittite Diplomatic Correspondence: Fact and Fiction', in A. Teffeteller (ed.), *Mycenaeans and Anatolians in the Late Bronze Age: the Aḫḫiyawa Question.*
Miller, J.L. 2006. 'Ein König von Ḫatti an einen König von Aḫḫijawa (der sogenannte Tawagalawa-Brief)', in B. Janowski and G. Wilhelm (eds.), *Texte der Umwelt des Alten Testaments, Neue Folge. Band 3: Briefe,* Gütersloh: 240-247.
Moran, W.L. 1992. *The Amarna Letters,* Baltimore – London.

Müller-Karpe, A. 2003. 'Remarks on Central Anatolian Chronology of the Middle Hittite Period', in M. Bietak (ed.), *The Synchronisation of Civilisations in the Eastern Mediterranean in the Second Millennium B.C. II. Proceedings of the SCIEM 2000 – Euroconference, Haindorf 2nd of May-7th of May, 2001*, Vienna: 383-394.

Neve, P. 1996. *Hattuša – Stadt der Götter und Tempel. Neue Ausgrabungen in der Hauptstadt der Hethiter* [2nd edition], Mainz.

Özyar, A. 2006. 'A Prospectus of Hittite Art Based on the State of our Knowledge at the Beginning of the 3rd Millennium AD', in D.P. Mielke, U.-D. Schoop and J. Seeher (eds.), *Strukturierung und Datierung in der hethitischen Archäologie / Structuring and Dating in Hittite Archaeology – Voraussetzungen – Probleme – Neue Ansätze / Requirements – Problems – New Approaches, Internationaler Workshop Istanbul, 16.-27. November 2004* (Byzas 4), Istanbul: 125-148.

Pedersén, O. 1998. *Archives and libraries in the ancient Near East, 1500-300 B.C.*, Bethesda.

Seeher, J. 2001. 'Die Zerstörung der Stadt Ḫattuša', in G. Wilhelm (ed.), *Akten des IV. Internationalen Kongresses für Hethitologie, Würzburg, 4.-8. Oktober 1999* (Studien zu den Studien zu den Boğazköy-Texten 45), Wiesbaden: 623-634.

Surenhagen, D. 2008. 'Schriftsysteme und Schriftgebrauch in der Ägäis, dem östlichen Mittelmeerraum und im Alten Orient während des 2. Jahrtausends v. Chr.', in A. Kyriatsoulis (ed.), *Austausch von Gütern, Ideen und Technologien in der Agäis und im östlichen Mittelmeer. Von der prähistorischen bis zur archaischen Zeit*: [*5. Internationale*] *Tagung, 19.-21.05 2006 in Ohlstadt Obb. Deutschland*, Weilheim: 245-282.

Thaler, U. 2007. 'Aḫḫiyawa und Ḫatti: Palatial Perspectives', in S. Antoniadou and A. Pace (eds.), *Mediterranean Crossroads,* Athens 2007: 291-323.

Van den Hout, Th.P.J. 2002. 'Another View of Hittite Literature', in S. De Martino and F. Pecchioli Daddi (eds.), *Anatolia antica. Studi in memoria di Fiorella Imparati* (Eothen 11), Firenze: 857-878.

Waal, W.J.I. 2011. 'They wrote on wood. The case for a hieroglyphic scribal tradition in Hittite Anatolia', *Anatolian Studies* 61: 21-35.

Waal, W.J.I. 2016. *Hittite Diplomatics. Studies in Ancient Document Format and Record Management* (Studien zu den Boğazköy-Texten 57), Wiesbaden.

West, M.L. 1966. *Hesiod. Theogony*, Oxford.

West, M.L. 1997. *The East Face of Helicon. West Asiatic Elements in Greek Poetry and Myth,* Oxford.

Wouters, W. 1989. 'Urḫi-Tešub and the Ramses-Letters from Boghazköy', *Journal of Cuneiform Studies* 41.2: 226-234.

What conclusions might be drawn from the archaeology of Mycenaean civilisation about political structure in the Aegean?

Oliver Dickinson

1. Preliminary comments

I begin with a warning: do not trust generalisations about archaeological material without question, even those made by specialists, especially if these generalisations are encountered in works that were published decades ago.[1] Archaeological material relating to a particular period or human society is usually so enormous in quantity that a sense of it can only be conveyed to the interested by generalisations; but in order to say something positive specialists often avoid lengthy expositions of the generally complex and inadequate state of the evidence, and concentrate more on the similarities than the dissimilarities, tending to ignore information that does not fit a broad picture. Also, the pace of archaeological discovery is such that any published generalisations run the risk of being made obsolete at any moment (examples appear in this paper).

It seems reasonable to start the discussion with Homer, the poet to whom the Iliad and Odyssey were attributed in antiquity, because Aegean archaeology effectively started with Schliemann's attempts to find a reality behind the legend of the Trojan War, the background of the Iliad. This took him from excavating the site certainly believed in antiquity to be Troy, in north-west Anatolia, to mainland Greece, where his excavations at Mycenae and Tiryns had even more spectacular results than those at Troy, and started the investigation of the series of advanced cultures based in the southern Aegean that is still continuing. This series had its first peak in the Minoan civilisation centred on Crete, which reached its height in the earlier part of the Late Bronze Age, around the 17th to 15th centuries BCE. At this time of greatest Cretan influence in the Aegean the

1 I have kept references to a minimum, concentrating on less publicised sites, material, and studies. Up-to-date general accounts of Mycenaean civilisation can be found in Shelmerdine 2008: chs. 10-15, and Cline 2010 (many chapters, including accounts of individual sites), also a very brief survey in Dickinson 2014c: 1874-9. Throughout, my references to absolute chronology will be following the conventional scheme, as outlined in Dickinson 2014c: 1860-1, not the higher chronology followed by Manning and others. Where unspecified, dates are always BCE.

in: Kelder, J.M. and Waal, W.J.I. (eds) 2019: *From 'LUGAL.GAL' to 'Wanax'. Kingship and Political Organisation in the Late Bronze Age Aegean*, Sidestone Press (Leiden), pp. 31-48.

Mycenaean civilisation began to develop on the southern Greek mainland, to spread after the collapse of Minoan civilisation and take in much of the Aegean in the 14th and 13th centuries BCE (hereafter referred to generally as the Palace Period), before it in turn collapsed around 1200 BCE.

It cannot be denied that the historical Greeks had no real perception of the length of human occupation in Greece before their own times. Their legends of the foundation of their cities and the exploits of the heroes cover only a few generations before the Trojan War, which was generally treated as having brought the age of heroes to an end, although the historical map of Greece was thought to be the result of population movements two or three generations after the War. Yet for a long time after Schliemann's discoveries great pioneers of Mycenaean archaeology like Tsountas, Wace and Blegen believed that the Greek legends and traditions preserved historical memories of the Greek Bronze Age and that the Homeric poems, the only genuinely 'archaic' element of the Greek legendary tradition, largely reflected the realities of the Mycenaean world, a view that has become embedded in popular accounts of the Greek Bronze Age and its sites. There is a small element of truth in this: although at least the central cores of the poems attributed to Homer were probably created in the late 8th or earlier 7th centuries BCE, they clearly belong to a tradition of orally created and performed epic poetry that must stretch back to Mycenaean times, since they include references to items characteristic only of that period and to places that were only important then, notably Troy and Mycenae itself. But what might be called the 'Mycenaean interpretation' of Homer has been increasingly questioned in recent years (e.g. Bennet 1997).

Although some of my colleagues continue to believe in some kind of real Trojan War, I hope they would concede that the world of the Homeric poems does not portray Mycenaean civilisation at its height. In fact, this world is best described as a quite unreal overlay of fairy tale magnificence on a violent and unstable society with limited resources and horizons. At best, this might be thought a partial reflection of the Mycenaean world in its final phase, between the ca. 1200 collapse of the palace civilisation and the 11th century BCE, so after the period with which this workshop is concerned. But many features of the Homeric world belong to the early Iron Age, and it has been well described as 'a poetic creation, what *some* eighth-century Greeks thought the heroic world *ought* to have been like' (Morris 1997: 558).

I think it important to make this point, because in my own work on the Aḫḫiyawa texts and their relevance to Mycenaean Greece I have become aware that this major change in attitudes towards the historical value of the Homeric poems seems to have escaped the notice of important Hittitologists such as Bryce and Singer, who present Aḫḫiyawa as an aggressive if not predatory power, for ever trying to subvert Hittite control of the western Anatolian kingdoms and bring them into an Aḫḫiyawan sphere of influence, and in doing so apparently treat the Homeric poems as containing an accurate depiction of the Mycenaean elite. This is patent in the publication of the Aḫḫiyawa texts, most clearly in the comment, significant because it is made without any suggestion that it might be questioned, '... the image presented in the Homeric epics of Mycenaean plundering enterprises ...' (Beckman, Bryce and Cline 2011: 99). I have argued forcefully elsewhere against the still commonly expressed view that 'the Mycenaeans' were an especially warlike civilisation (Dickinson 2014a), and in a Mycenaean Seminar at the Institute of Classical Studies, London (*The use and abuse of the Aḫḫiyawa texts*, December 7th 2016) I have argued equally strongly against the view of Aḫḫiyawa as an aggressive and would-be expansionary power, so I will merely state here that I think this a highly questionable interpretation of the evidence. Nevertheless, I have no doubt that the interpretation of the Aḫḫiyawa texts to suggest that there was a major power based in the Aegean in the Palace Period that the Hittites called Aḫḫiyawa, and that this must be part of Mycenaean Greece, is essentially correct.

A basic point relevant to this that needs to be made, because it reflects a very common error into which Beckman, Bryce and Cline fall like many others, is that 'the Mycenaeans' are not a *people*, as the Egyptians or Hittites or Assyrians might be thought to be. The term 'Mycenaean' is an archaeological label, applied primarily to a complex of recognisable material features. But the common tendency has been to assume that the Mycenaeans were an ethnic group based in the southern Greek mainland – although some want to identify them only as an elite or ruling class – and to suppose that where material or influences classifiable as Mycenaean appear in quantity elsewhere, e.g. in the Aegean islands or on the west coast of Anatolia at sites like Miletus, it is because immigrant 'Mycenaeans' have appeared there. But we have no reason to suppose that the populations of the various regions that make up the southern Greek mainland viewed themselves as a single ethnic group in the way that the historical Greeks did. In fact, there is every reason to believe that it was possible to 'become Mycenaean', and this is what the archaeological evidence suggests that the inhabitants of many Aegean islands did – but not Crete, a point that I shall come to – and also Miletus and the Anatolian coastal region to its south.

2. The supposed uniformity of Mycenaean culture

Almost certainly, there were in these regions 'Mycenaeans' who did not speak Greek as their first language, or maybe not at all, just as there may have been communities in the remoter parts of mainland Greece who did speak some form of Greek but were at best 'semi-Mycenaean' in their material culture (cf. Dickinson 2014b: 158). Miletus, which is surely the Millawanda of the Aḫḫiyawa texts, is a particularly interesting case. Like much of the east Aegean region that 'became Mycenaean' from the 14th century BCE, Miletus had previously been Minoan in material culture, but there is no reason to think that the change in material culture was accompanied by any wholesale change of population. Rather, for their own reasons the local inhabitants, whatever their origin, having previously presented themselves as 'Minoan', chose to adopt various traits that modern archaeologists call 'Mycenaean'. There may have been some influx of population from the mainland to this and other newly 'Mycenaean' regions; but it is striking that the name of Atpa, the local ruler or governor of Millawanda referred to in the famous Tawagalawa letter, is not Greek and apparently not Luwian either, a reminder of how diverse the populations of these regions may have been (the name of Awayana, like Atpa a son-in-law of the notorious Piyamaradu and apparently also based in Millawanda (Beckman, Bryce and Cline 2011: 105), also does not look Greek). So the appearance of features of Mycenaean material culture at Miletus, or anywhere else outside the original Mycenaean cultural area, does not necessarily represent the activity of 'Mycenaeans' moving around for whatever reason, let alone of the agents of a Mycenaean state trying to extend its authority. This is not to say that such things did not happen, simply that this is not a necessary inference from the simple appearance at a site of artefacts or features classifiable as Mycenaean. Craftworkers, in particular, might move simply to find work opportunities; one potting group certainly moved in the Palace Period to Troy, where much of the fine decorated Mycenaean pottery is of local fabric. But Troy never 'became Mycenaean'.

This leads on to the topic of the uniformity of Mycenaean material culture, which in the past has been cited as evidence for some version of political unity, often envisaged as an 'empire' under the control of Mycenae. Desborough (1972: 17-18) argued as much, in a passage worth quoting at length:

> But were the various mainland and Aegean areas knit into a single whole? The material culture, in its many aspects, is so uniform that one must at the very least conclude that links between one small kingdom and another were of the closest. Besides this, it must be pointed out that the Hittites knew of a land called Aḫḫiyawa, uncertainly located but very probably in the Aegean, of an importance suitable for a combined power, but less suitable for any of the lesser districts when taken separately; and Homer's Agamemnon would appear to have the role of a High King – though of course this may have been only for the purposes of the expedition against Troy. There is no solid proof that Greece and the Aegean formed a union of kingdoms under one overlord, but I think that the balance of probability is that such was the case. And if there was a High King, he would have had his seat at Mycenae.

Note the Homeric reference, which others have made, but I have to say, with regret (because Vincent Desborough was my mentor in work on the early Iron Age, especially the material at Lefkandi), that it is wrong. There is no suggestion anywhere in the Iliad that the other kings and princes owed any form of allegiance to Agamemnon. Rather, the forces assembled against Troy formed a purely temporary confederacy, made up of some rulers that could be imagined to be Agamemnon's firm allies, and others who came, as Achilles says in Book I, so that Agamemnon might be pleased, and to get recompense from the Trojans for his brother Menelaos (Il.1.158-9). In Thucydides's 'rational' interpretation, these rulers came out of fear rather than loyalty, because Agamemnon had greater power and a stronger fleet than any other king (Thuc. I.9).

On the basis of one line in the Iliad describing Agamemnon as lord of all Argos and many islands (Il.2.108), Thucydides was prepared to believe that he controlled islands far from the Argive coast; this was not hard for him to imagine, because in his day Athens did directly control several Aegean islands, both close and remote – indeed, for a while it effectively controlled most of the Aegean islands and coasts through the so-called Delian League. But his main use of the line is to prove that Agamemnon must have had a fleet, and he is very unspecific about what he thought to be the extent of Agamemnon's power. In general, the Greek legends were so specifically tied to a single city or state that they did not even allude to the strong likelihood that, as in historical times, cities formed alliances and leagues and might conquer each other. The absence of any real memory of a great state in the 'heroic age' based anywhere on the Greek mainland underlines what can be argued for on other grounds, that Greek tradition did not preserve any meaningful historical information about Mycenaean civilisation.

3. The development of Mycenaean 'uniformity'

What, then, of this argument from uniformity of material culture, as offered by Desborough and others since (cf. Kelder 2012: 42; Eder and Jung 2015: 113)? One might object, from the start, that there is no necessary link between cultural uniformity and political unity. It is not my impression that the generally short-lived 'empires' of antiquity imposed any such uniformity, although they might build monuments in their own style and set up inscriptions in their own language in subject territories, and the fashions and customs of the dominant power might be emulated in such territories. But as far as I know Egyptian control of Palestine and parts of Syria during the period of the Eighteenth and Nineteenth Dynasties, chronologically equivalent to much of the Late Bronze Age in Greece, did not involve any strong 'Egyptianisation' of local material culture, nor did Hittite control of northern Syria and much of Anatolia outside the Hittite homeland involve much of this kind. Thus, there is no reason to expect that, if an 'empire' centred on Mycenae was created, this would necessarily have resulted in the spread of cultural homogeneity, let alone its enforcement, and the argument backwards from supposed cultural uniformity to political union is illegitimate.

It must be admitted that, with the marked exception of Crete, the material culture of the southern Aegean in the Palace Period does appear uniform enough to allow the application of the term 'Mycenaean' to all of it without qualification. Walk into any substantial museum in what might be called the 'Mycenaean region', and you will probably see pottery, figurines and other artefacts that are of recognisable standard types. But how real and deep-rooted is this uniformity? This is where it pays to look at the evidence in detail.

For a start, it needs to be emphasised that, while Mycenaean material culture may look very homogeneous in the Palace Period, it did not begin that way. A rather romantic view of the beginning of the Mycenaean era is suggested by Vermeule's words: '... cities on remote rivers in Greece which are being settled by Mycenaeans in this period on top of a 'barbarous' peasant stock' (Vermeule 1964: 105), and 'The emergence of the early Mycenaean Age as an historical era thus involves movements of new princes or barons with small bands of followers, who take over fresh territory ...' (Vermeule 1964: 118).

Such comments reflect the already questioned idea that the 'Mycenaeans' were an elite who, coming with their immediate followers from a particular area in search of new territory, spread a uniform complex of material features and the beliefs that they embodied. I will state very firmly that as an account of how the archaeological evidence shows that Mycenaean culture developed this is quite simply wrong.

Rather, various elements that might be considered basic to the culture can be perceived either to develop almost simultaneously in several regions, or to originate in one and spread quickly to others, in a context of relatively rapid change that resulted in a strongly hierarchical arrangement of society, with a clearly marked elite. Previously, in the Middle Helladic culture of the southern mainland and adjacent islands, there had been at best only subtle indications of social differentiation, in a society whose communities were mostly of village type, relatively poor and rarely having strong contacts to the outside world beyond their own region. Such a portrait, I will comment, does not fit at all well with the notion that warlike invaders speaking the Indo-European ancestor of the Greek language conquered the southern mainland in the late 3rd millennium, but, although this idea is still not dead (cf. Feuer 2011), it deserves to be, as a wholly obsolete way of explaining cultural and linguistic change.

The contrast between the apparently rather egalitarian Middle Helladic society and the splendour of the Shaft Graves of Mycenae has in the past, even quite recently, led to a variant of this theory of 'the Greeks' as warlike invaders, which brings them into Greece at the end of the Middle Helladic period as conquerors who became the ruling elite of the Mycenaean civilisation (Drews 1988). But this quite ignores the evidence, not only from Mycenae but other centres in different parts of the southern mainland, notably Thebes in Boeotia and several in Messenia, for a *gradual* emergence of an elite, as shown most clearly in their graves. These only slowly begin to be distinguishable from the ordinary Middle Helladic pits, sometimes lined and roofed with stone, by being more substantial in size and construction and containing a greater number of 'grave-goods', including occasional daggers and metal ornaments. Such graves can be found at several centres in Mycenae's home province, the Argolid, and also elsewhere, as at Thebes and in the neighbourhood of Pylos in Messenia. As the graves became larger and more elaborate, they were often used for successive burials, the quantity and value of the goods placed with the dead increased considerably, and there are indications that graves might have markers and ceremonies might be held at them. At about the same time, there is evidence for increasing links with the towns of the Cyclades and the Minoan civilisation centred in Crete, which by this time had extended to include Kythera off the south coast of the Peloponnese and several islands of the south-east Aegean. These links show not only in the types of goods, including weapons, placed in the graves of the emerging elite, but in a whole range of styles of decorated pottery that began to be produced by the potters of different regions, of which the style that was to develop into Mycenaean decorated pottery was only one, closely related in its origins to the style of the local Minoan pottery of Kythera.

Also, appearing first in the south Peloponnese, domestic pottery types of Minoan origin such as tripod cooking pots and lamps began to be produced, as well as the 'conical cups' ubiquitous in Minoan and strongly Minoan-influenced cultures, and types of rock-cut and stone-built tomb that have Aegean parallels began to be constructed on the mainland. All include more or less the same basic plan of an open passageway (the dromos) leading to a partly or wholly subterranean chamber, very often through a narrower roofed entranceway (the stomion). The stone-built tholos tombs are the best known of these, but much commoner are the rock-cut chamber tombs. There remain questions about where these were produced first; on present evidence, they seem to appear in different parts of the Peloponnese more or less simultaneously and in varying forms, whereas there is a strong argument that tholos tombs were first developed in one province, Messenia (but recent discoveries may oblige us to revise this). There is a significant distinction between the types. Tholos tombs proper, nearly always circular and domed, with diameters of at least several metres, are normally found singly or in pairs (Mycenae is totally exceptional in having nine) and are clearly graves for an elite, to judge from their impressive size and architecture and the remains of the goods placed in them (most have been robbed). Chamber tombs vary considerably in size and shape, and can be found in large cemeteries, up to hundreds at major centres like Mycenae and Thebes, and although they certainly could be used for elite burials they were mostly used for a series of burials over a period, perhaps belonging to a single family, that might be described as 'sub-elite' or mildly prosperous, on the basis of the generally modest goods placed with the dead. Where we find the skeletal evidence, it is clear that tholos tombs were also used for several burials, an example of a custom shared by the elite and the general population.

It took generations for these novelties to spread and blend into a more homogeneous early Mycenaean culture. Significantly, tholos tombs spread all over Messenia in the first

Mycenaean phase, Late Helladic I, much of which predated the eruption of Santorini, but they did not arrive at Mycenae until the next phase, Late Helladic IIA, which definitely followed the eruption and during which tholos tombs were built at many sites in the Peloponnese and, rarely, outside it – but not, surprisingly, at Thebes or anywhere else in Boeotia, the most important province in central Greece. This development has always been taken as evidence for the establishment of a host of principalities, great and small, not all of them stable and some likely to be subordinate to others. No less than six tholoi seem to have been built at Mycenae during this phase, an indication of its pre-eminence. During the same phase the Mycenaean decorated pottery style, which seems to have been perfected in the Argolid, was widely adopted and the plain domestic wares of each region, which had previously had distinctive characters, began to become more homogeneous. But even when Minoan civilisation collapsed, around the middle of the 15th century BCE, this change had not taken place all over central Greece, to judge from the evidence of Lefkandi on Euboea and Kirrha in Phocis, nor in the most northerly 'Helladic' region of the mainland, Thessaly, and the simple form of Middle Helladic burial in pits was still quite widely practised. It was only in the following Palace Period that the Mycenaean pottery style and the chamber tomb really became common all over the Mycenaean region, and only then did the well-known types of small clay figurine develop and spread.

4. The rise of the Mycenaean culture to dominance, the spread of Linear B, and the nature of the early palaces

Following the collapse of the Minoan civilisation around the mid-15th century BCE, Mycenaean influence begins to be more markedly perceptible in the Aegean, although at first mainly in the form of imported decorated pottery, which when analysed chemically or spectrographically seems to come mainly from the Argolid. It was also in this period, the late 15th and much of the 14th centuries BCE, that on any chronology there was a 'final palace' at Knossos, which seems to have dominated much of central and western Crete, as can be determined from the Linear B documents found scattered in deposits all over the palace and in nearby buildings, which are written in generally intelligible Greek. This development, along with the sudden appearance of elite graves around Knossos, and also at Kydonia (modern Khania) in west Crete, that show marked similarities in burial customs with early Mycenaean elite graves, has led to the theory of a 'Mycenaean conquest' of Crete and to the quite common usage 'Mycenaean Crete' in referring to the following period.

But I believe that this usage is highly misleading. It does seem likely that the dominant element in the new ruling class of Crete originated from the mainland, but at least some of them could have been there before the collapse, and what happened need not have been anything as simple as a 'conquest'; all kinds of explanations for their rise to power could be created, on historical analogies. But, although their language was now used for administration, and they seem to have considerably influenced burial customs (chamber tombs of the mainland style began to become popular in Crete), and potters began to produce their favoured kind of drinking vessel, the stemmed goblet, in other respects they seem to have assimilated very much to Minoan ways, like other foreign groups that took over superior civilisations in the later Bronze Age (e.g. the Hyksos in Egypt and Kassites in Babylonia). For a while in the Palace Period the palace of Knossos was maintained very much in the old style, with no obvious Mycenaean features, and throughout the period Crete maintained distinctive traditions in architecture (no fortifications of mainland type are found), in its pottery and seals, in some important aspects of burial customs, and perhaps most significantly in religious practices and types of site. Thus, although there was a very old tradition of using figurines in ritual contexts in Crete, that might in fact have influenced the original development of the standard Mycenaean figurines, these Mycenaean types only appear very rarely in Cretan contexts and hardly ever seem to have been locally made. More significantly still, there are several distinctive and well-represented types of site used for ritual in Crete, none of which can be closely paralleled in the comparatively poorly represented and notably variable Mycenaean evidence for ritual sites. In fact, throughout the Palace Period Crete remained essentially a distinct if related world.

The above makes the devising of theories linking the distribution of the Linear B script with a hypothetical single great power in the Aegean difficult, for it would have to be argued that this power included two rather different styles of civilisation, and that the role of its supposed ruler would have changed when, as the theory would have it, he visited his Cretan dominions. This is not impossible, but I cannot help feeling that it is unlikely. The point has a considerable bearing on the development of Aḫḫiyawa. For in my view it is likely that Linear B was devised at Knossos; yet not only the ways that it was used administratively but a lot of technical terminology concerning official titles, types of land, etc. seem to be very similar to what is found in certainly later material from Pylos and other mainland sites. Would this not be an argument for making Knossos, not any Mycenaean centre, the capital of Aḫḫiyawa? It might seem so, but there is a major problem, that in the 13th century, the period in which most of the references in Hittite sources to Aḫḫiyawa can be dated, including those clearly calling its ruler a 'Great King', Knossos, though still a substantial settlement, was very much in decline. Even after its destruction by fire, parts of the palace remained in use, as did parts of other major buildings, but since large areas were left filled with rubble from previous destructions, they surely became increasingly unsafe, and all were eventually abandoned. But there were no new buildings to replace them, no more rich tombs at or near Knossos, nothing comparable to what can be found at Mycenae, Thebes, Pylos and several other mainland centres in the 13th century. Crete still had locally important centres, the greatest of them being Kydonia (Khania), which used Linear B for administration and played a role in Mediterranean-wide trade, but none of them exerted very significant influence in the Aegean.

We are still not clear about how Linear B and the administrative system that went with it spread to the mainland, but it seems very likely that this happened during the early part of the Palace Period when Knossos was still a centre of considerable importance. Even though Crete lost most of its influence in the Aegean following the collapse of the pure Minoan civilisation, Knossos would surely have retained immense prestige in the eyes of the mainland rulers, with a palace and other buildings far more impressive than any of theirs. In the circumstances, it seems only too likely that its system of administration, quite unlike anything current on the mainland before, was shown off by its new rulers and emulated by mainland princes. This was precisely the time when mainland princes, ambitious to play a role in the wider world, might choose to organise their principalities along more 'civilised' lines. In the mid-15th century Tuthmosis III of Egypt received embassies not just from rulers of Keftiu, generally taken to be Crete, but, after his attacks on Mitanni, from a country that is variously transliterated as Tanaya or Tinayu, which seems likely to be part of the Greek mainland. Also, we learn from the fragmentary letter KUB 26.91 preserved at Ḫattuša, now considered to have been sent by a king of Aḫḫiyawa, that his ancestor was gifted with some islands, perhaps as a dowry, by the king of Assuwa in northwest Anatolia, who was evidently ready to have diplomatic relations with Aḫḫiyawa around 1400, before the Hittite conquest (see some interesting comments on this in Melchert [forthc.]).

But the whole question of the transmission of Linear B must now be reconsidered in the light of new discoveries, which serve as a reminder of how much we do not know and how easily our perceptions and theories can be changed by new finds. For a long time, the large archive of Linear B material found in the 13th century palace of Pylos has been the most extensive known on the mainland, although smaller quantities have been discovered at Mycenae, Tiryns and Thebes in a variety of 13th century contexts. Very recent finds of particular significance have included a single tablet fragment from Mycenae in a mid-to-late 14th century context, another in a context no later than the 14th century at Iklaina south-east of Pylos, an important site but not of the first rank, and two from old excavation material from Volos (ancient Iolkos), the most important Mycenaean site in Thessaly, along with two inscribed items from a major 13th century building at Dhimini nearby.

But the most astonishing and unexpected find has been at Ayios Vasileios in Laconia, 11½ km south of Sparta (and 4½ km south-west of the Vapheio tholos site), where a large deposit of tablets and nodules (inscribed lumps of clay that accompanied livestock and goods) has been discovered in excavations that began as recently as 2009, associated with what is surely a palatial complex of 14th century date (I am extremely grateful to the excavator, Dr. Adamantia Vasilogamvrou, for copious information about the site, its material and its dating). With the possible exception of the Iklaina fragment this is the oldest find of Linear B on the mainland, certainly no later than the bulk of the deposit at Knossos, quite possibly earlier; unfortunately, this is not as widely known as it deserves to be (e.g. the site is not even mentioned in Eder and Jung 2015).[2] 119 items inscribed in Linear B had been found by the end of 2015 (and perhaps a few more since), which makes this the fourth largest source of Linear B material after Knossos, Pylos and Thebes. It seems to be a single group, fallen from an upper floor; the material is fragmentary and still largely unpublished, but already specific links with the Knossos material have been noticed.

Taken together with the early Mycenae and Iklaina finds, Ayios Vasileios's material seems to guarantee that Linear B spread to the mainland well before the final destruction of the Knossos palace, and was probably adopted in several regions of the Peloponnese more or less simultaneously. This is of considerable relevance to the argument that has recently been developed (cf. Kelder 2010: 11-2; Eder and Jung 2015: 113-8), that lays stress on the uniformity of the administrative and scribal practices involved in the use of the Linear B script, and maintains that this can only be explained if they are the products of a single administration. Quite apart from the problem inherent in the dating of the Knossos material, to which I have already referred, we now have a situation where Linear B could have been adopted in south Peloponnesian centres *before* Mycenae.[3] Moreover, Ayios

2 For brief accounts see *Archaeological Reports* nos. 57 (2010-11: 23), 59 (2012-13: 31) and 61 (2014-15: 10), and http://popular-archaeology.com/issue/spring-2017).

3 Since the time of writing this paper (2016), the situation has changed. Recent work at Ayios Vasileios indicates that the building (Delta) with the Linear B inscriptions should instead be dated to LH IIIA2, and its destruction may be late in the phase if not even just into LH IIIB (Kardamaki 2017, cf. conclusions on 111, 114 particularly, cf. also the Abstract on p. 73).

Vasileios Building Delta, the one with which the Linear B material is associated, is proving to have a noticeably 'Minoan' aspect, with stoa-like colonnades facing onto two sides of a large rectangular court, which may be flanked on the north by another major building, Alpha, where a range of extremely impressive finds has been found, including items from Crete and Egypt. So far no trace has been found of the central hall-and-porch 'megaron suite' of rooms that is supposedly a standard feature of a typical Mycenaean palace. Relatively enormous numbers of fresco fragments have been found in many parts of the site; reports suggest that they have a wide variety of themes and a good many are on a small scale, in that respect maybe closer to Knossos than to other Mycenaean sites, whose frescoes are mostly dated later in any case. Yet the pottery and other features of the site, including a cemetery of early Mycenaean stone-built graves, are entirely mainland in nature. The overall impression is that the power represented by these finds was independent and in no way dominated politically or culturally from Mycenae or anywhere else.

The above discovery gives added significance to an argument advanced by Nelson (2007), based on careful study of the remains of earlier buildings identified under the surviving palace at Pylos, that the immediately preceding building, destroyed in the 14th century, had a very different arrangement from the 13th century palace, although this incorporated some of its foundations. The older building may have been closer to a Minoan palace in its layout – there was a possible central court, and a row of magazines like those on the west side of the Knossos palace – and certainly has 'Minoan' features in its techniques of construction. Taken with the Ayios Vasileios evidence, this suggests that the first really impressive palaces might have been built in the south Peloponnese and have owed more to Cretan influence than to the supposedly standard Mycenaean palace plan, although buildings with something like a central 'megaron suite' can be documented at other less prominent sites in the south Peloponnese in early contexts (the Menelaion site near Sparta and Nichoria in Messenia). The central 'Great Megaron' of the Tiryns palace does seem to go back to the 14th century; however, the most recent investigations have uncovered evidence for something beneath this of quite different form, including a staircase and upper terrace (Maran 2017). Unfortunately, there is no way of telling what any similarly early structures at Mycenae itself would have looked like, for only a few scattered walls remain of anything earlier than what is now visible, which is likely to have been built late in the 14th century at earliest, and was further adapted and extended later (cf. French 2002: 47, 57-61).

The 'megaron suite' plan, then, seems to have become much more dominant in the later part of the Palace Period, and hence was used for the final versions of the Mycenae and Pylos palaces and in other buildings. But at Thebes, where several 13th century buildings that seem to have palatial functions have been discovered, they seem like those of Ayios Vasileios to be separate from each other, and no traces of a 'megaron suite' have ever been identified (Dakouri-Hild 2010: 698-9). To sum up, the development of palaces on the mainland, like the adoption of Linear B, is likely to have been a much more complex process than has tended to be imagined in the past. It seems impossible to maintain that in either case something was simply evolved at one site and adopted by, even imposed on the rest.

5. Possible political arrangements in Mycenaean Greece at the time of the palace civilisation

Whatever the type of building, it certainly seems that impressive complexes began to be built at several leading mainland centres in the 14th century; I have named the most obvious already, Mycenae, Tiryns, Pylos, and Thebes. Ayios Vasileios was clearly very important for a time, though it appears to have been destroyed towards the end of the 14th, or possibly in the very early 13th, century BC. The only other site that looks likely on present evidence to have been a really major centre is Orchomenos in western Boeotia, which historically was Thebes's major rival. But the arguments are rather inferential, depending partly on the discovery of palace-quality frescoes on the site and a tholos tomb that is a virtual duplicate of the largest and finest tholos of all, the so-called Treasury of Atreus, which is likely to have been built in the earlier 14th century; they are so similar that the same building team may have planned and constructed them. This is hard to understand, if, as the advocates of a single major Mycenaean state might want to contend, Orchomenos was subordinate to Mycenae; why should it alone have such a magnificent tomb, when other supposedly subordinate but major centres like Pylos and Thebes did not? But it might make sense if Mycenae and Orchomenos were separate powers, allied in their opposition to Thebes. Further evidence of this might be sought in the remarkable fortress of Gla, built in the 14th century in the middle of the area of Lake Copais in Boeotia, which was largely drained by a series of dykes built, like the fortress, in the well-known 'Cyclopean' style of fortification used for the walls of Mycenae and Tiryns, also 14th century in their beginning (Hope Simpson and Hagel 2006: 77-8, 187-209). Orchomenos was far better placed geographically than Thebes to undertake this work and to control the rich agricultural land that resulted, but it could well have had help, including a workforce expert in building 'Cyclopean' walls, from Mycenae.

Such suggestions are inevitably speculative, but I feel that they explain the evidence more plausibly than the 'single state' hypothesis, which also does not seem to take account of the early appearance and apparent disappearance of Ayios Vasileios as a major centre. It might be argued that the destruction of Ayios Vasileios represents Mycenae's ridding itself of a potentially dangerous rival. But if so, why is it not possible to identify any major Linear B-using centre in Laconia later, that might be understood as a seat of local government, whereas at Pylos, which also suffered a 14th century destruction, there is a major palace from which, to judge from the Linear B material, a considerable territory was administered? For that matter, why would complete 'Cyclopean' fortifications be built in the later 13th century not only at Midea, the third great fortress site of the Argolid, but at Athens and less significant sites like Krisa near Delphi and Teikhos Dymaion on the northwest tip of the Peloponnese, all of which, even Athens, might be argued with varying degrees of plausibility to be outposts of Mycenae's power – whereas they are conspicuously absent from Pylos and Thebes, the most important sites of territories that one might expect, if they were subject to Mycenae, to be carefully controlled by garrisoned fortresses?

Still on the topic of public works involving the use of 'Cyclopean' architecture, this seems a good point to mention the road system, involving terraces, bridges and culverts, that has been traced radiating from Mycenae, mostly heading for the passes into the Corinthia, but no further. The suggestion that the Greek mainland was linked by a network of such roads (Kelder 2012: 45) is quite simply not the case; there are potential roads within several provinces, but none between them (Hope Simpson and Hagel 2006: ch. 2). Overland travel would probably have been relatively arduous, especially through the Peloponnese, a point to remember when theories involving wars of conquest are offered.

I find it much easier to imagine Mycenaean Greece of the Palace Period as I have suggested elsewhere (e.g. Dickinson 2014b: 158), as a mosaic of principalities large and small, the leading ones 'palace societies' with a literate administration, others more simply organised but relatively stable 'chiefdoms', others again loose and potentially unstable tribal groupings. All of them surely had relations with their neighbours that could vary between alliance, dependence, indifference, and hostility – not too dissimilar from historical Greece, in fact. There is no reason why the greatest, like Mycenae itself, should not have had a circle of allies, some perhaps more like vassals but still technically independent, much as in the Hittite Empire. Without written information, the likely complexity of the situation and any changes over time will never be worked out.

Here we come to the major limitations of the Linear B material. It includes nothing that could throw light on the history, laws, diplomatic links or even trading connections of the centres using it. Instead it only informs us about items and commodities issued by, sent in to, or stored at each palace, including some evident taxes, on personnel of interest to the palace, including work groups who were employed in palace-supported industries and supported with rations, some based in distant settlements, and on livestock in which the palace had an interest, particularly sheep as producers of wool. Most of our information comes from Knossos and Pylos, which differ considerably in the approaches of the two administrations: the officials of Knossos seem to have dealt mainly with the local capitals of regions in Knossos's territory, though they might have information on individuals, but the Pylos scribes dealt with a much more developed system of territorial subdivision, in which there were two provinces, each with several subdivisions, and they were able to gather information about individual settlements in these subdivisions. The texts give us place names, some recognisable from historical times, which allow an estimation of the extent of the territories controlled, which seem to have been generally larger than those of the historical city states that occupied the same regions. We also learn something of how the territories were taxed, but the gaps in our information are such that, for example, we do not know where the Pylos palace got the barley and figs that it distributed as rations, or the olive oil sent as offerings to shrines.

Some of the perceptible differences between the two centres may well reflect their different dates, but there is enough similarity in the material from all sites to suggest that scribes and officials were trained in a particular tradition. However, this was not unchanging; there was room for quite a degree of variation in scribal practice between sites, and even within sites, in the way that signs were drawn, words were spelled, and texts arranged (cf. Duhoux 2013: 17; I am grateful to Dr. G. Flouda for sending me a copy of this). Even the clay from which tablets were made might differ quite considerably, as shown by study of the Pylos material, where one batch is so distinct that it might have been made and inscribed elsewhere in the territory. There are some clear indications that Linear B could be written outside the major palace centres, including the Iklaina find, but the general impression is that most administrative activity took place at the palace sites. At Knossos, tablets were written and stored in several different places within the palace and even in separate buildings, and this scattering of 'offices' seems to be typical at Mycenae, Tiryns and Thebes also; but at Pylos there was evidence of a significant innovation, for the great bulk of the material (80%) was stored in a two-room archives complex, and in this relatively late material improvements can be noticed in the way information was laid out on tablets and the use of different types of tablet for different stages in the process. These changes and differences make it hard to believe that even the mainland centres using Linear B were part of a single administration.

Much has been made of the fact that terminology for leading office-holders is found at both Knossos and Pylos, including what seems to be the highest position, the *wanax*, a word used in Homeric Greek to mean 'king'; derivatives from this word appear in Linear B material elsewhere too. But the references to the activities of the *wanax* and other figures are so few and often enigmatic that much that is often stated about their position and powers is no more than reasonable conjecture. It is easier to base a general conclusion on the archaeological evidence for impressive buildings and tombs, and finely made luxury goods, that there was a clearly marked elite, led by rulers, whether one calls them kings, princes or chiefs, both within the likely territories of the palaces and elsewhere. But it is noteworthy that very little representational material can be related to such persons and there is a complete lack of inscribed public monuments, in marked contrast with the Near Eastern civilisations (see also the contribution of Fritz Blakolmer in this volume).

6. The archaeological evidence for Mycenaean material culture and its variations in the Palace Period

What general picture do we get of the level of civilisation in the Aegean of the Palace Period? In this world Mycenae undoubtedly bulked large. It has the finest tholoi, the most impressive fortifications, chamber tomb cemeteries which held many exceptionally richly provided burials, and by the 13th century a series of impressive buildings had been built on the slopes inside the citadel and near it. Survey work has demonstrated the existence of a broad spread of settlement around the citadel (Maggidis and Stamos 2006); recent excavation has verified the existence of an outer circuit wall with more than one gate, so maybe Mycenae was more like a small city than has sometimes been imagined. The remains of Thebes also hint at a developed town at its centre, the hill called the Kadmeia; there is evidence of a spread of population over more than 30 hectares, a circuit wall, aqueducts, and fresco remains in 24 different plots, likely to belong to other major buildings beside the palace (Dakouri-Hild 2010: 696-700). There have been two recent discoveries of other Mycenaean sites which have a townlike aspect, both belonging to the Palace Period, the fortified township at Kalamianos in the eastern Corinthia (Tartaron et al. 2011) and a settlement covering perhaps 10 hectares near the ancient settlement mound of Dhimini, which has a very broad and clearly marked street off which buildings open, including a complex structure made up of two wings flanking a court that seems very likely to be the base of a local ruler or governor, although it lacks frescoes and elaborate architecture (Adrimi-Sismani 2007). In Messenia, Pylos may have been a town as extensive as Thebes, and Iklaina, which was probably the administrative centre of one of the subdivisions of the Pylos state, has some impressive structures; but Nichoria, likely to have been another administrative centre, seems more like a disorganised village, spread over a series of slopes; there are traces of a street in one part, but spaced houses without common orientation in another (McDonald and Wilkie 1992: ch. 7).

There seems to have been a wide spread of settlements over the landscape in the Palace Period, but very little is known about them; the impression is that the majority were most like villages, small or large. The variations in what is known remind us of the potential for different levels of sophistication between the different parts of the Mycenaean world, and lead on to the more general point, that discussions that try to draw general pictures inevitably tend to conceal evidence of local traditions and preferences. Thus, the centre of stylistic development for decorated Mycenaean pottery was undoubtedly the Argolid, and a great deal of the Mycenaean pottery found elsewhere, including in the Near East and central Mediterranean, has been shown by analysis to be from there. But potters in other regions did not follow the Argolid in all respects; they tended to limit their production to a few of the standard types, no doubt partly in response to customer demand, and when they innovated did so mostly in minor details. But in the fine plain and domestic wares, which make up far the greatest proportion of the pottery produced, there might be more scope for the preservation of traditional local types, especially in remoter provinces which 'became Mycenaean' late like Thessaly and the Cycladic islands (on which see Earle 2015: 382). Sometimes, as in the Pylos palace, strange decorated vessels may even appear, likely survivals of older local traditions.

Differences on this scale may not seem very significant, but when it comes to important parts of belief systems such as burial customs they deserve attention, since they could suggest different social structures and/or membership of different population groups. Thus, while chamber tombs are an extremely widespread form of burial in the Mycenaean world, there are areas where they were never popular, such as Thessaly, and they are hard to find in the Cycladic islands, but have been recognised on one or two. In the Dodecanese they are quite common but have distinctive features, being often used for single burials only, and show little evidence for the 'secondary burial' ritual well documented in the Argolid (Voutsaki 1993: especially ch. 9). Also, some of the Palace Period burials in the Dodecanese were cremations, exceptionally, no doubt under influence from Anatolia. On the mainland, one can perceive an insistence on continuing traditional local forms of tomb at Eleusis and Marathon in Attica, and a startling division within the putative territory of the Pylos state between central Messenia, where chamber tomb cemeteries were common, and western Messenia, where they have only been found at and near Pylos itself; elsewhere burials were made in groups of small stone-built tombs, often sunk in large mounds that may well derive from the local Middle Helladic tradition of burial tumuli. It is even possible to observe marked differences between different regions in the popularity of particular decorated vase shapes as grave-goods. If only more cemeteries were fully published – unfortunately, far too many have been excavated and only published in preliminary reports, if at all – further evidence of such local features would surely accumulate.

Another variation in local practice of potential significance concerns clay figurines, which are as standard Mycenaean items as the pottery. There continues to be debate over their precise purpose and meaning, but it is clear that they were important ritual items, which could be used as offerings at shrines and in graves, and to judge from their occurrences in settlement deposits could also play a role in household cult. They are notably common at Mycenae; Lisa French, the premier expert in figurines, has estimated that every basketful of pottery dug up at Mycenae contains six fragments on average. Yet at Nichoria, where Palace Period deposits were extensively investigated, a mere 122 fragments were recovered, and at Lefkandi, where admittedly most Mycenaean levels were Postpalatial, only 92. Also, they have barely been found in Rhodes before the

Postpalatial period. While in the case of pottery the rarity of types may simply reflect what local potters were ready to produce in quantity, the commonness or rarity of figurines (probably also made by potters) could reflect important differences in beliefs.

Since their purposes certainly included dedication at shrines, this introduces the topic of religion, an area where uniformity has been claimed. Given the sporadic nature of the references in Linear B material that clearly name gods, I do not believe it can be stated as certain or even probable that 'the same gods were worshipped throughout the Mycenaean world' (Kelder 2010: 115). On the contrary, I would suggest that, lacking religious texts, we know virtually nothing. We do not know what hierarchy was recognised among the gods, which the most important were, and which god(s) were honoured at the relatively few shrines and sacred places that have been identified. We do not even understand why the popular figurines, when human-shaped, were largely female, which led to theories of a presiding 'great goddess', as often suggested for Minoan religion, before the decipherment of Linear B showed that male gods were as prominent as female in Mycenaean religion.

The archaeological material can in fact be described as extraordinarily variable, to the extent that every time a new place of public worship is identified, it shows major differences from those already known. A case in point is the open-air site on Mt. Lykaion in Arcadia, which seems to have been maintained continually from at least the later Mycenaean period into Hellenistic times; in the historical period, it was a well-known sanctuary of Zeus.[4] Throughout, the specific form of animal sacrifice that involved burning part of the body on the altar (in this case, an 'ash altar' built up from previous sacrifices) was commonly practised, a rite which was central to historical Greek religion, as described from the Homeric poems onwards, but has only rarely been recognised at Mycenaean sites previously (cf. Hamilakis and Konsolaki 2004) and is not clearly referred to in the Linear B texts. It may be noted, however, that the animals sacrificed at Mt. Lykaion were mainly sheep and goats, rather than the cattle which are typical in historical times, and there is also plentiful evidence for the more usual practices of offering figurines and foodstuffs, presumably in pottery containers, and making libations. As I have already noted, there is a marked contrast between the extreme variability of the Mycenaean Palace Period material and the recognisable and recurrent patterns of religious practice in Crete at the same period, much of which derives from the Minoan civilisation, when Cretan religion clearly developed considerably.

7. Final comments

To sum up, the Mycenaean civilisation began in local variety, and even though its material culture had become superficially quite homogeneous by the Palace Period, there is still evidence for a sometimes surprising degree of local variability, which may reflect differences within the population of the mainland and Aegean islands that would have been important at the time. Although Mycenae was surely pre-eminent among the 'palace sites', and is much the most likely candidate to be capital of Aḫḫiyawa, there is little evidence to suggest that it ever controlled the others. In fact, the other obvious centres of power are sufficiently distant geographically for it to seem likely that Mycenae would have had great difficulty in controlling them, and since there is no evidence that Mycenae

4 See the Wikipedia entry on Mount Lykaion and http://lykaionexcavation.org; I am grateful to Prof. M. Voyatzis, co-director of the project, for much information.

had better armed, more disciplined, or overwhelmingly larger forces than the other major mainland centres, it might not enjoy consistent success in attempting to subjugate other centres. It seems worth pointing out that in historical times the regions where Linear B was in use have never been under the control of a single power, unless that was completely external and considerably superior in strength, like the Roman and Ottoman empires.

But these remarks do not apply to those parts of the Aegean region that 'became Mycenaean' in the Palace Period, the majority of the islands and part of the west Anatolian coast. These are notable for their lack of potential centres of power (apart from Miletus), as is particularly the case on Rhodes. This has sometimes been argued to have been the centre of Aḫḫiyawa, but no major citadel has been identified and none of the numerous cemeteries excavated has proved to be very rich. Here, the predominance of decorated pottery of Argive origin could be seen as a sign that Mycenae was extending its influence and control, to make itself the centre of Aḫḫiyawa, a power to be reckoned with by the west Anatolian kingdoms and eventually by the Hittite empire.

The basic problem that the Hittites evidently had with Aḫḫiyawa was that its power centre was far from the Anatolian coast, but it had interests more or less throughout the west Anatolian coastal region, from Wiluša in the north to the Lukka lands in the south, reflecting probably long-standing links with local kingdoms. This meant that there was always the possibility that, if the king of Aḫḫiyawa felt he had sufficient reason, he might support movements anywhere within western Anatolia to throw off Hittite control and cause serious problems, at a time when the Hittite king might wish to concentrate on Egypt or Assyria or was troubled by a relative's claim to the throne. Maybe, also, the Hittites were not entirely clear about the power and resources of the king of Aḫḫiyawa; and the indications from texts like the Tawagalawa letter that there could be some kind of special relationship between the Hittite and Aḫḫiyawan royal families should not be overlooked.

But it is going beyond my brief to discuss the Hittite material, so I will end with the comment that, while Mycenae probably did not have a dominant position on the Greek mainland, it could well have had extensive power and influence in the Aegean, and for this reason, and because they could not get at it easily, the Hittite kings found it advisable to deal with it diplomatically rather than, as seems to have been their customary manner, by force.

Bibliography

Adrimi-Sismani, V. 2007. 'Mycenaean Northern Borders Revisited: New Evidence from Thessaly', in M.L. Galaty and W.A. Parkinson (eds.), *Rethinking Mycenaean Palaces II*, Los Angeles.

Beckman, G.H., T.R. Bryce and E.H. Cline. 2011. *The Ahhiyawa Texts* (Writings from the Ancient World 28), Atlanta.

Bennet, J. 1997. 'Homer and the Bronze Age', in I. Morris and B. Powell (eds.), *A New Companion to Homer*, Leiden: 511-534.

Cline, E.H. (ed.) 2010. *The Oxford Handbook of the Bronze Age Aegean*, Oxford.

Dakouri-Hild, N. 2010. 'Thebes', in E.H. Cline (ed.), *The Oxford Handbook of the Bronze Age Aegean*, Oxford: 690-711.

Desborough, V.R.d'A. 1972. *The Greek Dark Ages*, London.

Dickinson O. 2014a. ‘How warlike were the Mycenaeans, in reality?’, in Y. Galanakis, T. Wilkinson and J. Bennet (eds.), *ΑΘΥΡΜΑΤΑ. Critical Essays on the Archaeology of the Eastern Mediterranean in Honour of E. Susan Sherratt*, Oxford: 67-72.

Dickinson O. 2014b. ‘The Mainland Bronze Age’, *Pharos* 20.1: 145-161.

Dickinson O. 2014c. ‘The Aegean’, in C. Renfrew and P. Bahn (eds.), *The Cambridge World Prehistory, Vol. 3,* Cambridge: 1860-1884.

Drews, R. 1988. *The Coming of the Greeks. Indo-European Conquests in the Aegean and the Near East,* Princeton.

Duhoux, Y. 2013. *Paradeigmata: Recueil d'Inscriptions Grecques Dialectales: Tome 1, Le mycénien* (Études anciennes 53), Paris.

Earle, J.W. 2015. ‘Mycenaeanization on Melos: a view from the Phylakopi pantries’, in Chr. Stampolidis, Ç. Maner, and K. Kopanias (eds.), *NOSTOI. Indigenous Culture, Migration and Integration in the Aegean Islands and Western Anatolia during the Late Bronze and Early Iron Age,* Istanbul: 369-386.

Eder, B. and R. Jung. 2015. “Unus pro omnibus, omnes pro uno’: the Mycenaean Palace System’, in J. Weilhartner and F. Ruppenstein (eds.), *Tradition and Innovation in the Mycenaean Palatial Polities,* Vienna: 113-140.

Feuer, B. 2011. ‘Being Mycenaean: A View from the Periphery’, *American Journal of Archaeology* 115: 507-536.

French, E. 2002. *MYCENAE. Agamemnon's Capital. The Site in its Setting,* Stroud.

Hamilakis, Y. and E. Konsolaki. 2004. ‘Pigs for the gods: burnt animal sacrifices as embodied rituals at a Mycenaean sanctuary’, *Oxford Journal of Archaeology* 23: 123-151.

Hope Simpson, R. and D.K. Hagel. 2006. *Mycenaean Fortifications, Highways, Dams and Canals,* Sävedalen.

Kardamaki, E. 2017. ‘The Late Helladic IIB to IIIA2 pottery sequence from the Mycenaean palace at Ayios Vasileios’, Archaeologia Austriaca 101: 73-142.

Kelder, J. 2010. *The Kingdom of Mycenae. A Great Kingdom in the Late Bronze Age Aegean,* Bethesda.

Kelder, J. 2012. ‘Ahhiyawa and the world of the Great Kings: a re-evaluation of Mycenaean political structures’, in A. Papadopoulos (ed.), *Recent Research and Perspectives in the Late Bronze Age Eastern Mediterranean,* Amsterdam (= *Talanta* 44): 41-52.

Maggidis, Chr. and A. Stamos. 2006. ‘Detecting Mycenae: Systematic Remote Sensing Survey in the ‘Lower City’ – Towards the Discovery of the Mycenaean Settlement Outside the Citadel’, in S. Campano and M. Forte (eds.), F*rom Space to Place: Proceedings of the 2nd International Workshop, CNR, Rome, Italy, December 4-7, 2006* (British Archaeological Reports International Series 1568), Oxford: 157-166.

Maran, J. 2017. ‘Tiryns: From the rise of its palace to the post-palatial resurgence’ (Ventris Lecture, Institute of Classical Studies, London 17/5/2017).

McDonald, W.A. and N.C. Wilkie (eds.). 1992. *Excavations at Nichoria in Southwest Greece Vol. II: The Bronze Age Occupation,* Minneapolis.

Melchert, H.C. [forthc.]. ‘Mycenaean and Hittite Diplomatic Correspondence: Fact and Fiction’, in A. Teffeteller (ed.), *Mycenaeans and Anatolians in the Late Bronze Age: the Aḫḫiyawa Question.*

Morris, I. 1997. 'Homer and the Iron Age', in I. Morris and B. Powell (eds.), *A New Companion to Homer*, Leiden: 535-559.

Nelson, M.C. 2007. 'Pylos, block masonry and monumental architecture in the Bronze Age Peloponnese', in J. Bretschneider, J. Driessen and K. van Lerberghe (eds.), *Power and Architecture: Monumental Public Architecture in the Bronze Age Near East and Aegean*, (Orientalia Lovaniensia Analecta), Leuven: 143-59.

Shelmerdine, C.W. (ed.) 2008. *The Cambridge Companion to the Aegean Bronze Age*, Cambridge.

Tartaron, T.F., L. Tzortzopoulou-Gregory, D.J. Pullen, A. Dill, R.K. Dunn, and J.I. Boyce. 2011. 'The Saronic Harbors Archaeological Research Project (SHARP). Investigations at Mycenaean Kalamianos, 2007-2009', *Hesperia* 80: 559-634.

Vermeule, E.B. 1964. *Greece in the Bronze Age*, Chicago.

Voutsaki, S. 1993. *Society and Culture in the Mycenaean World. An Analysis of Mortuary Practices in the Argolid, Thessaly and the Dodecanese* (Ph.D. thesis, Cambridge).

No kings, no inscriptions, no historical events? Some thoughts on the iconography of rulership in Mycenaean Greece

Fritz Blakolmer

1. Introduction

If one were to try to epitomise the Aegean Bronze Age to an Egyptologist by a catchy characterisation, one could say: imagine pharaonic Egypt, but without pyramids and other splendid tombs of rulers, without the great temples along the Nile, without public monuments bearing inscriptions carved in stone, without the information provided by the lists of dynasts and the books of the dead, and without the monumental propaganda of rulership by the Pharaohs! [1] Although such a striking characterisation of the Aegean civilisation certainly falls short, it is remarkable that the absence of these and further significant markers of dynastic empires is not due to our fragmentary knowledge of the monuments themselves, but basically applies to the cultural mechanisms of Minoan and Mycenaean societies and politics. Indeed, this is a highly precarious point of departure, when we approach the question of an iconography of rulership in this civilisation.

The character of the arts in the Aegean Bronze Age is *per se* an 'official' one in the sense that it is difficult to detect a non-official, private and thus individual iconography. We are also not able to distinguish any regional patterns of predilection of distinct pictorial subjects in the Aegean. These phenomena apply, on the one hand, to large-scale images of semi-public character such as mural-paintings in 'palaces' as well as in other élite mansions and, on the other hand, to minor arts. By the palatial periods of the Aegean, both categories shared a common 'palatial' iconography that essentially originated in Neopalatial Crete. In Late Palatial Crete (LM II-IIIA/B) as well as possibly during the entire development of the Late Helladic Greek mainland, Aegean iconography never achieved, or even intended, any abrupt change or shift entailing fundamental innovations; only minor, gradual developments can be detected (Shaw 1997: 484, 500f.; Blakolmer 2015a). These

1 I am grateful to Maria Anastasiadou, Artemis Karnava and Jörg Weilhartner for important advice and to Sarah Cormack for revising the language of this paper.

in: Kelder, J.M. and Waal, W.J.I. (eds) 2019: *From 'LUGAL.GAL' to 'Wanax'. Kingship and Political Organisation in the Late Bronze Age Aegean*, Sidestone Press (Leiden), pp. 49-94.

observations suggest that the artists as well as the patrons, including the Late Mycenaean kings (*wanaktes*) themselves, were forced to select their iconographic themes from a rather restricted thematic corpus of highly impersonal imagery.

In this study, I will focus upon the iconography of the Mycenaean palatial periods, although for this purpose it is indispensable to refer to the earlier Mycenaean periods and particularly to Minoan Crete as well. Three distinct phenomena of 'dynastic' modes of self-presentation, which were well-known in the neighbouring Near Eastern civilisations, constitute the point of departure of this analysis: the pictorial representation of rulers, the use of inscriptions and the depiction of historical events. In the subsequent analysis of the Mycenaean iconography of rulership we will focus on the pictorial programs themselves in order to approach an adequate understanding of the Mycenaean 'iconography of power'.

2. The missing king

In Egypt and other regions of the Near East the iconography of the ruler has a long tradition reaching back to the 3rd millennium,[2] be it the individual portrait or a generic image of a king.[3] In the first case, this was achieved by reproducing personal features of the distinct physical appearance of the face, the body or other unmistakable signs of singularity of a person. In the second case, we have to expect the image of a non-individual ruler characterised by a distinct head-gear, a typical garment, a sceptre and further insignia, his/her position as seated on a throne or standing in a chariot and, in particular, by an iconographic context which allows us to distinguish this figure from common members of the élite. In Mesopotamia, for example, the ruler was represented, in iconography as well as in inscriptions, essentially by the following four central roles: as a constructor, as hunting a lion, as a conqueror victorious against his enemies and as the recipient of tribute gifts (see, e.g., Muller 2005: 43). Finally, we might expect the depiction of a ruler on prestigious objects such as stone stelae and signet-rings or in the iconographic program of a mural decoration.

In contrast, in the Aegean Bronze Age, we can at first glance speak of the phenomenon of 'the missing ruler' in the sense that individual portraits and other forms of depicting any sovereign were broadly absent from Aegean iconography.[4] Even though, in recent years, fresh new studies have brought some new impetus into this discussion (see esp. N. Marinatos 2010: 14-26, 50-65; Whittaker 2015), one indeed gains the impression that the depiction of the ruler was a very neglected pictorial subject in Minoan and Mycenaean palatial civilisations.

2.1. Minoan Crete

Although the iconography of Minoan Crete appears slightly more prolific in examples of ruler images than Mycenaean imagery, this does not mean that there is any clear evidence to an extent and with a character comparable to that in the Near East. Instead, there only exist more images worthy of discussion in Neopalatial Crete than in Mycenaean Greece (cf. E. Davis 1995). In Minoan iconography human figures generally possess an anonymous,

---

2 Winter 1986; Assmann 1996; Heinz 2002: 80-91; Bonatz 2007.

3 See in general Gauer 1968; Metzler 1971 and Jaeggi 2008.

4 See the discussions in E. Davis 1995; Rehak 1995, esp. 113-7; Shelmerdine 1999; Blakolmer 2007: 214-5; Greco 2014, esp. 305-7 and Whittaker 2015.

almost 'faceless' character mainly guided by uniformity with no physiognomic individualisation ever being intended. Even the so-called 'portrait gems' hardly reflect real individual portraits.[5] Human heads could well be marked by a distinct hair-style, a beard or headgear as belonging to a special group within society. However, in no single case can we recognise any specific physical characteristics which might indicate the portrait of a concrete individual.

Although, recently, it has been claimed that no king or queen was depicted in Aegean seal glyptic (Crowley 2013: 350-1), in a series of Minoan seal images, several of them found at Mycenaean mainland sites and partly in later contexts, we can indeed identify a ruler iconography in Neopalatial Crete. These mostly present the ruler as an unspecified, anonymous man depicted in distinct activities. A symbolic scene of investiture is probably depicted on seal-impressions of the 'Mother of the Mountain' ring from Knossos (Fig. 1) which show a goddess in the centre holding a sceptre in her outstretched arm (*CMS* II 8, no. 256). As this 'commanding gesture' is directed to an adoring male which corresponds with the palatial building at the opposite side of the seal image, this could well be interpreted as the encounter of a ruler with a goddess and his reception of divine power (N. Marinatos 1995: 46; 2010: 83-4).[6] The so-called 'Runner's Ring' from Kato Symi (Lebessi et al., 2004, see Fig. 2) may reflect the demonstration of physical strength of the Minoan ruler as this was the case also in the investiture ritual of the Egyptian Pharaoh (Blakolmer and Hein 2018). A series of Neopalatial seal images can be tentatively reconstructed as what the author has named a 'Special procession' which may be part of a ritual of inauguration of a political leader (Blakolmer 2016; 2018a; forthc. a; Blakolmer and Hein 2018). Amongst them are included the motif of a signet-ring which possibly shows a Minoan ruler in a fringed cloak proceeded by another man transporting a sceptre-like *insignium* (*CMS* II 6, no. 11, see fig. 3); it is perhaps no coincidence that this constitutes the most frequently attested seal impression of Minoan Crete so far. A seal-image from Kato Zakros (Fig. 4) can hardly be interpreted as other than depicting a proskynesis scene, i.e. the veneration of a ruler surrounded by dignitaries.[7] On the Minoan signet-ring from the 'Tiryns treasure' a procession of four Minoan genii approaches an enthroned male figure who holds a LM I chalice (Fig. 5) – an image that exhibits several details typical of royal presentation scenes in Near Eastern iconography (*CMS* I, no. 179; Rehak 1995: 107-8; Dubcová 2016: 265).

These and other seal images demonstrate that we indeed encounter an imagery of rulership in LM I Crete, namely in an abstract, over-individual manner which reflects a kind of divine kingship and, obviously, served to reinforce a hierarchy of dominance.[8] Most of these seal images were inspired by Near Eastern iconographic models and they reflect nearly universal codes of expressing power and authority. Although one could object that these and further seal motifs from Neopalatial Crete merely constitute isolated examples and hardly any of them possesses successors in the iconography of the Mycenaean palatial periods, this impression may be deceiving, as will be shown below. Additional examples are provided by the iconographic motifs of the so-called 'Knossos replica rings' which clearly underline that the thematic spectrum of Minoan images of

5 Biesantz 1958; Pini 1999; Younger 1995: 165-8, pls. LVII – LIX; Foster 1997.

6 See furthermore Krattenmaker 1995a: 50-1, 57-8; Drappier and Langohr 2004: 36-8; Boulotis 2008: 52.

7 *CMS* II 7, no. 3; N. Marinatos 2007; 2010: 182-4.

8 See also N. Marinatos 2010: 14-26, 50-65; Drappier and Langohr 2004: esp. 28-9; Dubcová 2009.

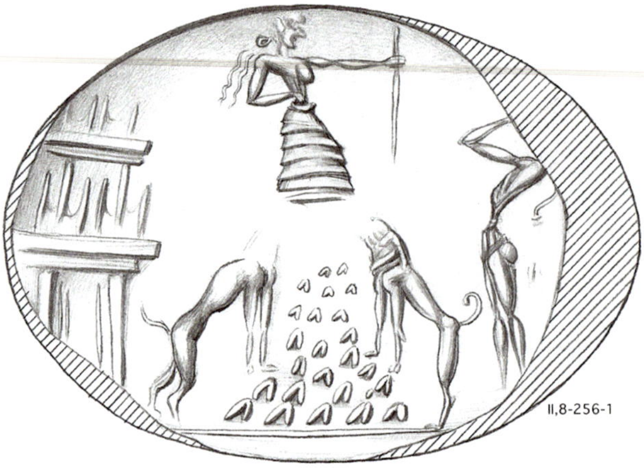

Fig. 1: Seal image of the ‚Mother of the Mountain' from Knossos (after *CMS* II8, no. 256).

Fig. 2: 'Runner's Ring' from Kato Symi (after Lebessi et al. 2004, pl. 2).

Fig. 3: Seal image from Ayia Triada (after *CMS* II6, no. 11).

authority in fact exhibited typical traits of a 'ruler imagery' reflecting the deeds of glorified, anonymous male humans in fighting, hunting and agonistic activities such as bull-leaping.[9] Furthermore, insignia of power and sovereignty are well attested in Minoan Crete, most of them stimulated by the Near East: as has often been convincingly demonstrated, attributes such as a staff or a sceptre, the fenestrated axe of Syrian type, a special headgear, distinct

9 See esp. Betts 1967; Hallager 1996: 205-24; Schoep 1999; Goren and Panagiotopoulos 2009; Weingarten 2010.

Fig. 4: Seal image from Kato Zakros (after *CMS* II7, no. 3).

Fig. 5: Signet-ring from Tiryns (after *CMS* I, no. 179).

forms of dress and further elements might constitute insignia of Minoan rulership.[10] Therefore, when J. Driessen concluded in 1988: 'Either the ruler iconography does exist, but we have failed to recognize it as such [...], or it was not a habit to depict actually living people' (Driessen 1988: 121), both assumptions seem to be valid for Minoan Crete. On the one hand, several iconographic motifs which can hardly be interpreted other than as ruler images certainly exist. On the other hand, these examples are remarkably few in number and, even more strikingly: we search in vain for the depiction of any individual ruler. Thus, K. Krattenmaker and others have spoken, with good reason, of an 'iconography of legitimacy' in Minoan Crete, instead of 'ruler images'.[11]

2.2. The Mycenaean mainland

When searching for the depiction of a ruler, in a broader sense, on the Mycenaean mainland, one might be tempted to start with the metal masks from the Shaft Graves at Mycenae (Kopcke 1976).[12] However, in hardly any example do the variable and indistinct facial features permit us to understand these human faces as the reflection of an individual

10 See esp. Otto 1987; 2000; Drappier and Langohr 2004: 26-7, 34-8; Boulotis 2008: 50-3; Dubcová 2009; Buchholz (ed.) 2012; Blakolmer and Dubcová [forthc.].

11 Krattenmaker 1995a, see also Drappier and Langohr 2004: 37 ('iconographie de la légitimité') and Boulotis 2008: 52.

12 Cf. further Dickinson 2005; Hristova 2012: 417-22.

portrait. At least the majority of them appear as a compilation of all essential components of the human face without creating any concretising portrait of the deceased (see esp. Kopcke 1976). More fruitful for our query are the Shaft Grave stelae from Mycenae.[13] At least five of them show, in variable versions, a warrior standing in his chariot and fighting a foot soldier (Fig. 6). These motifs may have been adapted from Near Eastern models for the specific necessities of the 'dynasties' of the Shaft Grave warrior-chiefs at Mycenae. In this sepulchral context, the iconographic motifs of the warrior in a chariot suggest an interpretation of the rulers buried in these tombs. Thus, these public images on the stelae erected atop several Shaft Graves obviously reflect an ideal vision of military strength, a rhetorical statement of the victorious ruler and, on other stelae, possibly also of the successful hunter. Nothing in these images points to a legendary battle of historical character or even to a divine status of these warrior-chiefs. Additionally, the diverse spiral ornaments and some Minoan pictorial elements on these stelae may have expressed the affiliation to the palatial realm of Minoan Crete.[14]

Instead of interpreting the male figures in the chariot in the pictorial pottery of LH IIIA-B as a *wanax*, the central authority of a Mycenaean palace state, we should rather speak of members of the palatial élite, in a more general sense (Rystedt 1999: 94-6; Karageorghis 1959). When a hunter in a chariot and in association with a dog is depicted as belonging to the élite, such as on a LH IIIB ivory plaque from Thebes (Fig. 7),[15] we can describe him only as an unspecific male who is scarcely distinguishable from the chariot-driver positioned beside him. When we adduce the 'commanding gesture' – according to the Minoan pictorial formula (Figs. 1 and 17) – as a criterion for the depiction of a ruler (or a deity), two examples come into consideration, both found on the Mycenaean Cyclades. The first example, the warrior on an ivory relief plate from Delos (Fig. 8)[16] signifies more than a simple statement of status and power, probably a Cypro-Mycenaean origin has to be attributed to this piece.[17] The second example is a cushion-seal from the LH IIIC necropolis of Aplomata on Naxos which shows a man holding a spear in front of ritual equipment and a palm tree; this seal probably constitutes an heirloom from Minoan Crete.[18]

Similar to Neopalatial Crete, the iconography of the mural paintings in Mycenaean palaces delivers little unequivocal evidence of the depiction of a Mycenaean king. Among the fresco fragments from the LH IIIB battle-frieze in the throne-room of Mycenae[19] one figure with Mycenaean outfit depicted in front of Aegean style architecture (Fig. 9) stands out because of his size: he is larger than all other warriors preserved on the fragments of this frieze, and thus he constitutes the 'exception to the Aegean rule of anonymity' (Chapin 2016a: 464). A substantial problem in identifying this figure as the *wanax* of Mycenae, though, results from the fact that he is depicted as falling. Therefore, he most probably belongs to the 'others', that is, the adversaries of the postulated armed forces of Mycenae.

---

13 Heurtley 1921-23; S. Marinatos 1968; Mylonas 1951; Younger 1997.

14 Evans 1928: 195-202, figs. 105-10B; Heurtley 1921-23: esp. 144-5; Vermeule 1975: 6, 16, 32.

15 Aravantinos 2000: 55-60, figs. 15, 20-1; 1996: 187-9, fig. 5 bottom.

16 Poursat 1977: 157, 160, pl. XIV,1; Tournavitou 1995: 491-2, 527; Hiller 2011: 140.

17 See Poursat 1977: 163; Krzyszkowska 1991:116 with n. 40; Tournavitou 1995: esp. 527; P. Rehak and J.G. Younger 1998: 251-2.

18 *CMS* V, no. 608. For its dating to LM IIIA, see Dionisio, Jasink and Weingarten 2014: 220, cat. no. 200.

19 Rodenwaldt 1911: 231-48, pls. X – XII; Rodenwaldt 1921: 21-45; Lamb 1921-23: 249-55, pls. XLII – XLIII; Immerwahr 1990: 123-5, 192 (My no. 11); Vonhoff 2008: 49-58, 287-90, cat. nos. 58-80.

Fig. 6: Stele from Shaft Grave IV at Mycenae (after Evans 1935, fig. 190 facing p. 255).

Fig. 7: Ivory plaque from Thebes (after Aravantinos 2000: 99, fig. 21).

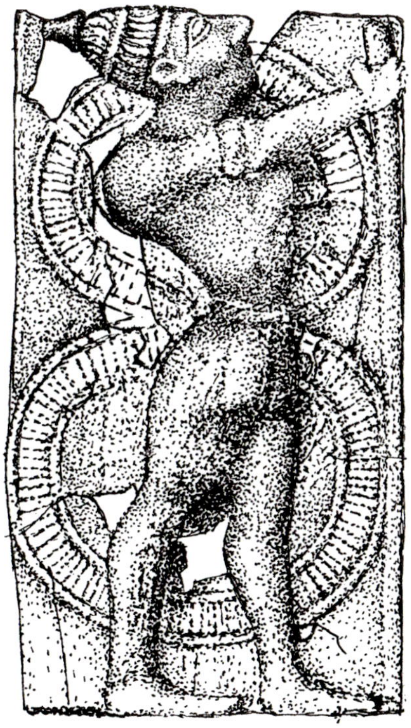

Fig. 8: Ivory relief plate from Delos (after Buchholz and Wiesner 1977: 8, fig. 2).

Fig. 9: Fallen warrior from the *megaron* frieze at Mycenae (after Rodenwaldt 1921, col. pl. after p. 30).

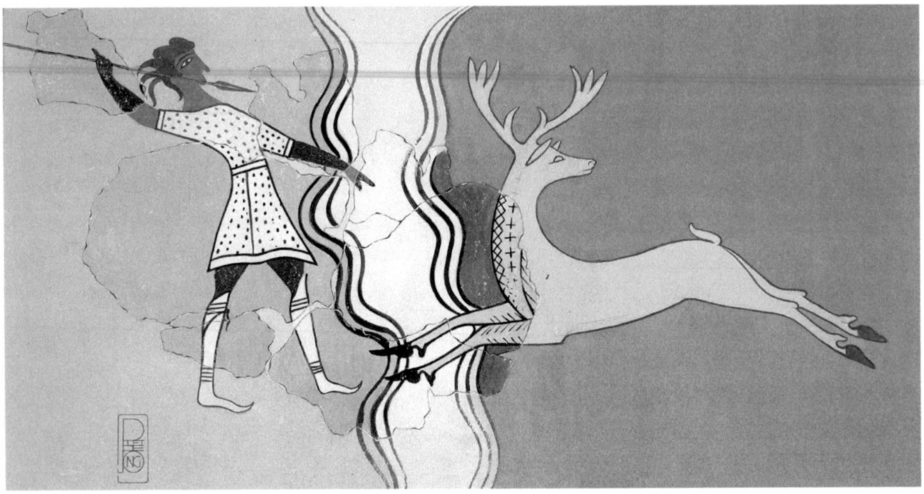

Fig. 10: Fresco fragment with hunting scene from Pylos (after Lang 1969, pl. 121 [16 H 43]).

Although one could speculate that this is the depiction of a prominent duel of the *wanax* of Mycenae against an adversary, both being distinguished by their larger scale,[20] such a scenario would be unparalleled in the Aegean. As far as can be assessed by the preserved mural fragments of hunting scenes, the main hunter killing a boar or a stag (Fig. 10) remains indistinct and is not marked by any special insignia as a ruler.[21]

Nevertheless, M. Cultraro has expressed a positive view concerning a ruler depicted in palatial mural scenes (Cultraro 2000; Otto 2011; Dubcová 2009: 22). By analysing the mural paintings of the throne-room at Pylos (Fig. 15), he defined the lyre-player as the king himself, being the only human figure which is clearly highlighted by his larger size.[22] From his seated position on a rock, his distinctive garment and the fact that he holds a lyre, Cultraro concludes that this figure, as well as the one wearing a similar dress in front of the large-scale bull in the procession scene of the vestibule, represent the *wanax* who presides over the banquet and in his sacerdotal function in a supposed investiture ceremony (Cultraro 2000: esp. 12-26). This interpretation, however, cannot be supported by any parallels and remains doubtful.

In the iconography of the Mycenaean palatial periods, in no single example can any individual figure be convincingly defined as a *wanax*. Although, on the Shaft Grave stelae, we can observe images of the warrior-chiefs, at least in a very general, non-individualised manner, in the subsequent Mycenaean periods we are not able to discern any individual portraiture, and no glorification of any figure who is clearly marked as the sovereign can be singled out. Although one could argue that in Mycenaean mural paintings depicting scenes of war and hunt, the image of a ruler is missing due to the fragmentary state of preservation of the painted plaster fragments, it must be stressed that the depiction of a ruler is absent in all other iconographic media as well. Obviously, in contrast to most Near

20 Cf. the reconstruction in Lurz 1994: 78, fig. 26.

21 See in general Morris 1990; Cultraro 2004; Vonhoff 2011.

22 For the throne-room of the palace at Pylos and its mural program, see Blegen 1956: 95, pl. 40,2; Blegen and Rawson 1966: 76-92; Lang 1969: 180, 194-6, pls. 53, 111, 134, 136; McCallum 1987: 108-41; Immerwahr 1990: 133-7, 199 (Py no. 18).

Eastern rulers, the Mycenaean *wanax* did not explicitly define his hierarchical position in the interplay of dominance and integration in the society by means of iconography (cf. Heinz 2002: 84-5). Only in the case of the Shaft Grave stelae the following line in a Sumerian epic comes to mind: 'May the people look at me admiringly!'[23] In the Late Mycenaean periods, however, ideological messages communicated by imagery made no use of the sovereign himself.

It is obvious that, in Mycenaean palatial iconography, the *wanax* functioned as the 'author' of the images, but in no single case was he the subject of the depiction (cf. Winter 1981: 2). Based on the pairs of griffins (and lions respectively) flanking the throne in the mural paintings of the throne-rooms at LM I-II Knossos and LH IIIB Pylos (Fig. 12), J. Bennet (2007: 12-5; 2015: 29-30) argued that the ruler was not represented because when he took his place on the throne, in fact, he was physically present (see also Greco 2014: 331-2). 'There is no need, then, to look for the Mycenaean *wanax* in these frescoes, since the room decoration served as the backdrop – the stage set – for its star, the enthroned king himself' (Chapin 2016a: 465). Thus, Bennet explained the absence of the *wanax* in the iconography of the throne-room and in procession scenes at Pylos by the existence of a 'first person iconography' in contrast to a 'third person' representation of the ruler, in other words: a 'participatory' or 'inclusive' representation in contrast to a 'panoptic' representation (Bennet 2015: 30-1). Nonetheless, one might ask whether the Aegean understanding of imagery, in fact, was so fundamentally different from that in all other civilisations of the Eastern Mediterranean. Are we really confronted with a basically incomplete iconography in Aegean images, also the small-scale ones?

Additionally, the great majority of Aegean mural paintings reflect scenery in an outdoor setting[24] and, therefore, they were perceived as 'images' in the proper sense. Bennet's concept doubtlessly applies to the eastern wall of the throne-room of Pylos and to that in the palace of Knossos, which show 'creatures of power' flanking and protecting the throne and, thus, the real (or imagined) person seated on it – comparable to the colossal statues of fantastic creatures guarding the entrances to the citadels in the Near East. However, this model of 'the *live icon* of the ruler seated on the throne' (Greco 2014: 332) is hardly appropriate to explain the absence of any *wanax*, his wife and his entourage of noble-men from other mural images, and those in additional rooms of these and other palaces and mansions, unless one postulates that the palatial mural iconography of Mycenaean Greece was addressed, in its entirety, exclusively to one person, the *wanax* of the respective palatial region.[25] Moreover, in other artistic media, such as seals and ivory relief plaques on portable objects, the absence of any ruler and additional aspects of a propagandistic iconography certainly cannot be explained by the general assumption of a 'first person iconography'. Instead of presuming such a basically different Mycenaean approach to the imagery *per se*, one instead gets the impression that the depiction of the ruler – as an individual as well as the holder of this office – was deliberately avoided for ideological reasons. The answer therefore has to be sought elsewhere.

---

23 Quoted after Winter 1996: 20.

24 For this important point, see Shank 2008: 101; Blakolmer 2014: 121-4.

25 Cf. also the criticism by Thaler 2015: 351.

3. The missing inscriptions

Other elements of dynastic behaviour may include inscriptions complementing or explaining what is depicted in the image and related textual means, comparable to the addition of the inscribed name of a ruler in a cartouche. This phenomenon, well-known in the ancient Near East, is doubtless connected with additional questions of literacy, such as that of the existence of public inscriptions of official character, i.e. monumental texts presenting the *res gestae* of a ruler or the codification of laws cut in stone and erected in a public place (Baines 1989; Winter 1998; Thomas 1995). The 'standard inscription' in the throne-room of the Northwest Palace of Aššurnaṣirpal II at Nimrud constitutes a remarkable, yet not untypical, example. These repetitive texts were carved upon every block of the relief images and praised the king by his four royal attributes: as 'attentive prince', 'keeper of the gods', 'fierce predator' and 'hero in battle' (Winter 1998: 67). The exact meaning of the dynastic inscriptions and the question of who was able to read and to understand these texts is of secondary relevance here.[26] Of major importance, however, is the fact that literacy itself was used (or not) as a supplementary medium for transmitting messages in a manner comparable to, or completing an iconographic scene.

3.1. Minoan Crete

In Minoan Crete only a few examples of a kind of 'monumental inscription' chiselled in stone can be cited, such as an ashlar block with three Linear A signs from the north-west court of the palace at Malia.[27] A large-scale block at the north-west corner of the palace at Knossos shows an enigmatic linear design which has been connected with script.[28] The fragment of another stone block from Knossos – possibly of an unusual five-sided form – exhibits three signs of Linear A (or Linear B?) script and was tentatively interpreted as belonging to a LM IA sepulchral monument (Hood 1997: esp. 115-6). At the entrance to the chamber of the tholos tomb of Kephala at Knossos an ashlar block bears two signs of Linear A or Linear B script and its chronological attributions vary from MM III until LM IIIA (Hutchinson 1956: 76-7, pl. 10b; Preston 2005: 62, fig. 2; p. 73, fig. 8). Although, in this case, the reuse of an older Neopalatial block cannot be ruled out, its assignment to a LM II sepulchral context has recently been favoured (Preston 2005: 83-6).

On several wall plaster fragments from Knossos and Ayia Triada engraved or painted signs of Linear A script are preserved,[29] among them an engraved sign which was part of a Knossian mural composition depicting plants (Cameron 1968b).[30] Although, in these examples, a speculative interpretation as captions of the images could be considered, only in the case of a plaster fragment from the 'Area of the Taureador Frescoes' bearing a singular Linear B (?) sign, accurately painted parallel to a border band, might one think of a real inscription of deeper meaning.[31] While seals were a common medium bearing inscriptions in the Cretan Hieroglyphic script during the Middle Minoan period, by the

26 On literacy in the Aegean Bronze Age, see Palaima 1987; Michailidou 2000-1; Whittaker 2005.

27 Godart 1973; Olivier 1980: 224 no. 301; Faure 1996: 134-5.

28 Evans 1921: 132, fig. 98; Boulotis 1986: 10-1, figs. 3a – b; Faure 1996: 134, pls. XII – XV.

29 Evans 1921: 636-7, figs. 473a – b; 1928: 440-3, figs. 257-9; Cameron 1965a, 1968a and 1968b. See furthermore Cameron 1965b. For the inscriptions on plaster fragments from Ayia Triada, see also Godart and Olivier 1982: 130-5 (HT Zd 155-7).

30 This sign does not belong to any Aegean script. For this mural painting, see Morgan 2005a: 42, pl. 3,2.

31 Evans 1921: 637; Cameron 1965a: 12-5, pl. 10; Palaima 1981.

LM I period Linear A signs occur extremely rarely on seals.[32] This indicates a restriction of the literality in this medium (cf. Schoep 1999: 119-20). In the Late Minoan seals and signet-rings no script at all was used for supplementing an iconographic scene. Even though the 'floating objects' which occur in ritual scenes on Minoan signet-rings no doubt possess a distinct meaning, they certainly do not constitute signs of script in the narrow sense (see esp. Kyriakidis 2005: esp. 147-8).

Although the social and symbolic meanings of the Linear A script were significantly enlarged by the Neopalatial period, as is reflected by inscribed libation tables and further precious objects of ritual and votive character (Whittaker 2005; B. Davis 2014), its general employment remains limited. An example worth mentioning in this context is the lower part of a female terracotta statuette from Poros showing a painted Linear A inscription: A-SA-SA-RA (Dimopoulou et al. 1993). This votive statuette derives from a ritual LM IIIA1-2 context and can be typologically dated to LM II-IIIA. That this example of a Minoan inscribed figurine was not a unique case is demonstrated by a male clay figurine from LM I Tylissos with three Linear A signs symbolically engraved upon its schematic body.[33] On the bronze figurine of a bull from Ayia Triada two signs of script were engraved on a small gold disc on its forehead (Kanta and Perna 2011). This is part of an inscription of Linear A or B, which probably originally consisted of four signs and conformed to the votive character of this miniature figurine. Finally, in the northern part of the central court of the palace at Knossos, in front of the throne-room area, A. Evans found the lower part of an Egyptian stone statuette of User, ca. 20 cm in height with an incised funerary inscription on the 'throne'.[34] This archaeological evidence is of great significance for our question, as it clearly indicates that – despite the clear knowledge of statuettes with inscriptions carved in stone coming from Egypt and even their presence at Knossos – the Minoan rulers categorically did not make any use of this medium for official propaganda.

3.2. Mycenaean mainland

In Mycenaean Greece, writing was much more restricted to utilitarian bureaucratic purposes than in Minoan Crete. It is obvious that the occasional social and symbolic meaning of the Linear A script in Neopalatial Crete was not adopted into Linear B (see, e.g., Whittaker 2005: 29). On a stone beam atop the entrance to the tholos tomb of Kazanaki in Volos a repetition of seven times the same sign (possibly attributable to the Linear B script) was engraved; this can hardly be interpreted as an inscription in the narrow sense.[35] Although the character of an inscription has been attributed to several signs on the surfaces of Mycenaean stone blocks from Argos, Mycenae and Malthi, none of these interpretations appears conclusive.[36] As far as can be judged, no Linear B sign on any mural plaster fragment has ever been reported from the Mycenaean mainland. The painted Linear B inscription (*pi-ra-ki*) on the border fragment of a LH IIIB deep bowl with dotted rim from Mycenae possibly denotes the name of the donor or of a deity (Iakovidis 1986: 240, pl. 20b; Pliatsika 2015: 608-9, fig. 13) and constitutes one of the few examples of

32 *CMS* II2, no. 213b; II3, no. 38; XI, no. 311b; Krzyszkowska 2005: 127; Crowley 2013: 296; Olivier 1999: 422-6 (ARM Zg 1, CR (?) Zg 3, KN Zg 55). See most recently Perna 2014: esp. 256-8.

33 Hazzidakis 1921: 71-3, fig. 37, no. 17; Olivier 1981; Hooker 1992: 105.

34 Gill and Padgham 2005; Phillips 2008: 92-4, cat. no. 158, fig. on p. 320; Aruz 2008: 126-7.

35 Adrimi-Sismani and Alexandrou 2001-4, 2006 (2009): 133.

36 See, e.g., Protonotariou-Deilaki 1990a: 81-2, figs. 27-8, 1990b: 88 with n. 29; Valmin 1953: 41-3, pl. III.

an inscription on a clay vessel (except for the stirrup-jars).[37] Thus, it goes without saying that in the palatial imagery we should not expect any addition of the personal name of a Mycenaean *wanax*, such as the name *e-ke-ra$_2$-wo* (Echelaos), which perhaps can be attributed to the king in the last palace of Pylos.[38]

3.3. Summary

A consequence of the above is that neither in Minoan Crete nor on the Mycenaean mainland any clear evidence of the use of script for propagandistic royal purposes exists. This applies to monumental inscriptions of public character as well as to inscribed texts or names in iconographic scenes. While in the iconography of the ancient Near East inscriptions were used for both accompanying and parallelising the images as well as celebrating the deeds of a king without any direct relation to the image itself (cf. Winter 1981: 25), the rulers of the Aegean Bronze Age categorically neglected the combination of image and script. It might even be assumed that the Linear scripts of the Aegean Bronze Age excluded the function of recording information of 'historical' character.[39] In light of the information provided by the Linear B tablets, A. Farnoux (1995: 232) aptly concluded that 'on peut parfaitement connaître les noms des vaches qui passent dans un royaume et ignorer ceux des rois qui y règnent'.

As a sort of substitute for public inscriptions, two alternative strategies of dynastic communication have been proposed for the Aegean Bronze Age: firstly, that of a basically non-literate culture in which public affairs such as the glorification of the ruler were communicated by oral transmission via rhapsodes to the community (Jasink 2005: esp. 64-6; Greco 2014: esp. 308-33), and secondly, by the realm of visual symbols and imagery (Jasink 2005: 66-7; Hiller 1995). Although it has been suggested that in the Aegean this role was fulfilled by images, emblems, rituals and performances (Bennet 2004, 2015: 31; Greco 2014: 308), this was certainly the case in the Near East as well, and this despite the very existence of epigraphs in images there. Given the absence of any inscription complementing images such as, later on, in the Neo-Assyrian palace of Aššurnaṣirpal II mentioned above, in the palaces of the Aegean Bronze Age one could spontaneously draw the following conclusion: either there existed no kings with a similarly high authority in the Aegean, or other qualities were attributed to them than those of Near Eastern potentates. If both assumptions fail, though, the reason for this obvious absence could be the particular character and use of script in the Aegean.

4. The missing historical events

Irrespective of the methodological differentiation between the depiction of a contemporary event or of an event of the historical past, it is beyond doubt that in Near Eastern civilisations narrative images of historical content, identifiable by inscriptions, constituted an important propagandistic vehicle for commemorating the ruler at a significant event in visualised form. This may be achieved by depicting a particular event of political

37 See furthermore Palaima 1987: 502-3.

38 See Lindgren 1973: 153-5, Leukart 1992: 404-5; Palaima 1995: 129-35; Deger-Jalkotzy 1996: esp. 16-7.

39 See Duhoux 2000; Facchetti 2002; Jasink 2005. See furthermore Driessen 2000: 186-7.

character, a unique official state affair, a specific war or the like, that is, a unique event that cannot be repeated.[40]

Due to the absence of individual or generic portraits as well as the deficiency of inscriptions in Aegean images, as discussed above, our interpretation of the historical character of an image is *a priori* restricted to the iconography itself. When searching for images of historical character in the Aegean, we should avoid the mistake of prematurely deducing the character of a distinct battle at a distinct place and at a distinct time, from the depiction of a non-specific town, arbitrary landscape elements, ships on the sea and formula-like warrior scenes. If we wish to argue in favour of, for example, the depiction of a historical battle, we have to expect some individual narrative features, such as a distinct location, warriors of individual identity or ethnicity and other specific elements which could point to a particular war-like event (Blakolmer 2007).

A good illustration of our methodological problems in detecting a historical image in Aegean art are the warlike scenes depicted on the 'Siege rhyton' from Shaft Grave IV at Mycenae (Fig. 11).[41] In early research, the iconography of this silver vessel, probably of Minoan origin, was categorised as the illustration of 'some critical episode of Minoan colonial history' (Evans 1930: 106) and thus as '*a* historic piece in the modern sense' (Evans 1930: 89)[42] as reflecting the heroic deeds of the tomb owner (Stais 1915: esp. 51) and as 'the first historical representation in European art' (Meyer 1928: 233). At a later stage, the indistinct character of the pictorial elements on the 'Siege rhyton' became apparent and, with good reason, more general interpretations were favoured: 'a generalized tradition of battle imagery, which may be attached to different historical events through succeeding generations' (Vermeule 1964: 102) and 'quintessential distillations of all the great sieges' (Vermeule 1975: 42).[43] Given our actual knowledge of battle scenes in the Aegean Bronze Age, we should favour the viewpoint of P. Militello who characterised the combatants depicted in images such as this as 'anonymous and collective, devoid of heroes and protagonists' (Militello 2003: 384). There is no indication that these sea and inland battle scenes exhibited any clear focus of the action, any unmistakable definition of the identity and ethnicity of the groups of combatants, any individualised warriors or even a ruler and any depiction of a distinct town and its territory. Even in Egyptian iconography, battle scenes should by no means automatically be understood as historical representations; even these could (also) have possessed a predominant magical-mythical aspect.[44]

The ongoing discussion of the iconography of the mural paintings from the 'West House' at Akrotiri enables a better understanding of individuality and historicity which were of negligible importance in Minoan art (Morgan 1988: 88-92, 155-65; Blakolmer 2007: 215-7). Nevertheless, in the south frieze the topographic details of both settlements are presented in such an individual manner that it is difficult to interpret them as anything other than the reproduction of distinct places, most probably on the island of Thera itself. Beyond that, however, we are not able to define any individual features which might allow us to speak of the deliberate pictorial reproduction of a concrete event at a distinct time. Additionally, although abundant evidence exists of depictions of architectural complexes

40 Smith 1965: 147-79; Kantor 1957; Groenewegen-Frankfort 1951; Moscati 1963; Winter 1981, esp. 2-3.

41 See Evans 1930: 89-106, figs. 50-2, 54-6; Hooker 1967; Sakellariou 1975.

42 See also Evans 1930: 98-9; Rodenwaldt 1912: 203, n. 2; 1921: 51.

43 See also Hooker 1967: 271 and Döhl 1980.

44 Cf. Groenewegen-Frankfort 1951: 116; R. Schulz 2002: esp. 41. See in general Heinz 2001.

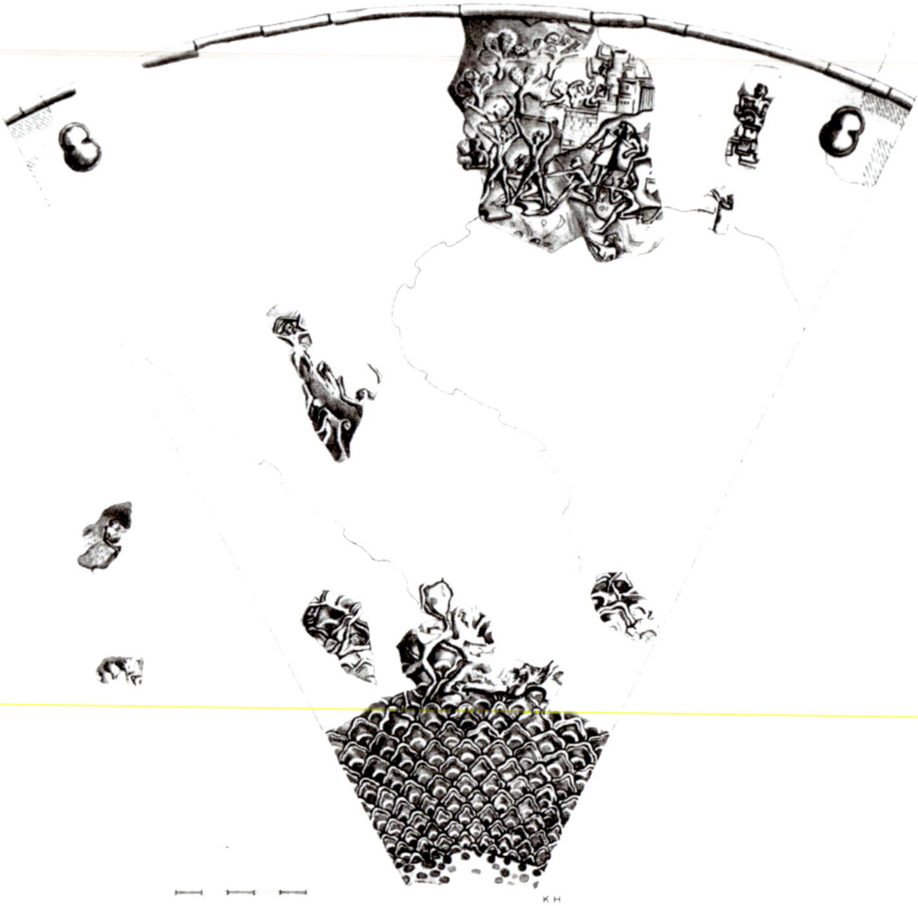

Fig. 11: 'Siege rhyton' from Shaft Grave IV at Mycenae (after Sakellariou 1975: 196, fig. 1).

in Minoan art, they mostly seem to represent variable types of palatial as well as non-palatial architecture rather than individual buildings at distinct places.[45] We should therefore agree with the statement by N. Marinatos (1984a: 119) that 'historical events are absent from Theran and Minoan art and [...] political history was insignificant'.

4.1. Mycenaean iconography: generic or specific?

When considering the problem of defining historical events in Mycenaean iconography, we may ask: did battle and hunting scenes reflect particular war scenes and unique events of royal hunt worth remembering? As far as can be judged, at least the majority of the examples appear broadly indistinctive and of a generic character. The extensive, although poorly preserved mural friezes with battle scenes from the *megaron* at Mycenae,[46] from

45 See in general Boulotis 1990; Krattenmaker 1995b; Nörling 1995; Pavúk 2002: 567-83.

46 See n. 19 above.

Hall 64 of the palace at Pylos[47] and possibly further examples from Orchomenos and Ayios Vasileios[48] could well be the outcome of the introduction of a new pictorial genre, one that can be defined as specifically Mycenaean.[49]

However, the question arises: was the message sent by the Late Mycenaean kings really different from that of earlier Minoan battle images? As demonstrated above, no representation of a current ruler (or his ancestors) going into battle or being glorified as victorious commander-in-chief can be observed in Mycenaean mural images. Landscape elements were reduced to a minimum and the architecture of the settlements depicted in these friezes does not permit us to deduce any intended definition of individual places.

Combatants of contrasting ethnicity can until now only be detected in the battle frieze from Hall 64 in the LH IIIB palace of Pylos, which shows soldiers in Mycenaean outfit fighting men clad in animal-skin.[50] This led J. Bennet and J. Davis to the interpretation of a historical image depicting a military confrontation of the palatial state of Pylos against its non-Mycenaean enemies in the course of the territorial expansion to eastern Messenia during LH IIIA, i.e. the depiction of a historical event in the past.[51] Although this reading of the Pylian image correlates with – and was deduced from – our actual understanding of the historical development of the kingdom of Pylos, it does not constitute more than an attractive hypothesis built on the basis of an otherwise largely indistinct iconography. Given the widespread absence of any individualising iconographic means, with the exception of the group of skin-clad and non-helmeted warriors, the interpretation as a commemorative reflection of a real territorial expansion and the integration of neighbouring regions into their own empire, as argued by Davis and Bennet, remains at least a seductive model. In all other examples of Mycenaean warlike images, though, nothing permits us to propose any interpretation that a *wanax* celebrated a historical victory in a specific battle against distinct enemies. As the battle frieze from Pylos also includes a naval scene, this image may well point to the military power of the *wanax* encompassing both the sea off the coast of Messenia as well as the hinterland;[52] if so, this message was transmitted in a remarkably symbolic and only superficially suggestive manner. As a consequence, the more cautious interpretation by A. Chapin, saying that Late Mycenaean battle friezes reflect 'an official ideology of military aggression and victory through the mythic illumination of their own heroic past', may better conform to the widely generic character of these images (Chapin 2016a: 465).[53]

The vast absence of historical depictions in Mycenaean Greece is further demonstrated by the fact that almost no images of foreigners and delegations from neighbouring territories or palatial kingdoms can be observed (Blakolmer 2012a). An important exception seems to be a procession of Egyptians in mural paintings from Pylos which present male figures with red-brown but also black skin colour and wearing variable

47 Lang 1969: 71-4, 214-5 (22-30 H 64), pls. 16-21, 117, 123-4, A, M; Immerwahr 1990: 128, 197 (Py no. 10); Brecoulaki, Stocker, Davis and Egan 2015.

48 Bulle 1907: 74-9, pls. XXVIII 2-6.; Spyropoulos 2015: 366; Petrakos 2010: 38-9, figs. 36a – c.

49 Hiller 1999: 326-7; Blakolmer 2018 b; forthc. b.

50 Lang 1969: 44-5, 71-2 (22 H 64), pl. M. For a new reconstruction of this part of the mural frieze by H. Brecoulaki, see *To Vima*, March 13, 2016, fig. on p. 20-1.

51 J. Davis and Bennet 1999: 107-11, 115; Bennet 2007: 15-17. See already Yalouris 1989.

52 For Near Eastern comparanda, see Winter 1981: 25.

53 See also Chapin 2014: 44-5, 51-2.

dress and headgear, among them a feline skin and a cap reminiscent of the Egyptian *Nemes* headscarf.[54] This reminds us, at least in its general character, of the assumption of 'an Egyptian royal embassy to Mycenae' (Wiener 2015: 136; Hankey 1981), based on the fragments of faience wall plaques bearing the cartouche of Amenophis III.[55] However, the question whether this mural painting reflects the singular event of a distinct visit of a delegation coming from Egypt to deliver gifts to the *wanax* of Pylos, at that time, remains unanswered. If this mural painting was meant as a variable series of exotic foreigners which visited Pylos at different times, we can hardly talk of an individual historical event.

One may conclude that the absence of individual figures, epigraphs of historical content and distinct pictorial information in narrative images of the Aegean Bronze Age points to the fact that, despite their supposedly prominent propagandistic meaning, these scenes depicted supra-individual and non-historical stories. As far as can be judged by the images known to date on the Mycenaean mainland, historical categories such as temporality and an individual locality do not seem to have been indicated. Although several exceptions may have existed, it is clear that Mycenaean rulers did not make any use of such iconographic tools of sovereignty. In concluding our observations, the assessment by A. Furumark (1941: 430) is still valid: 'There is little or nothing in Aegean art that can be justly claimed to be individual, historical, or mythological.'[56]

5. Further hints of a Mycenaean 'iconography of power'

It is obvious that all three essential aspects of dynastic modes of self-presentation discussed above were strongly underrepresented in the Aegean Bronze Age. In the Mycenaean palatial periods this absence may have been even more glaring than in Neopalatial Crete. It is noticeable that several aspects of the missing iconography of rulership in the Aegean are reminiscent of the cultural behaviour of non-monarchical political systems such as the democracy (*isonomia*) of classical Athens.[57] This comparison, however, definitely fails due to the completely different Late Mycenaean political system of the '*wanax* kingship'.[58] Nevertheless, this juxtaposition shows quite plainly the idiosyncratic character of the mechanisms of Aegean iconography by suppressing or masking the office of the Mycenaean rulers as well as their identity. However, the remarkably anonymous and non-personal character of Mycenaean iconography should not lead us to the premature conclusion of the absence of any 'iconography of power'. Is it really true that neither Minoans nor Mycenaeans practiced a 'political' propagandistic art, as has been stated by M. Benzi (1977: 3)? Could it be that political propaganda simply was expressed in a different way than in the Near East?

Further evidence of a Mycenaean iconography of power and authority may be delivered by seal images. Based on seal motifs from Early Mycenaean Greece, R. Laffineur defined the following pictorial motifs as symbolically reflecting a 'ruler iconography': fighting men, a man on a chariot, a boar's tusk helmet, a man fighting a lion, a wounded lion and a wounded wild goat (Laffineur 1990: esp. 154, 1992). One could argue that, on the

54 Lang 1969: 41-2, 61-2, 91-4 (54-9 H nws), pls. 41-4, 117, 129-30, D; Blakolmer 2012a: 59-60 with n. 15, figs. 4-5.

55 Hankey 1981; Phillips and Cline 2005; Phillips 2007.

56 See also Karageorghis 1958: 383.

57 See esp. Rodenwaldt 1933: 1045-8.

58 Kilian 1988; Wright 1994: 56-60, 2006: 7-52; Palaima 1995: 129-35; 2016. See already Puhvel 1958.

one hand, this selection seems very subjective. However, on the other hand, it would be difficult to imagine a completely different outcome if the Mycenaeans would have selected iconographic topics reflecting their affiliation to the palatial élite. Nonetheless, these and other subjects on seals did not allude to the ruler alone and, therefore, they should be categorised as an 'iconography of power' related to activities of war and hunt amongst the élites of Mycenaean Greece as well as those of Minoan Crete.[59] When looking to the Late Mycenaean mainland, it has been suggested that the motifs on seal impressions from Pylos reflect the mural iconography of the palace at this site, both forms of art showing griffins, octopus, hunting and bull-leaping scenes, and thus these iconographic motifs were defined as 'the currency of élite solidarity' (Bennet 2001: 34-5).[60] Although this reasoning appears sound, a considerable amount of seal imprints attested by the sealings from Pylos derive from seals and signet-rings which constitute heirlooms, and many of them were probably imports from Minoan Crete (see Pini 1997: 82-91). Even though this does not exclude a connection with the iconographic program of the mural-paintings in the LH IIIB palace of Pylos, examples such as these probably merely reflect the continuity of Minoan pictorial subjects, which extended until the end of the Mycenaean palatial period.

6. The pictorial programs of the Mycenaean palaces

More detailed information can be gained from the thematic repertory of the mural paintings in the palaces on the Mycenaean mainland; these will be presented here in cursory fashion in order to filter out any possible propagandistic messages. A pair of lions and griffins flanking the throne, such as in the murals of the throne-room of Pylos (Fig. 12),[61] constitute a strong rhetorical statement of the super-natural status of the *wanax* and a suitable back-drop for ceremonial activities connected with Mycenaean kingship. It is interesting to note that the motif of the griffin in front of a palm-tree, well known from the LM I or LM II mural paintings in the throne-room of the palace at Knossos,[62] already occurs on the impressions of a seal-stone from Kato Zakros which possibly dates as early as MM III/LM I.[63] Large-scale protective animals such as griffin or sphinx are also known from House A at LM I Ayia Irini on Kea (E. Davis 2007: 148-9, pl. 17.1), from Thebes (Keramopoullos 1909: 93, pl. 2.6; Immerwahr 1990: 138, 201, Th No. 3), Tiryns (Rodenwaldt 1912: 160-1; Immerwahr 1990: 137-8, 203, Ti No. 9) and further from halls at Pylos as well as possibly from Orchomenos (Shaw 1997: 496-7; Spyropoulos 2015: 367) and Mycenae (Cameron and Mayer 1995: 283; Pliatsika 2015: 605-6, fig. 9). Not only did griffins occupy prominent positions in the murals of Mycenaean palaces; the flame-like 'notched-plume decoration', typical of griffin's wings, occurs also as ornament of the central hearths in

59 For the Minoan origin of many of these subjects, see esp. W.-D. Niemeier 1990.

60 See also Panagiotopoulos 2010: esp. 305-7, 2014: esp. 124-33, 142-6.

61 For the griffins in the throne-room of Pylos, see Blegen 1956; Lang 1969: 180, 194-6, pls. 53, 111, 134, 136; McCallum 1987: 97-101, pl. IX; Immerwahr 1990: 136-7, 199 (Py No. 18); Hiller 1996: esp. 79, pl. VI; Shank, 2007: 160-1.

62 See esp. Cameron 1987: 322-5, figs. 3, 7; Immerwahr 1990: 96-8, 176 (Kn No. 28), pls. 47-8; Hiller 1996: 78-81; Shank 2007: esp. 162-4, figs. 19, 4-5.

63 *CMS* II7, no. 87. For its dating to 'MM IIIB – LM IA', see Morgan 1988: 50, fig. 37. See the dating to MM II in Morgan 2010, 310-1, fig. 10.

Fig. 12: Central part of the northeast wall of the throne-room of Pylos, reconstruction as envisioned by Piet de Jong (after C.W. Blegen 1956, pl. 40, fig. 2).

Fig. 13: Lion gate at Mycenae (after Amandry 1995, fig. on p. 9 above).

Mycenaean palace *megara*.[64] Thus, a symbolic association of the griffin with the power of Minoan rulership as well as that of the Mycenaean *wanaktes* is obvious.

The monumental stone relief block from the Lion Gate at Mycenae, visible for a wider social arena (Fig. 13),[65] seems to belong to the same 'iconographic cycle' as the griffins

64 Evans 1930: 550-1, figs. 401A – B; 1935: 179-81; D'Albiac 1995: 63-72; Wace 1949: 77, pls. 96-7a.; Blegen and Rawson 1966: 85-7, fig. 66 (R. 6); p. 199-200 (R. 46); Lang 1969: 186-9 (1 T nw, 3-4 T 23, 7 T sw, 8 T ne), pls. 114-5, L; Darcque 2005: 174-7.

65 Wace 1921-23a: 9-38; Aström and Blomé 1964: 159-191; Shaw 1986; Blackwell 2014.

depicted in the murals of the throne-room of the palace at Knossos – as the author has pointed out elsewhere (Blakolmer 2011a: 69-72; 2015a: 93-4). Thus, this large-scale emblem is iconographically and semantically also connected with the lions and griffins flanking the throne in the palace at Pylos (Fig. 12) and, possibly, in other palaces such as that of Mycenae, although this has to remain conjectural.[66] J. Maran and E. Stavrianopoulou (2007: 286) rightly stated: 'An impressive architectural monument like the Lion Gate [...] would have presented an excellent place for an image of the king under whose reign it was built, or for a monumental inscription.' One could also wonder why no large-scale chariot motif – highly popular in contemporary pictorial pottery – was depicted at the entrance into the citadel of Mycenae. However, such propagandistic strategies obviously did not conform to the Mycenaean 'language of rulership'. Instead, the highly symbolic relief image of the Lion Gate perfectly reflects the religious legitimation of the palatial authority,[67] and the interpretation by F. Matz as 'an invocation and a prayer set in stone' may come close to its original message.[68] Although the motif of griffins and lions flanking or accompanying a male (or female) figure is well attested in seal-images,[69] it is astonishing that, given their prominent position in Aegean throne-rooms, lion and griffin were not represented more often. This may lie, at least partly, in the scarcity of Late Mycenaean seal production, and we should not forget that the crouching griffin or sphinx was a popular subject on Late Mycenaean ivory plaques (Poursat 1977: 57-68) which is possibly even reflected by Linear B tablets of the Ta series from Pylos.[70]

It is worth highlighting that the stone relief blocks from the Atreus tholos tomb which show scenes of bulls,[71] which is by no means untypical of Late Mycenaean royal ideology, are also counted amongst the very few examples of large-scale images presented in the public space. That this Minoan-rooted imagery of the bull in monumental format was not a unique case in Late Mycenaean art is well exemplified by a life-sized bull in stucco relief from the house at Plakes, outside the citadel of Mycenae (Fig. 14).[72]

A further pictorial theme in throne-room 6 of the palace of Pylos is a ritual scene depicted on the Northeast wall to the far right of the throne. Although some erroneous reconstruction has to be discarded (Stocker and J. Davis 2004: 70), the fragments show male figures transporting objects in a procession(?), at least two pairs of men at small tables and the lyre-player seated on a rock (Fig. 15) already mentioned above.[73] Despite their fragmentary character, these scenes have convincingly been associated with ceremonial banquets alluded to in Linear B texts such as Un 2.[74] In Vestibule 5 a procession of men and women and a large-scale bull were depicted, also underlining the ceremonial character.[75] Although – given the prominent position of these ritual

66 For the assumed reconstruction of guarding creatures flanking the throne in the *megaron* at Mycenae, see Lurz 1994: 78; Boulotis 2013: 148; Thaler 2015: 353.

67 See also Wright 1994: 51, 54.

68 Matz 1958: 423: 'eine Beschwörung und ein Gebet aus Stein'.

69 Spartz 1962; Müller 2000; Barclay 2001; Crowley 2010. See furthermore Laffineur 1992: 105-12.

70 Ta 714.2 (instr. pl. *po-ni-ki-pi*) and 722.1 (*po-ni-ke-qe*): either 'palm tree' or 'griffin'. See Aura Jorro and Adrados 1993: 138.

71 Wace 1921-23b: 338-57, pl. LVI; Younger 1987; Hiller 2009; Blakolmer 2011b.

72 Iakovidis 2013: 239, 312, pl. 66a – b.

73 Lang 1969: 79-81, 110-1, 194-6, pls. 125-6; McCallum 1987: 87-107, pls. IX – X.

74 Säflund 1980; Killen 1994; Wright 2004: 41-3; Bennet 2007:13.

75 Lang 1969: 38-40, 192-3, pls. 119-20; McCallum 1987 : 77-87, 109-23, pls. VIII a – c; Shank 2008: 99-100.

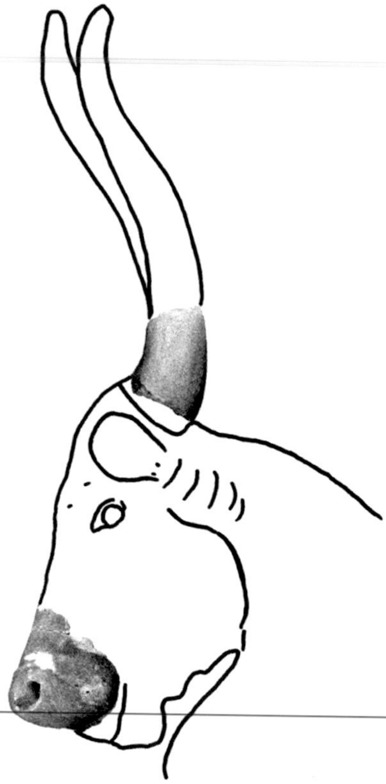

Fig. 14: Stucco relief fragments of a bull from the house at Plakes, Mycenae (after Iakovidis 2013, pl. 66b).

themes in the *megaron* unit at Pylos, their association with the enthroning ritual of the *wanax* is a sounding hypothesis – we have to keep in mind that the evidence of ceremonial subjects such as the preparation for feasting and banqueting remains meagre in the iconographic programs of the Mycenaean palaces.[76]

Female processions are a prominent topic of Mycenaean palatial iconography.[77] In the 'Vestibule procession' in the *megaron* of Pylos the figures were orientating the visitor towards the left side, to the entrance into the throne room. (McCallum 1987: 122-3; Thaler 2015: 343). A comparable position of processional figures in the vestibule, and possibly on the walls of further rooms of the *megaron* complex, was suggested for the large-scale female procession paintings in the palace of Tiryns as well (Maran 2012: 156-7; Thaler 2015: 344). The character of the processions in Mycenaean wall paintings appears highly multifunctional and possibly even ambiguous and by no means should be associated exclusively with ceremonies of rulership (Blakolmer 2008). Furthermore, it is remarkable that, with the possible exception of several procession scenes, hardly any depiction of religious character and deities can be observed in the mural paintings of Mycenaean palaces, although the main function of many of the decorated rooms was of ritual purpose (Blakolmer 2000: 400-1).

Extensive battle friezes held a prominent position in the throne-room of Mycenae (Fig. 9), in Hall 64 at Pylos and possibly in further Mycenaean palaces; their character has been discussed already above. This pictorial subject, reflecting the military ideology, seems to have been restricted to a few selected halls in palaces and, despite some iconographic predecessors in Neopalatial Crete, narrative, small-scale images of warfare could well have been created out of the distinct needs of some 'political' propaganda of Late Mycenaean kingship.[78] The iconographic motif of the predominant warrior in the chariot fighting an enemy on foot on the stone stelae of the Shaft Graves (Fig. 6) has no successors in the iconography of later Mycenaean periods. Apparently, this pictorial *topos* of the LH I warrior-chiefs at Mycenae did not fit the requirements of the *wanax* kingship,

76 Cf. Shaw 1997: 496. See also Pini 2008.

77 Peterson 1981; Immerwahr 1990: 114-21; Blakolmer 2008.

78 See n. 49 above.

Fig. 15: Mural scene from the *megaron* at Pylos (after Wright 2004: 43, fig. 13).

and this is despite the fact that several of these stone stelae, attributable to some noble but nebulous ancestors, were re-erected and visible to the public in LH IIIB Mycenae.[79]

Fragments of mural paintings assignable to hunting scenes decorated several important halls in Mycenaean palaces, although they do not stem from the *megara* themselves (Immerwahr 1990: 129-32). In contrast to warrior scenes, the subject of hunting boar and deer was not confined to the palaces of Pylos (Fig. 10), Tiryns, Thebes and Orchomenos, but is attested also at wealthy mansions outside the citadel of Mycenae (Cameron and Mayer 1995: 280-3; Tournavitou 2009: 647-72; 2012: 725-7), at Argos (Tournavitou and Brecoulaki 2015: 214-24) as well as at Ayia Irini on Kea (N. Marinatos and Morgan 2005). Additional pictorial subjects in Mycenaean palaces are marine motifs such as octopus and dolphin painted on the floors of palatial *megara* (Hirsch 1977: 23-42; Egan and Brecoulaki 2015), as well as in a mural painting in Building H at Gla (Boulotis 2015), and monumental friezes with large-scale figure-of-eight shields (Immerwahr 1990: 138-40). Ornamental motifs such as running spirals, so-called half-rosette motifs, series of rosettes and the waz-lily or papyrus motifs occur not only in decorative zones in mural paintings but also in stone relief friezes in Mycenaean palatial architecture,[80] at the façades of the most monumental tholos tombs and even on the podium of the throne at Tiryns (Th. Schulz 1988). This symbolic ornamental vocabulary was more or less limited to the palatial sphere and can be defined as royal or high-status emblems (see esp. Hiller 2005). In this context, we can point to the decoration of the so-called 'palace style' jars of LM II Crete, because of the monumentalisation of Minoan 'palatial' motifs such as the figure-of-eight shield, the helmet, papyrus, octopus and symbolic ornament motifs such as rosette and triglyph. It

79 See Woodard 1968; Gates 1985; Laffineur 1995; Wardle 2015: 587-9.

80 See, e.g., Moser von Filseck 1986.

is at least highly probable that all of them possessed a deeper meaning connected with power,[81] and this could be the case for the 'palace style' amphorae on the Early Mycenaean mainland as well (Kalogeropoulos 1998: 85-179).

6.1. Concluding observations

With this short (and incomplete) overview we can conclude that, based on present knowledge, the griffins and lions flanking the throne in the palace of Pylos are the only iconographic evidence that unequivocally supports the existence of a Mycenaean king of divine or semi-divine character, as indicated by the Linear B texts. With the possible exception of the ceremonial scenes in the Pylian *megaron*, no other pictorial evidence of the mural programs of Mycenaean palaces clearly points to the office of the *wanax* himself. Further iconographic themes of exclusively palatial character could have been battle friezes and emblems such as the 'half-rosette motif', whereas other mural themes occur also in élite mansions outside palaces. Thus, in Late Mycenaean mural paintings we can roughly draw a distinction between an iconography of elevated status and affiliation to the palatial sphere, on the one hand, and an even more exclusive palatial symbolism of the *wanaktes* by heraldic 'creatures of power', extensive battle friezes and 'metaphysical' emblems, on the other hand. When in recent studies, emphasis was placed on the connection of the '*wanax* kingship' with ancestral veneration,[82] this could be reflected, at best, indirectly by the continuity of the symbolism in iconography. As a consequence, only general aspects of the '*wanax* kingship' were communicated in a metaphorical way by the iconographic programs of the Mycenaean palaces: control, order, stability and continuity by the divine power of the sovereign.

Additionally, this itemisation demonstrates that 'Minoan-ness' was an important indicator of power on the Mycenaean mainland.[83] This elitist attitude started already in the Shaft Grave period and was even intensified during the palatial periods (Blakolmer 2015a: esp. 93-101). The Mycenaean indebtedness to the iconography of the palace at Knossos becomes most obvious in the depiction of activities related to the bull (Fig. 14), such as bull-leaping which occur relatively frequently in Mycenaean mural decoration (Immerwahr 1990: 111-3; Shaw 1997: 497-9, 501); the example in the palace of Tiryns derives from Light-well X beside the *megaron* (Rodenwaldt 1912: 162-5, pl. XVIII; Maran 2012: 152, n. 17). The phenomenon of the recurrence to the LM I palace of Knossos can be observed also in post-Neopalatial Crete itself, as was pointed out by J. Driessen and Ch. Langohr (2007: 179): 'the local, "Minoan" past was used, during the advanced Late Bronze Age [...], to consolidate power as part of a strategy of legitimation in the formation and maintenance of a new regime.' This underlines the fact that the iconography of the Mycenaean palaces, and the Mycenaean era in general, was by no means contradictory to Neopalatial Crete but, instead, it was characterised by continuity in the iconographic themes and in their meanings.

Can we detect any dichotomy in the Mycenaean iconographic programs between the palace and the religious sphere? The only way to answer this question is via a comparison of the mural iconography of the LH IIIB Cult Centre at Mycenae with that of contemporary

81 See esp. Hiller 1995: 562-72. See furthermore Briault 2007.

82 See esp. Lupack 2014; Palaima 2016.

83 See esp. Whittaker 2002; 2014, esp. 147-206; Maran and Stavrianopoulou 2007; Blakolmer 2011a.

Fig. 16: Sketchy drawing of the mural paintings in the Room with the Fresco at Mycenae (slightly altered version of the drawing by L. Papageorgiou published in: N. Marinatos 1988: 251, fig. 3).

palaces at Mycenae, Pylos and other sites. On the one hand, they clearly shared several pictorial topics, such as female processions, figure-of-eight shields and even chariot scenes (Kritseli-Providi 1982; Morgan 2005b). On the other hand, we know of no depiction of large-scale griffins or lions and battle-scenes from the Cult Centre, although the symbolism of warfare and power is included in these mural paintings as well (see esp. Rehak 1984, 1999: 227-8). Additionally, a further link between both spheres can possibly be observed at Mycenae: although hardly any successor of the symbolic iconography of rulership on signet-rings of Neopalatial Crete (Figs. 1-5) can be detected in the imagery of the Mycenaean palatial periods, the murals of the Room with the Fresco in the Cult Centre may form an

Fig. 17: 'Chieftain cup' from Ayia Triada, side A (after Kaiser 1976, fig. 25a).

exception (Fig. 16).[84] Here, a large-scale scene shows a female figure clad in a flounced skirt and a bodice and holding a long staff in her right hand; she faces another female figure with a long decorated dress holding a large sword in front of her, all contained in an architectonic frame. A closer inspection suggests that this may be the 'female version' of the main scene depicted on the LM I 'Chieftain cup' from Ayia Triada (Fig. 17): [85] here, the superordinate divine figure holding a sceptre at the right side is symbolically assigning divine power and authority to the figure at the left side, who exhibits a warlike character. As has been observed already by P. Rehak (1992: 50), the female figure with the staff in the fresco of the Cult Centre is reminiscent of the central goddess in the seal-image of the 'Mother of the Mountain' from Knossos (Fig. 1), while the long dress of the figure to the left side is similar to that worn by the seated ruler on the Genii Ring from Tiryns (Fig. 5). This assumed indebtedness of the mural painting in the Cult Centre to ruler images of Neopalatial Crete is all the more likely as the female figure in the dado zone to the left side of this mural (Fig. 16) derives from another sacral motif well known in Neopalatial Crete: a goddess holding bunches of grass(?) in both raised hands, accompanied by a quadruped.[86]

84 N. Marinatos 1988; Rehak 1992, esp. 47-50; Morgan 2005b: 168-9; Chapin 2016b.

85 S. Marinatos and Hirmer 1973: pls. 100-2; Kaiser 1976: 28-9 ('Hagia Triada 3'), fig. 25a; Koehl 1986.

86 *CMS* II6, nos. 30-1; V Suppl. 1A, no. 175. Cf. Blakolmer 2012b: 95-6, figs. 39-40; 2015b. Recently, a different view was expressed by Chapin 2016b.

Thus, irrespective of the female sex of the figure to the left side of the upper zone, the painting in this shrine may represent a symbolic investiture scene with a possible emphasis on the warlike character of kingship. Although it has recently been suggested that the Room with the Fresco antedates the extension of the citadel walls and thus its closer interrelation with the palatial authorities at Mycenae has been cast into doubt,[87] this LH IIIB1 mural image seems to underline the entanglement of sovereignty and religion in the Mycenaean palatial periods. Furthermore, this example may demonstrate that hardly any dichotomy of, or contradiction between, the religious and the palatial spheres existed in the ideology of Late Mycenaean kingship.

7. An explanatory model

What conclusions can be drawn from these observations and interpretations of the 'missing features' of dynastic expression in Mycenaean iconography? The main question is: what strategy was chosen by the Mycenaean *wanaktes* in order to legitimise their rule over their subordinates and their territories? As can be judged by the iconographic evidence, their decision was deliberately different from that of the rulers in other regions of the Eastern Mediterranean. The rulers of the Bronze Age Aegean made use of only a limited spectrum of 'cultural rhetorics' in iconography by selecting merely those pictorial motifs which symbolised their power in a very general, abstract, hyper-individual and anonymous manner. It has been argued that the absence of rulers, inscriptions and historical events in Aegean iconography was substituted and compensated by oral, non-written poetry, by actually experienced performances and by the inclusion of all human senses.[88] This, however, does not explain the absence of ruler imagery in the Aegean, since all of these aspects – verbal, visual, performative – were indeed present, as well, in Near Eastern iconography. In other words, the existence of an oral tradition does not automatically negate the existence of a dynastic iconography. Nonetheless, could the Aegean strategy of the 'missing concreteness' lie in an idiosyncratic system of kingship which did not allow for dynastic mechanisms? Based upon the information provided by the Linear B texts, this explanation appears unlikely for the Late Mycenaean '*wanax* kingship', whereas an 'untypical' system of sovereignty often was ascribed to Neopalatial Crete.

It is noteworthy that in the seal images from Neopalatial Crete presented above (Figs. 1-5) the postulated ruler is by no means depicted as an individual; instead, he is reflected as a kind of archetypical, hero-like *topos*, as the 'profession' of a sovereign. Thus, one explanation of the impersonal character of iconography in Mycenaean palaces could be that the office of the '*wanax* kingship' counted, instead of the individual king himself.[89] This would mean that the position of the *wanax* was of such outstanding dominance in its spiritual and cosmological meaning that it was believed to be counterproductive to depict an individual person of this rank. This assumption can possibly be supported by the fact that the representation of rulers on the Shaft Grave stelae at prepalatial Mycenae (Fig. 6) was not pursued in the subsequent periods; this may well be explained by the contrasting functions and by a different understanding of the distinct position of the *wanax* during

87 Iakovidis 2004: 14, 28-9; Wardle 2015, esp. 578-9, 586. For a differing position, see Maran 2006: 77.

88 See esp. Bennet 2007: 14-6; Greco 2014: 305-40.

89 For the functions of the *wanax*, see esp. Carlier 1998; Palaima 1995, 2006.

LM II/LH IIB-LH IIIB.[90] Thus, the holder of this highest office in a Late Mycenaean (regional) state was defined neither by his individual characteristics nor as an anonymous ruler *per se* in a dynastic succession of kings.

As we have seen above, a Mycenaean *wanax* was represented not even as an indistinct holder of this position, that means as a non-individual deified ruler, as was mostly the case in the depiction of the Egyptian Pharaoh. This leads us to a further thought: if the Mycenaean *wanax* was perceived as a heroised or deified king and given the fact that, in the Aegean Bronze Age, deities were mostly depicted in an indistinct, non-individualised form (Blakolmer 2010, esp. 37-61) why should we expect that greater attention was paid to the representation of a distinct ruler in Aegean imagery? Thus, the following question arises: could our problem of the 'invisible ruler' in the iconography of the Aegean Bronze Age be due to the equally indistinct and generalised character of deities which were depicted as devoid of attributes, individuality and age, and possibly even of exchangeable sex?

In order to explain the peculiar iconography of rulership in Mycenaean Greece, we probably have to return to Minoan Crete. As Neopalatial Crete did not provide any models for a dynastic ruler imagery, Mycenaeans adopted symbolic creatures, procession scenes and the symbolism of ritual, as is best demonstrated by the relief blocks of the Lion Gate (Fig. 13) and the Atreus tholos tomb at Mycenae. These are powerful expressions, on the one hand, of the sacral kingship and, on the other hand, of the symbolism of the palace of Knossos and its 'glory of the past'.

As W.-D. Niemeier (1987: 90-1) convincingly argued, the mural painting programs of the Minoan palaces deliver not a single hint for the assumption that a sovereign functioned as a patron. Instead, broadly anonymous images of rituals, festivities and 'religious landscapes' are depicted on Minoan murals (see esp. Cameron 1987: 321-8; N. Marinatos 1996). The most convincing model to date which perhaps enables a better understanding of the religious ideology in the society of Neopalatial Crete is the 'monastery model' by J. Bintliff (1977: 160-4).[91] By comparing the socio-political strategy of Neopalatial Crete with that of Byzantine Greece, Bintliff postulated that Minoan rulers exerted political power based on their religious authority on the highest priestly level. Social integration, cohesion and identity were created by means of religion and commonly shared rituals, resulting in the effect that Minoan religious symbols functioned also as political insignia.[92] In this theocratic system, all of public life was strongly pervaded by religion as propagated by the palatial authorities that are otherwise largely invisible to us. Given the fact that religious rituals constituted the primary binding force of society, this mechanism may not have required or permitted the depiction of any distinct sovereign. Thus, Minoan iconography masks the individual rulers and they, for their part, profited by this strategy of 'threskeiocracy' (N. Marinatos 1984b; 1995). This model matches exceptionally well with the 'non-personal, collective image of power' (Greco 2014: 307) in Minoan Crete, when we consider the striking absence of many components typical of dynastic kingship in the Near East. Given the receptive character of Mycenaean iconography, it is no wonder that these

90 This change was already pointed out by Maran and Stavrianopoulou 2007: 287.

91 See also Cadogan 2012: 103-4; Blakolmer [forthc. c].

92 See, e.g., Hood 1995; Betancourt 2002: 207-11; N. Marinatos 1995; Adams 2004; Boulotis 2008: 52; Whittaker 2015.

elementary aspects of a 'religio-political' imagery created in Neopalatial Crete were never fundamentally changed. We may therefore conclude that in Minoan Crete no iconography of rulership was ever developed and on the Late Mycenaean mainland nothing was added in order to conform to the Mycenaean '*wanax* ideology' (see also Rehak 1995: esp. 115-6) which might have possessed, at least partly, quite similar traits of sacral kingship.[93]

8. Lawagetas and wanax in iconography?

Finally, two issues, both regarding the political system according to the Linear B texts, have to be addressed. Given the definition of the office entitled *ra-wa-ke-ta* as the second rank in the hierarchy of a Mycenaean palace state with a supposed military significance, and thus tentatively attributed to the Southwest-wing of the palace at Pylos,[94] we may ask: can we distinguish between an iconography of the *wanax* and a contrasting one attributable to the *lawagetas*? Although the warlike pictorial theme of the mural paintings in Hall 64 at Pylos constitutes the primary argument in favour of its ascription to the *lawagetas*, in the palace of Mycenae the battle frieze decorated the main *megaron*. This could have been the case at Orchomenos as well.[95] The supposed association of the possible warlike functions of the *lawagetas* with the 'secondary' *megara* of Mycenaean palaces cannot be supported by the mural iconography of any palace other than Pylos. Additionally, we can neither define different competitive dynasties, kin groups or 'factions' on the basis of contrasting iconographic concepts, strategies or contents, nor can we detect any distinct iconography attributable to the *e-qe-ta*, the *da-mo* or other groups of functionaries such as *da-mo-ko-ro*, *qa-si-re-u* or *ko-re-te-re* in Aegean images. With the exception of the few pictorial subjects defined above, the same iconographic themes occur in palaces as well as in larger mansions outside the citadel of Mycenae (cf. Tournavitou 2012, 2015) and at other sites.

The second question is that of the existence of a pan-Mycenaean 'super-*wanax*', a super-imposed central authority which encompassed the entire Mycenaean Aegean (either including Crete or not) and possessed the top position among the rulers of regional palace states (cf. esp. Kelder 2010; Eder and Jung 2015). Due to the absence of the depiction of any Mycenaean king, it is problematic to find an iconographic definition of a plurality of *wanaktes* of unequal rank. Furthermore, our knowledge of the pictorial programs of Mycenaean palaces does not allow for the recognition of any hierarchy of palaces. Although, based on the mural paintings in the respective throne-rooms, contrasting ways of articulating legitimacy of power were assumed for the palaces in the Argolid and that at Pylos (Whittaker 2001: 360), the state of preservation and the variability of the attribution of a pictorial theme to a distinct type of hall hardly allow this conclusion to be confirmed. The site of Mycenae may well have taken an outstanding position in the formation and development of an 'iconography of power' during the entire Late Bronze Age, from the time of the Shaft Grave stelae (Fig. 6) up to that of the *megaron* frieze (Fig. 9) and the Cult Centre (Fig. 16). However, we are not able to define any unique pictorial subject or any preeminent iconographic feature restricted to this site which could point to an outstanding top position of the rulers of Mycenae.[96] Nonetheless, despite a certain

93 See esp. Palaima 1995; Whittaker 2001; Maran and Stavrianopoulou 2007; Hiller 2011; Blakolmer 2011a: 71-3.

94 See Kilian 1987, esp. 32. For the functions of the *lawagetas*, see esp. Palaima 1995: 129; Wyatt 1994-95.

95 See n. 48 above.

96 A very useful overview of the mural paintings at Mycenae is presented by Boulotis 2013.

variability of the thematic programs in the Mycenaean palaces, they appear homogeneous to an extent which permits us to postulate a common 'master plan' in the formation of the pictorial schemes and – in spite of the obvious iconographic models in the LM I-II palace of Knossos – this prototype of Mycenaean palatial mural paintings has to be postulated on the Greek mainland itself. Nevertheless, the mural images do not deliver any explicit argument in favour of the assumption that the palace of Mycenae, or any other palace such as that at Thebes, exercised a superordinate hegemony and functioned as the capital of a politically unified 'Mycenaean Great Kingdom'.

9. Summary

In concluding our observations on the iconography of kingship in Mycenaean Greece, it has to be emphasised that, when considering images of rulers, the use of script, the depiction of historical events and other forms of iconographic expression of dynastic politics, the Aegean Bronze Age followed very particular paths. While, during the Early Mycenaean period, an independent manifestation of rulership can be defined in the motifs of the warrior in his chariot on the Shaft Grave stelae at Mycenae, by the palatial periods of LH IIIA-B the Mycenaean 'iconography of power' became more strongly orientated towards that of (earlier) Knossos. Therefore, hardly any depiction of a ruler can be recognised. Late Mycenaean iconography points to a palatial élite identity and widely suppressed the identity of the *wanax* himself in both meanings: as the highest office of authority and as an individual person. Paradoxical as this sounds, the more powerful the rulers at Mycenaean centres became, the more they disappeared from iconography.

According to the information provided by the Linear B texts as well as by the iconography of protective griffins and lions, the Mycenaean '*wanax* kingship' (similar to the rulership in Neopalatial Crete) possessed a strong theocratic component. This could be an important reason why – according to the general rules of indistinct divine figures in the Aegean – Mycenaean iconography masks the identity of the *wanaktes* as well as that of individual deities and heroes. The main reason for the 'missing ruler' in Late Mycenaean iconography, though, might be the absence of any adequate models in Minoan imagery and, as a consequence, this elementary phenomenon has to be explained in the light of Neopalatial Crete.

Indeed, these results are by no means satisfactory and further methodological and comparative approaches may enable deeper insight into this problem. As is frequently the case in Late Mycenaean Greece, it is difficult to decide whether we may trust in what is depicted in the images or whether Mycenaean iconography has to be understood at a symbolic meta-level by simulating 'Minoanised' subjects and messages. Did Mycenaean religion really function as a major tool for constructing and propagating elitist status and social cohesion to the same extent as in Neopalatial Crete? Alternatively, could it be that the Mycenaean reality was over-shadowed by the Minoan-rooted imagery and by the deficiency of any independent iconographic tools developed by Mycenaeans for their own political demands? In any case, the iconographic 'rhetoric' of Late Mycenaean state ideology did not allow the representation of the person of a *wanax*, or made it appear unnecessary. The mechanisms of justification, legitimisation and symbolisation of political dominance and power pursued quite different paths: on a symbolic level, by general pictorial themes of elitist character and, last but not least, by the indebtedness, affiliation and legacy of Minoan Crete.

Bibliography

Adams, E. 2004. 'Power and ritual in Neopalatial Crete: a regional comparison', *World Archaeology* 36.1: 26-42.

Adrimi-Sismani, V. and S. Alexandrou. 2001-04. 'Μυκηναϊκός θολωτός τάφος', *Archaiologikon Deltion* 56-59: 506-8.

Adrimi-Sismani, V. and S. Alexandrou. 2006 (2009). 'Μυκηναϊκός θολωτός τάφος στη Θέση Καζανάκι', in A. Mazarakis Ainian (ed.), Αρχαιολογικό έργο Θεσσαλίας και Στερεάς Ελλάδας 2, Volos: 133-149.

Amandry, P. 1995. 'Schliemann, marchand et archéologue', *Dossier d'Archéologie* 206: 2-13.

Aravantinos, V. 1996. 'Tebe micenea: recenti scoperte epigrafiche ed archeologiche (1993-1995)', *Studi micenei ed egeo-anatolici* 38: 179-190.

Aravantinos, V. 2000. 'Νέα μυκηναϊκά ελεφαντουργήματα από την Καδμεία (Θήβα)', in V. Aravantinos (ed.), *Γ΄ Διεθνές Συνέδριο Βοιωτικών Μελέτων, Θήβα, 4-8 Σεπτεμβρίου 1996* (Επετηρίς της Εταιρείας Βοιωτικών Μελέτων III.1), Athens: 31-120.

Aruz, J. 2008. *Marks of Distinction. Seals and Cultural Exchange between the Aegean and the Orient (ca. 2600-1360 B.C.)* (CMS Beiheft 7), Mayence.

Assmann, J. 1996. 'Preservation and presentation of self in ancient Egyptian portraiture', in P. der Manuelian (ed.), *Studies in Honor of William Kelly Simpson. Vol. I*, Boston: 55-81.

Aström, P. and B. Blomé. 1964. 'A reconstruction of the Lion relief at Mycenae', *Opuscula Atheniensia* 5: 159-191.

Aura Jorro, F. and F.R. Adrados (eds). 1993. *Diccionario griego – español. Diccionario Micénico, Vol. II*, Madrid.

Baines, J. 1989. 'Communication and display: the integration of early Egyptian art and writing', *Antiquity* 63: 471-482.

Barclay, A.E. 2001. 'The Potnia Theron: adaptation of a Near Eastern image', in R. Laffineur and R. Hägg (eds.), *POTNIA. Deities and Religion in the Aegean Bronze Age, Proceedings of the 8th International Aegean Conference, Göteborg, Göteborg University, 12-15 April 2000* (Aegaeum 22), Liège and Austin: 373-386.

Bennet J. 2001. 'Agency and bureaucracy: Thoughts on the nature and extent of administration in Bronze Age Pylos', in S. Voutsaki and J. Killen (eds.), *Economy and Politics in the Mycenaean Palace States. Proceedings of a Conference held on 1-3 July 1999 in the Faculty of Classics, Cambridge*, Cambridge: 25-37.

Bennet, J. 2004. 'Iconographies of value: words, people and things in the Late Bronze Age Aegean', in C. Barrett and P. Halstead (eds.), *The Emergence of Civilisation Revisited* (Sheffield Studies in Aegean Archaeology 6), Oxford: 90-106.

Bennet, J. 2007. 'Representations of power in Mycenaean Pylos. Script, orality, iconography', in F. Lang, C. Reinholdt and J. Weilhartner (eds.), ΣΤΕΦΑΝΟΣ ΑΡΙΣΤΕΙΟΣ. *Archäologische Forschungen zwischen Nil und Istros. Festschrift für Stefan Hiller zum 65. Geburtstag*, Vienna: 11-22.

Bennet, J. 2015. 'Telltale depictions: a contextual view of Mycenaean wall paintings', in H. Brecoulaki, J.L. Davis and Sh.R. Stocker (eds.), *Mycenaean Wall Painting in Context: New Discoveries, Old Finds Reconsidered* (Meletemata 72), Athens: 21-34.

Benzi, M. 1977. 'Gli affreschi dell'ammiraglio a Thera', *Prospettiva* 10: 3-15.

Betancourt, Ph.P. 2002. 'Who was in charge of the palaces?', in J. Driessen, I. Schoep and R. Laffineur (eds.), *Monuments of Minos. Rethinking the Minoan Palaces. Proceedings of the International Workshop "Crete of the hundered Palaces?" held at the Université Catholique de Louvain, Louvain-la-Neuve, 14-15. December 2001* (Aegaeum 23), Liège: 207-212.

Betts, J.H. 1967. 'New light on Minoan bureaucracy. A re-examination of some Cretan sealings', *Kadmos* 6: 15-40.

Biesantz, H. 1958. 'Die minoischen Bildnisgemmen', *Marburger Winckelmann-Programm* 1958: 9-25.

Bintliff, J.L. 1977. *Natural Environment and Human Settlement in Prehistoric Greece* (BAR Supplementary Series 28), Oxford.

Blackwell, N.G. 2014. 'Making the Lion Gate relief at Mycenae: Tool marks and foreign influence', *American Journal of Archaeology* 118: 451-488.

Blakolmer, F. 2000. 'The Functions of Wall Painting and Other Forms of Architectural Decoration in the Aegean Bronze Age', in S. Sherratt (ed.), *Proceedings of the First International Symposium 'The Wall Paintings of Thera', Petros M. Nomikos Conference Centre, Thera, Hellas, 30 August – 4 September 1997, Vol. I*, Athens: 393-412.

Blakolmer, F. 2007. 'The Silver Battle Krater from Shaft Grave IV at Mycenae: Evidence of fighting "heroes" on Minoan palace walls at Knossos?', in R. Laffineur and S.P. Morris (eds.), *EPOS. Reconsidering Greek Epic and Aegean Bronze Age Archaeology. Proceedings of the 11th International Aegean Conference, Los Angeles, UCLA – The J. Paul Getty Villa, 20-23 April 2006* (Aegaeum 28), Liège – Austin: 213-224.

Blakolmer, F. 2008. 'Processions in Aegean iconography II: Who are the participants?', in L.A. Hitchcock, R. Laffineur and J. Crowley (eds.), *DAIS. The Aegean Feast, Proceedings of the 12th International Aegean Conference, University of Melbourne, Centre for Classics and Archaeology, 25-29 March 2008* (Aegaeum 29), Liège – Austin: 257-268.

Blakolmer, F. 2010. 'A Pantheon without attributes? Goddesses and gods in Minoan and Mycenaean iconography', in J. Mylonopoulos (ed.), *Divine Images and Human Imaginations in Ancient Greece and Rome* (Religions in the Graeco-Roman World 170), Leiden – Boston: 21-61.

Blakolmer, F. 2011a: 'Vom Thronraum in Knossos zum Löwentor von Mykene: Kontinuitäten in Bildkunst und Palastideologie', in F. Blakolmer, C. Reinholdt, J. Weilhartner and G. Nightingale (eds.), Österreichische Forschungen zur Ägäischen Bronzezeit 2009. Akten der Tagung vom 6. bis 7. März 2009 am Fachbereich Altertumswissenschaften der Universität Salzburg, Vienna: 63-80.

Blakolmer, F. 2011b. 'Creto-Minoan art abroad or Mycenaean imitation? The case of the bull reliefs from the Treasury of Atreus at Mycenae', in *Πεπραγμένα Ι΄ Διεθνούς Κρητολογικού Συνεδρίου (Χανιά, 1-8 Οκτοβρίου 2006)*, Vol. I.3, Chania: 461-482.

Blakolmer, F. 2012a. 'The Missing "Barbarians": Some thoughts on ethnicity and identity in Aegean Bronze Age iconography', in A. Papadopoulos (ed.), *Recent Research and Perspectives in the Late Bronze Age Eastern Mediterranean* (= *Talanta* 44), Amsterdam: 53-77.

Blakolmer, F. 2012b. 'Image and architecture: reflections of mural iconography in seal images and other art forms of Minoan Crete', in D. Panagiotopoulos and U. Günkel-Maschek (eds.), *Minoan Realities. Approaches to Images, Architecture, and Society in the Aegean Bronze Age* (Aegis 5), Louvain: 83-114.

Blakolmer, F. 2014. 'Meaningful landscapes: Minoan "landscape rooms" and peak sanctuaries', in G. Touchais, R. Laffineur and F. Rougemont (eds.), *PHYSIS. L'environnement naturel et la relation homme-milieu dans le monde égéen protohistorique, Actes de la 14e Rencontre égéenne internationale, Paris, Institut National d'Histoire de l'Art (INHA), 11-14 décembre 2012* (Aegaeum 37), Leuven – Liege: 121-128.

Blakolmer, F. 2015a. 'Was there a 'Mycenaean art'? Or: Tradition without innovation? Some examples of relief art', in J. Weilhartner and F. Ruppenstein (eds.), *Tradition and Innovation in the Mycenaean Palatial Polities, Proceedings of an International Symposium held at the Austrian Academy of Sciences, 1-2 March, 2013* (Mykenische Studien 34), Vienna: 87-112.

Blakolmer. F. 2015b. 'Zu einem Götterbild im Kultzentrum von Mykene: *si-to-po-ti-ni-ja*, ›Potnia Aigon‹ oder etwas anderes?', in H. Meyer (ed.), *Drahdiweiberl. Ansichten aus der alten und neueren Kunst- und Kulturwissenschaft. Φιλικόν Δῶρον – Munus Amicorum. Freundesgabe für Michaela Fuchs zum 4. August 2015* (Gephyra 9), Bonn: 9-14.

Blakolmer, F. 2016. 'Eine 'spezielle Prozession' in minoischen Siegelbildern: Evidenz für ein Herrschaftsritual im neopalatialen Kreta?', in G. Grabherr and B. Kainrath (eds.), *Akten des 15. Österreichischen Archäologentages in Innsbruck, 27. Februar – 1. März 2014* (Ikarus 9), Innsbruck: 33-39.

Blakolmer, F. 2018a. 'A 'Special procession' in Minoan seal images: Observations on ritual dress in Minoan Crete', in P. Pavúk, V. Klontza-Jaklová and A. Harding (eds.), *EUDAIMON. Studies in Honour of Prof. Jan Bouzek, Conference, Prague, 19-23 of May 2015*, Prague – Brno: 29-50.

Blakolmer, F. 2018b. 'Die Ikonographie des Krieges im spätmykenischen Griechenland', in K. Tausend (ed.), *Untersuchungen zum spätmykenischen Militärwesen* (Geographica Historica 39). Stuttgart: 33-67.

Blakolmer, F. [forthc. a]. 'Processions in Aegean iconography IV: A "Special procession" in seal images from Minoan Crete', in A.-L. Schallin and H. Whittaker (eds.), *Mycenaean Processions and Ceremonies in Context.*

Blakolmer, F. [forthc. b]: 'Mycenaean period wall-painting', in L. Hitchcock and B. Davis (eds.), *Blackwell Companion to Aegean Art and Architecture.*

Blakolmer, F. [forthc. c]. 'Palatial objects of prestige, "priest-kings" and the gold of the sanctuary: wealth and religion in the Minoan and Mycenaean world', in J. Masquelier-Loorius, J. Cornillon and J.-M. Salamito (eds.), *L'argent des dieux. Religions et richesses en Méditerranée dans l'Antiquité et au Moyen Âge. Colloque international, Université Paris-Sorbonne Paris IV, Paris 5e, 16, 17 & 18 octobre 2014.*

Blakolmer, F. and V. Dubcová. [forthc.]. 'Orientalische Götterkronen und das Problem 'fremder Götter' in der Ikonographie des minoischen Kreta', in G. Selz and K. Wagensonner (eds.), *Mesopotamische Kunstgeschichte(n). Festschrift für Erika Bleibtreu.*

Blakolmer, F. and I. Hein. 2018. 'A 'Special procession' in Minoan Crete as a ritual of rulership? A view from Egypt', in *Proceedings of the 10th International Congress on the Archaeology of the Ancient Near East (ICAANE), 25-29 April 2016, OREA, Austrian Academy of Sciences,* Wiesbaden: 195-208.

Blegen, C.W. 1956. 'The palace of Nestor. Excavations of 1955', *American Journal of Archaeology* 60: 95-101.

Blegen, C.W. and M. Rawson. 1966. *The Palace of Nestor at Pylos in Western Messenia, Vol. I*, Princeton.

Bonatz, D. 2007. 'The divine image of the king: Religious representation of political power in the Hittite Empire', in M. Heinz and M.H Feldman (eds.), *Representation of Political Power. Case Histories from Times of Change and Dissolving Order in the Ancient Near East*, Winona Lake: 111-136.

Boulotis, Ch. 1986. 'Στοιχεία μαγείας στη Μινωϊκή Κρήτη', *Archaiologia* 20: 8-15.

Boulotis, Ch. 1990. 'Villes et palais dans l'art égéen du IIe millénaire av. J.-C.', in P. Darcque and R. Treuil (eds.), *L'habitat égéen préhistorique. Actes de la Table Ronde internationale organisé par le CNRS, l'Université de Paris I et l'École française d'Athènes (Athènes, 23-25 juin 1987)* (Bulletin de correspondance hellénique supplément 19), Athens: 421-459.

Boulotis, Ch. 2008. 'From mythical Minos to the search for Cretan kingship', in M. Andreadaki-Vlazaki, G. Rethemiotakis and N. Dimopoulou-Rethemiotakis (eds.), *From the Land of the Labyrinth. Minoan Crete, 3000-1100 B.C., Essays*, New York: 44-55.

Boulotis, Ch. 2013. 'Από το ανάκτορο των Μυκηνών στο Θρησκευτικό Κέντρο: ο σηματοδοτικός λόγος των τοιχογραφιών', *O Mentor* 105: 117-160.

Boulotis, Ch. 2015. 'A dolphin frieze and argonauts from the Mycenaean citadel of Gla', in H. Brecoulaki, J.L. Davis and Sh.R. Stocker (eds.), *Mycenaean Wall Painting in Context: New Discoveries, Old Finds Reconsidered* (Meletemata 72), Athens: 371-403.

Brecoulaki, H., Sh. Stocker, J. Davis, and E. Egan. 2015. 'An unprecedented naval scene from Pylos: First considerations', in H. Brecoulaki, J.L. Davis and Sh.R. Stocker (eds.), *Mycenaean Wall Painting in Context: New Discoveries, Old Finds Reconsidered* (Meletemata 72), Athens: 260-291.

Briault, C. 2007. 'High fidelity or Chinese whispers? Cult symbols and ritual transmission in the Bronze Age Aegean', *Journal of Mediterranean Archaeology* 20: 239-265.

Buchholz, H.-G. (ed.). 2012. *Erkennungs-, Rang- und Würdezeichen im Zeitalter Homers* (Archaeologia Homerica D), Göttingen.

Buchholz, H.-G and J. Wiesner. 1977. *Kriegswesen I: Schutzwaffen und Wehrbauten* (Archaeologia Homerica E.I), Göttingen.

Bulle, H. 1907. *Orchomenos I. Die ältesten Ansiedelungsschichten*, Munich.

Cadogan, G. 2012. 'Γνωρίζουμε τους Μινωίτες 134 χρόνια μετά τις πρώτες ανασκαφές, του Μίνωα Καλοκαιρινού, στην Κνωσό', *Ariadne* 18: 91-117.

Cameron, M.A.S. 1965a. 'Four fragments of wall paintings with linear A inscriptions', *Kadmos* 4: 7-15.

Cameron, M.A.S. 1965b. 'The wall paintings with linear signs from the "House of the Frescoes"', *Kadmos* 4: 170-171.

Cameron, M.A.S. 1968a. 'The painted signs on fresco fragments from the "House of the Frescoes"', *Kadmos* 7: 45-64.

Cameron, M.A.S. 1968b. 'A graffito related to a myrtle composition on a Minoan fresco from Knossos', *Kadmos* 7.1: 97-99.

Cameron, M.A.S. 1987. 'The 'palatial' thematic system in the Knossos murals. Last notes on Knossos frescoes', in R. Hägg and N. Marinatos (eds.), *The Function of the Minoan Palaces. Proceedings of the Fourth International Symposium at the Swedish Institute in Athens*, Stockholm: 321-328.

Cameron, M. and A. Mayer. 1995. 'Wall Paintings', in I. Tournavitou (ed.), *The 'Ivory Houses' at Mycenae*, (British School at Athens Supplement 24), Athens: 281-284.

Carlier, P. 1998. '*wa-na-ka* derechef. Nouvelles réflexions sur les royautés mycéniennes', *Bulletin de correspondance hellénique* 122: 411-415.

Chapin, A. 2014. 'Aegean painting in the Bronze Age', in J.J. Pollitt (ed.), *The Cambridge History of Painting in the Classical World*, New York: 1-65.

Chapin, A.P. 2016a. 'Mycenaean mythologies in the making: the frescoes of Pylos hall 64 and the Mycenae megaron', in E. Alram-Stern, F. Blakolmer, S. Deger-Jalkotzy, R. Laffineur and J. Weilhartner (eds.), *METAPHYSIS. Ritual, Myth and Symbolism in the Aegean Bronze Age. Proceedings of the 15th International Aegean Conference, Vienna, Institute for Oriental and European Archaeology, Aegean and Anatolia Department, Austrian Academy of Sciences and Institute of Classical Archaeology, University of Vienna, 22-25 April 2014* (Aegaeum 39), Leuven: 459-466.

Chapin, A.P. 2016b. 'The performative body and social identity in the Room of the Fresco at Mycenae', in M. Mina, S. Triantaphyllo and Y. Papadatos (eds.), *An Archaeology of Prehistoric Bodies and Embodied Identities in the Eastern Mediterranean*, Oxford – Philadelphia: 81-88.

Crowley, J.L. 2010. 'The Aegean Master of Animals. The evidence of the seals, signets, and sealings', in D.B. Counts and B. Arnold (eds.), *The Master of Animals in Old World Iconography*, Budapest: 75-91.

Crowley, J.L. 2013. *The Iconography of Aegean Seals* (Aegaeum 34), Leuven – Liège.

Cultraro, M. 2000. 'L'affresco del cantore di Pilo e l'investitura del potere', *Ostraka* 9.1: 9-30.

Cultraro, M. 2004. 'Exercise of dominance. Boar hunting in Mycenaean religion and Hittite rituals', in M. Hutter and S. Hutter-Braunsar (eds.), *Offizielle Religion, lokale Kulte und individuelle Religiosität. Akten des religionswissenschaftlichen Symposiums Kleinasien und angrenzende Gebiete vom Beginn des 2. bis zur Mitte des 1. Jahrtausends v. Chr. (Bonn, 20.-22. Februar 2003)*, Münster: 117-135.

D'Albiac, C. 1995. 'The 'diagnostic' wings of monsters', in Ch. Morris (ed.), *Klados. Essays in Honour of J.N. Coldstream* (Bulletin of the Institute of Classical Studies of the University of London Supplement 63), London: 63-79.

Darcque, P. 2005. *L'habitat mycénien. Formes et fonctions de l'espace bâti en Grèce continentale à la fin du IIe millénaire avant J.-C.* (Bibliothèque des Ecoles Françaises d'Athènes et de Rome 319), Athens.

Davis, B. 2014. *Minoan Stone Vessels with Linear A Inscriptions* (Aegaeum 36), Leuven – Liege.

Davis, E.N. 1995. 'Art and politics in the Aegean: The missing ruler', in P. Rehak (ed.), *The Role of the Ruler in the Prehistoric Aegean. Proceedings of a Panel Discussion Presented at the Annual Meeting of the Archaeological Institute of America, New Orleans, Louisiana, 28 December 1992* (Aegaeum 11), Liège – Austin: 11-20.

Davis, E.N. 2007. 'Brush work', in Ph.P. Betancourt, M.C. Nelson and H. Williams (eds.), *Krinoi kai Limenai. Studies in Honor of Joseph and Maria Shaw* (Prehistory Monographs 22), Philadelphia: 145-150.

Davis, J.L. and J. Bennet. 1999. 'Making Mycenaeans: warfare, territorial expansion, and representations of the other in the Pylian kingdom', in R. Laffineur (ed.), *POLEMOS. Le contexte guerrier en Égée à l'âge du Bronze, Actes de la 7e Rencontre égéenne internationale, Université de Liège, 14-17 avril 1998, Vol. I* (Aegaeum 19), Liège – Austin: 105-120.

Deger-Jalkotzy, S. 1996. '"Hier können wir Achäer nicht alle König sein." Zur Geschichte des Frühgriechischen Königtums', in W. Leschhorn, A.V.B. Miron and A. Miron (eds.), *Hellas und der griechische Osten. Studien zur Geschichte und Numismatik der griechischen Welt. Festschrift für Peter Robert Franke zum 70. Geburtstag*, Saarbrücken: 13-30.

Dickinson, O. 2005. 'The 'face of Agamemnon'', *Hesperia* 74: 299-308.

Dimopoulou, N., J.-P. Olivier and G. Rethemiotakis. 1993. 'Une statuette en argile MR IIIA de Poros / Irakliou avec inscription en linéaire A', *Bulletin de correspondance hellénique* 117: 501-521.

Dionisio, G., A.M. Jasink and J. Weingarten. 2014. *Minoan Cushion Seals. Innovation in Form, Style, and Use in Bronze Age Glyptic*, Rome.

Döhl, H. 1980. 'Mykenische Kampfdarstellungen. Bild und Deutung im prähistorischen Griechenland', in Th. Krüger and H.-G. Stephan (eds.), *Beiträge zur Archäologie Nordwestdeutschlands und Mitteleuropas. Festschrift Klaus Raddatz* (Materialhefte zur Ur- und Frühgeschichte Niedersachsens 16), Hildesheim: 21-33.

Drappier, G. and Ch. Langohr. 2004. 'Iconographie du pouvoir en Crète minoenne. Vers la mise au point d'une méthodologie', in Y. Perrin and T. Petit (eds.), *Iconographie impériale, iconographie royale, iconographie des élites dans le monde gréco-romain*, Saint-Étienne: 19-47.

Driessen, J. 1988. 'The Scribes of 'The Room of the Chariot Tablets'', in J.-P. Olivier and T. G. Palaima (eds), *Texts, Tablets and Scribes: Studies in Mycenaean epigraphy and economy offered to Emmett L. Bennett, Jr.* (Minos Supplement 10), Salamanca: 123-165.

Driessen, J. 2000. *The Scribes of the Room of the Chariot Tablets at Knossos. Approach to the study of a Linear B deposit* (Minos Suplementos 15), Salamanca.

Driessen, J. and Ch. Langohr 2007. 'Rallying 'round a "Minoan" past'. The legitimation of power at Knossos during the Late Bronze Age', in M.L. Galaty and W.A. Parkinson (eds.), *Rethinking Mycenaean Palaces* II, Los Angeles: 178-189.

Dubcová, V. 2009. 'Zur Problematik der herrscherlichen Ikonographie im minoisch-mykenischen Griechenland', *Anodos. Studies of the Ancient World* 9: 17-32.

Dubcová, V. 2016. 'Divine power from abroad. Some new thoughts about the foreign influences on the Aegean Bronze Age religious iconography', in E. Alram-Stern, F. Blakolmer, S. Deger-Jalkotzy, R. Laffineur and J. Weilhartner (eds.), *METAPHYSIS. Ritual, Myth and Symbolism in the Aegean Bronze Age. Proceedings of the 15th International Aegean Conference, Vienna, Institute for Oriental and European Archaeology, Aegean and Anatolia Department, Austrian Academy of Sciences and Institute of Classical Archaeology, University of Vienna, 22-25 April 2014* (Aegaeum 39), Leuven: 263-274.

Duhoux, Y. 2000. 'Le linéaire B: une sténographie de l'âge du Bronze', Živa Antika 50: 37-57.

Eder, B. and R. Jung. 2015. ''Unus pro omnibus, omnes pro uno': the Mycenaean palace system', in J. Weilhartner and F. Ruppenstein (eds.), *Tradition and Innovation in the Mycenaean Palatial Polities, Proceedings of an International Symposium held at the Austrian Academy of Sciences, 1-2 March, 2013* (Mykenische Studien 34), Vienna: 113-140.

Egan, E.C. and H. Brecoulaki 2015. 'Marine iconography at the Palace of Nestor and the emblematic use of the argonaut', in H. Brecoulaki, J.L. Davis and Sh.R. Stocker (eds.),

Mycenaean Wall Painting in Context: New Discoveries, Old Finds Reconsidered (Meletemata 72), Athens: 292-313.

Evans, A. 1921. *The Palace of Minos at Knossos, Vol. I.* London.

Evans, A. 1928. *The Palace of Minos at Knossos, Vol. II.* London.

Evans, A. 1930. *The Palace of Minos at Knossos, Vol. III.* London.

Evans, A. 1935. *The Palace of Minos at Knossos, Vol. IV.* London.

Facchetti, G.M. 2002. 'La lineare B: una scrittura contabile e largamente imperfetta', *Kadmos* 41: 141-147.

Farnoux, A. 1995. 'La fondation de la royauté minoenne: XXème siècle avant ou après Jésus-Christ?', in R. Laffineur and W.-D. Niemeier (eds.), *POLITEIA. Society and State in the Aegean Bronze Age. Proceedings of the 5th International Aegean Conference, University of Heidelberg, Archäologisches Institut, 10-13 April 1994, Vol. II* (Aegaeum 12), Liège – Austin: 323-334.

Faure, P. 1996. 'Des chiffres et des lettres', *Cretan Studies* 5: 131-136.

Foster, K.P. 1997. 'Visage and likeness in Minoan art', in R. Laffineur and Ph.P. Betancourt (eds.), *TEXNH. Craftsmen, Craftswomen, and Craftmanship in the Aegean Bronze Age, Proceedings of the 6th International Aegean Conference, Philadelphia, Temple Univ., 18-21 April 1996, Vol. I* (Aegaeum 16), Liège – Austin: 127-140.

Furumark, A. 1941. *Mycenaean Pottery. Analysis and Classification*, Stockholm.

Gates, Ch. 1985. 'Rethinking the building history of Grave Circle A', *American Journal of Archaeology* 89: 263-274.

Gauer, W. 1968. 'Die griechischen Bildnisse der klassischen Zeit als politische und persönliche Denkmäler', *Jahrbuch des Deutschen Archäologischen Instituts* 83: 118-179.

Gill, D. and J. Padgham. 2005. "One find of capital importance': a reassessment of the statue of User from Knossos', *British School at Athens Annual* 100: 41-59.

Godart, L. 1973. 'Una nuova iscrizione in lineare A a Mallia', in *Antichità Cretesi. Festschrift D. Levi, Vol. I*, Catania: 197-198.

Godart, L. and J.-P. Olivier. 1982. *Recueil des Inscriptions en Linéaire A, 4. Autres documents* (Études Crétoises 21.4), Paris.

Goren, Y. and D. Panagiotopoulos. 2009. 'The 'Lords of the Rings': An analytical approach to the riddle of the 'Knossian replica rings'', *Bulletin of the Institute of Classical Studies of the University of London* 52: 257-258.

Greco, A. 2014. 'The art of propaganda in Aegean iconography: when art must be sung', in S. Gaspa, A. Greco, D. Morandi Bonacossi, S. Ponchia and R. Rollinger (eds.), *From Source to History. Studies on Ancient Near Eastern Worlds and Beyond. Dedicated to Giovanni Battista Lanfranchi on the Occasion of His 65th Birthday on June 23, 2014* (Alter Orient und Altes Testament 412), Münster: 305-340.

Groenewegen-Frankfort, H.A. 1951. *Arrest and Movement. An Essay on Space and Time in the Art of the Ancient Near East*, Cambridge.

Hallager, E. 1996. *The Minoan Roundel and Other Sealed Documents in the Neopalatial Linear A Administration, Vol. I* (Aegaeum 14), Liège – Austin.

Hankey, V. 1981. 'The Aegean interest in El Amarna', *Journal of Mediterranean Anthropology and Archaeology* 1: 38-49.

Hazzidakis, J. 1921. *Tylissos à l'époque minoenne*, Paris.

Heinz, M. 2002. 'Bild und Macht in drei Kulturen', in M. Heinz and D. Bonatz (eds.), *Bild – Macht – Geschichte. Visuelle Kommunikation im Alten Orient*, Berlin: 71-93.

Heinz, S.C. 2001. *Die Feldzugsdarstellungen des Neuen Reiches. Eine Bildanalyse*, Vienna.

Heurtley, W. 1921-23. 'Excavations at Mycenae. The grave stelai', *British School at Athens Annual* 25: 126-146.

Hiller S. 1995. 'Der SM II-Palaststil. Ausdruck politischer Ideologie?', in R. Laffineur and W.-D. Niemeier (eds.), *POLITEIA. Society and State in the Aegean Bronze Age. Proceedings of the 5th International Aegean Conference, University of Heidelberg, Archäologisches Institut, 10-13 April 1994, Vol. II* (Aegaeum 12), Liège -Austin: 561-572.

Hiller, S. 1996. 'Knossos and Pylos. A case of special relationship?', *Cretan Studies* 5: 73-83.

Hiller, S. 1999. 'Scenes of warfare and combat in the arts of Aegean Late Bronze Age. Reflections on typology and development', in R. Laffineur (ed.), *POLEMOS. Le contexte guerrier en Égée à l'âge du Bronze, Actes de la 7e Rencontre égéenne internationale, Université de Liège, 14-17 avril 1998, Vol. II* (Aegaeum 19), Liège: 319-330.

Hiller, S. 2005. 'The spiral as a symbol of sovereignty and power', in A. Dakouri-Hild and S. Sherratt (eds.), *Autochthon. Papers Presented to O. T. P. K. Dickinson on the Occasion of his Retirement, Institute of Classical Studies, University of London, 9 November 2005* (BAR-IS 1432), Oxford: 259-270.

Hiller, S. 2009. 'The façade of the so-called 'Treasure of Atreus' at Mycenae. Reflections on the iconography of the ornamental and figural reliefs', in D. Danielidou (ed.), *Δώρον. Τιμητικός τόμος γιά τον καθηγητή Σπύρο Ιακωβίδη*, Athens: 291-308.

Hiller, S. 2011. '*E-ke-ra$_2$-wo* 'Der Mann mit der Lanze': Wortetymologie, Herrschertitulatur und Bildtopos', in F. Blakolmer, C. Reinholdt, J. Weilhartner and G. Nightingale (eds.), Österreichische Forschungen zur Ägäischen Bronzezeit 2009. Akten der Tagung vom 6. bis 7. März 2009 am Fachbereich Altertumswissenschaften der Universität Salzburg, Vienna: 137-146.

Hirsch, E.S. 1977. *Painted decoration on the floors of Bronze Age structures on Crete and the Greek Mainland* (Studies in Mediterranean Archaeology 53), Göteborg.

Hood, S. 1995. 'The Minoan palace as residence of gods and men', in *Acts of the 7th International Cretological Congress, Vol. I.2*, Rethymno: 393-407.

Hood, S. 1997. 'A monumental Linear inscription from Knossos', *Kadmos* 36: 111-117.

Hooker, J.T. 1967. 'The Mycenae Siege Rhyton and the question of Egyptian influence', *American Journal of Archaeology* 71: 269-281.

Hooker, J. 1992. 'Early Balkan 'scripts' and the ancestry of Linear A', *Kadmos* 31: 97-112.

Hristova, P. 2012. 'Overlaying Mycenae's masks in funerary and living contexts of symbolic action: jewellery for body adornment, portraits, or else?', in M.-L. Nosch and R. Laffineur (eds.), *KOSMOS. Jewellery, Adornment and Textiles in the Aegean Bronze Age. Proceedings of the 13th International Aegean Conference, University of Copenhagen, Danish National Research Foundation's Centre for Textile Research, 21-26 April 2010* (Aegaeum 3), Leuven – Liege: 417-424.

Hutchinson, R.W. 1956. 'A tholos tomb on the Kephala', *British School at Athens Annual* 51: 74-80.

Iakovidis, S. 1986. 'Destruction horizon at Late Bronze Age Mycenae', in *Φίλια Έπη εις Γεώργιον Ε. Μυλωνάν, Vol. I.* (Library of the Athens Archaeological Society 103), Athens: 233-260.

Iakovidis, S.E. 2004. 'The Cult Centre of Mycenae', in L. Godart (ed.), *Culti primordiali della Grecità. Convegno internazionale alla luce delle scoperte di Tebe, Roma, 24-25 febbraio 2000*, Rome: 14-29.

Iakovidis, S.E. 2013. *Ανασκαφές Μυκηνών IV, Η οικία στις Πλάκες*, Athens.
Immerwahr, S.A. 1990. *Aegean Painting in the Bronze Age*, University Park PA – London.
Jaeggi, O. 2008. *Die griechischen Porträts: antike Repräsentation – moderne Projektion*, Berlin.
Jasink, A.M. 2005. 'Mycenaean means of communication and diplomatic relations with foreign royal courts', in R. Laffineur and E. Greco (eds.), *EMPORIA. Aegeans in the Central and Eastern Mediterranean. Proceedings of the 10th International Aegean Conference, Athens, Italian School of Archaeology, 14-18 April 2004, Vol. I* (Aegaeum 25), Liège – Austin: 59-67.
Kaiser, B. 1976. *Untersuchungen zum minoischen Relief*, Bonn.
Kalogeropoulos, K. 1998. *Die frühmykenischen Grabfunde von Analipsis (südöstliches Arkadien)*, Athens.
Kanta, A. and M. Perna. 2011. 'A Late Minoan IIIA-B bull bearing a Linear inscription from the «Piazzale dei Sacelli» of Haghia Triada', in F. Carinci, N. Cucuzza, P. Militello and O. Palio (eds.), *Kretes Minoidos. Tradizione e identità minoica tra produzione artigianale, pratiche cerimoniali e memoria del passato. Studi offerti a Vincenzo La Rosa per il Suo 70° compleanno* (Studi Cretese 10), Padova: 285-296.
Kantor, J.J. 1957. 'Narration in Egyptian art', *American Journal of Archaeology* 61: 44-54.
Karageorghis, V. 1958. 'Myth and epic in Mycenaean vase painting', *American Journal of Archaeology* 62: 383-387.
Karageorghis, V. 1959. 'Les personnages en robe sur les vases mycéniens', *Bulletin de correspondance hellénique* 83: 193-205.
Kelder, J. 2010. *The Kingdom of Mycenae: A Great Kingdom in the Late Bronze Age Aegean*, Bethesda.
Keramopoullos, A.D. 1909. 'Η οικία του Κάδμου', *Archaiologike Ephemeris*: 57-122.
Kilian, K. 1987. 'Zur Funktion der mykenischen Residenzen auf dem griechischen Festland', in R. Hägg and N. Marinatos (eds.), *The Function of the Minoan Palaces. Proceedings of the Fourth International Symposium at the Swedish Institute in Athens*, Stockholm: 21-38.
Kilian, K. 1988. 'The emergence of *wanax* ideology in the Mycenaean palaces', *Oxford Journal of Archaeology* 7: 291-302.
Killen, J.T. 1994. 'Thebes sealings, Knossos tablets and Mycenaean state banquets', *Bulletin of the Institute of Classical Studies of the University of London* 40: 67-84.
Koehl, R.B. 1986. 'The Chieftain Cup and a Minoan rite of passage', *Journal of Hellenic Studies* 106: 99-110.
Kopcke, G. 1976. 'Zum Stil der Schachtgräbermasken', *AM* 91: 1-13.
Krattenmaker, K. 1995a 'Palace, peak and sceptre: the iconography of legitimacy', in P. Rehak (ed.), *The Role of the Ruler in the Prehistoric Aegean. Proceedings of a Panel Discussion Presented at the Annual Meeting of the Archaeological Institute of America, New Orleans, Louisiana, 28 December 1992* (Aegaeum 11), Liège – Austin: 49-58.
Krattenmaker, K. 1995b. 'Architecture in glyptic cult scenes: the Minoan examples', in W. Müller (ed.), *Sceaux minoens et mycéniens. IVe symposium international, 10-12 septembre 1992, Clermont-Ferrand* (Corpus der minoischen und mykenischen Siegel Beiheft 5), Berlin: 117-133.
Kritseli-Providi, I. 1982. Τοιχογραφίες του Θρησκευτικού Κέντρου των Μυκηνών, Athens.

Krzyszkowska, O.H. 1991. 'The Enkomi warrior head reconsidered', *British School at Athens Annual* 86: 107-120.

Krzyszkowska, O. 2005. *Aegean Seals. An Introduction* (Bulletin of the Institute of Classical Studies of the University of London Supplement 85), London.

Kyriakidis, E. 2005. 'Unidentified floating objects on Minoan seals', *American Journal of Archaeology* 109.2: 137-154.

Laffineur, R. 1990. 'The iconography of Mycenaean seals and the status of their owner', *Aegaeum* 6: 117-160.

Laffineur, R. 1992. 'Iconography as evidence of social and political status in Mycenaean Greece', in R. Laffineur and J.L. Crowley (eds.), *EIKΩN. Aegean Bronze Age Iconography: Shaping a Methodology. Proceedings of the 4th International Aegean Conference, University of Tasmania, Hobart, Australia, 6-9 April 1992* (Aegaeum 8), Liège: 105-112.

Laffineur, R. 1995. 'Aspects of rulership at Mycenae in the Shaft grave period', in P. Rehak (ed.), *The Role of the Ruler in the Prehistoric Aegean. Proceedings of a Panel Discussion Presented at the Annual Meeting of the Archaeological Institute of America, New Orleans, Louisiana, 28 December 1992* (Aegaeum 11), Liège – Austin: 81-94.

Lamb, W. 1921-23. 'The frescoes from the walls', *British School at Athens Annual* 25, 1921-23: 249-55.

Lang, M.L. 1969. *The Palace of Nestor at Pylos in Western Messenia II. The Frescoes*, Princeton.

Lebessi, A., P. Muhly. and G. Papasavvas. 2004. 'The Runner's Ring, a Minoan athlete's dedication at the Syme sanctuary, Crete', *Mitteilungen des Deutschen Archäologischen Instituts, Athenische Abteilung* 119: 1-31.

Leukart, A. 1992. 'Les signes *76 (ra_2, «rja») et *78 (ro_2, «rjo») et le nom du grand prêtre de Poséidon (sinon du roi) à Pylos', in J.-P. Olivier (ed.), *Mykenaïka. Actes du IXe Colloque international sur les textes mycéniens et égéens organisé par le Centre de l'Antiquité Grecque et Romaine de la Fondation Hellénique des Recherches Scientifiques et l'École française d'Athènes (Athènes, 2-6 octobre 1990)* (Bulletin de correspondance hellénique Supplément 25), Paris: 387-405.

Lindgren, M. 1973. *The People of Pylos, Vol. II* (Boreas 3), Uppsala.

Lupack, S. 2014. 'Offerings for the *wanax* in the Fr tablets: Ancestor worship and the maintenance of power in Mycenaean Greece', in D. Nakassis, J. Gulizio and S.A. James (eds.), KE-RA-ME-JA. *Studies Presented to Cynthia W. Shelmerdine* (Prehistory Monographs 46), Philadelphia: 163-177.

Lurz, N. 1994. *Der Einfluß Ägyptens, Vorderasiens und Kretas auf die Mykenischen Fresken. Studien zum Ursprung der Frühgriechischen Wandmalerei*, Frankfurt.

Maran, J. 2006. 'Mycenaean citadels as performative space', in J. Maran, C. Juwig, H. Schwengel and U. Thaler (eds.), *Constructing Power. Architecture, Ideology and Social Practice*, Hamburg: 93-116.

Maran, J. 2012. 'Architektonischer Raum und soziale Kommunikation auf der Oberburg von Tiryns – Der Wandel von der mykenischen Palastzeit zur Nachpalastzeit', in F. Arnold, A. Busch, R. Haensch and U. Wulf-Rheidt (eds.), *Orte der Herrschaft. Charakteristika von antiken Machtzentren*, Rahden: 149-162.

Maran, J. and E. Stavrianopoulou. 2007. 'Πότνιος Ανήρ – Reflections on the ideology of Mycenaean kingship', in E. Alram-Stern and G. Nightingale (eds.), *Keimelion. The Formation of Elites and Elitist Lifestyles from Mycenaean Palatial Times to the Homeric*

Period. Akten des internationalen Kongresses vom 3. bis 5. Februar 2005 in Salzburg (DenkschrWien 350), Vienna: 285-298.

Marinatos, N. 1984a. *'Art and Religion in Thera. Reconstructing a Bronze Age Society'*, Athens.

Marinatos, N. 1984b. 'Minoan threskeiocracy on Thera', in R. Hägg and N. Marinatos (eds.), *The Minoan Thalassocracy. Myth and Reality. Proceedings of the Third International Symposium at the Swedish Institute in Athens, 31 May – 5 June, 1982*, Stockholm: 167-178.

Marinatos, N. 1988. 'The fresco from room 31 at Mycenae: Problems of method and interpretation', in E.B. French and K.A. Wardle (eds.), *Problems in Greek Prehistory. Papers Presented at the Centenary Conference of the British School of Archaeology at Athens, Manchester, April 1986*, Bristol: 245-251.

Marinatos, N. 1995. 'Divine kingship in Minoan Crete', in P. Rehak (ed.), *The Role of the Ruler in the Prehistoric Aegean. Proceedings of a Panel Discussion Presented at the Annual Meeting of the Archaeological Institute of America, New Orleans, Louisiana, 28 December 1992* (Aegaeum 11), Liège – Austin: 37-48.

Marinatos, N. 1996. 'The iconographical program of the palace of Knossos', in M. Bietak (ed.), *Haus und Palast im alten Ägypten. Internationales Symposium 8. bis 11. April 1992 in Kairo* (DenkschrWien Gesamtakademie 14), Vienna: 149-157.

Marinatos, N. 2007. 'Proskynesis and Minoan theocracy', in F. Lang, C. Reinholdt and J. Weilhartner (eds.), *Stephanos Aristeios. Archäologische Forschungen zwischen Nil und Istros. Festschrift für Stefan Hiller zum 65. Geburtstag*, Vienna: 179-185.

Marinatos, N. 2010. *Minoan Kingship and the Solar Goddess. A Near Eastern* Koine, Chicago.

Marinatos, N. and L. Morgan. 2005. 'The dog pursuit scene from Tell el Dab[c]a and Kea', in L. Morgan (ed.), *Aegean Wall Painting. A Tribute to Mark Cameron* (British School at Athens Studies 13), London: 119-122.

Marinatos, S. 1968. 'The stelai of Circle B at Mycenae', *Athens Annals of Archaeology* 1: 175-177.

Marinatos, S. and M. Hirmer. 1973. *Kreta, Thera und das mykenische Hellas* [2nd edition], Munich.

Matz, F. 1958. *Göttererscheinung und Kultbild im minoischen Kreta* (AbhMainz 7), Wiesbaden.

McCallum, L.R. 1987. *Decorative Program in the Mycenaean Palace of Pylos: The Megaron Frescoes* (Ph.D. thesis, University of Pennsylvania).

Metzler, D. 1971. *Porträt und Gesellschaft.* Über die Entstehung des griechischen Porträts in der Klassik, Munich.

Meyer, E. 1928. *Geschichte des Altertums II(1)*, Stuttgart.

Michailidou, A. 2000-1. 'Indications of literacy in Bronze Age Thera', *Minos* 35-36: 7-30.

Militello, P. 2003. 'Il *Rhytòn* dei Lottatori e le scene di combattimento: battaglie, duelli, agoni e competizioni nella Creta neopalaziale', *Creta Antica* 4: 359-401.

Morgan, L. 1988. *The Miniature Wall Paintings of Thera. A Study in Aegean Culture and Iconography*, Cambridge.

Morgan, L. 2005a. 'New discoveries and new ideas in Aegean wall painting', in L. Morgan (ed.), *Aegean Wall Painting. A Tribute to Mark Cameron* (British School at Athens Studies 13), London: 21-44.

Morgan, L. 2005b. 'The Cult Centre at Mycenae and the duality of life and death', in L. Morgan (ed.), *Aegean Wall Painting. A Tribute to Mark Cameron* (British School at Athens Studies 13), London: 159-171.

Morgan, L. 2010. 'An Aegean griffin in Egypt: the hunt frieze at Tell el-Dab[c]a', *Ägypten und Levante* 20: 303-323.

Morris, Ch. 1990. 'In pursuit of the white tusked boar: aspects of hunting in Mycenaean society', in R. Hägg and G. Nordquist (eds.), *Celebrations of Death and Divinity in the Bronze Age Argolid*, Stockholm: 149-156.

Moscati, S. 1963. *Historical Art in the Ancient Near East* (Studi Semitici 8), Rome.

Moser von Filseck, K. 1986. 'Der Alabasterfries von Tiryns', *Archäologischer Anzeiger:* 1-32.

Muller, B. 2005. 'De Mari à l'Egée: La peinture Proche-Orientale au 2e millénaire av. J.-C.', in A. Villing (ed.), *The Greeks in the East* (British Museum Research Publication 157), London: 37-45.

Müller, W. 2000. 'Zu Stil und Zeitstellung des Bildthemas Herr der Löwen', in I. Pini (ed.), *Minoisch-mykenische Glyptik. Stil, Ikonographie, Funktion. V. Internationales Siegel-Symposium, Marburg, 23.-25. September 1999* (CMS Beiheft 6), Berlin: 181-194.

Mylonas, G.E. 1951. 'The figured Mycenaean stelai', *American Journal of Archaeology* 55: 134-147.

Niemeier, W.-D. 1987. 'Das Stuckrelief des "Prinzen mit der Federkrone" aus Knossos und minoische Götterdarstellungen', *Mitteilungen des Deutschen Archäologischen Instituts, Athenische Abteilung* 102: 65-98.

Niemeier, W.-D. 1990. 'Mycenaean elements in the miniature fresco from Thera?', in D.A. Hardy, C.G. Doumas, J. A. Sakellarakis and P.M. Warren (eds.), *Thera and the Aegean World III. Proceedings of the Third International Congress, Vol. I*, London: 267-284.

Nörling, Th. 1995. *Altägäische Architekturbilder* (Archaeologica Heidelbergensia 2), Mayence.

Olivier, J.-P. 1980. 'Catalogue des marques de carriers', in O. Pelon (ed.), *Le palais de Malia*, Paris: 175-238.

Olivier, J.-P. 1981. 'Inscription en linéaire A sur une statuette en terre cuite de Tylissos (HM 6585)', *L'Antiquité classique* 50: 621-627.

Olivier, J.-P. 1999. 'Rapport 1991-1995 sur les textes en écriture hiéroglyphique Crétoise, en linéaire A et en linéaire B', in S. Deger-Jalkotzy, S. Hiller and O. Panagl (eds.), *Floreant Studia Mycenaea, Akten des X. Internationalen Mykenologischen Colloquiums in Salzburg vom 1.-5. Mai 1995, Vol. II*, Vienna: 419-435.

Otto, B. 1987. 'Minoische Bildsymbole', in *Kolloquium zur Ägäischen Vorgeschichte, Mannheim, 20.-22. 2. 1986* (Schriften des Deutschen Archäologen-Verbandes 9), Mannheim: 9-27.

Otto, B. 2000. 'Hoheitszeichen in der altkretischen Kunst', in F. Blakolmer (ed.), *Österreichische Forschungen zur Ägäischen Bronzezeit 1998. Akten der Tagung am Institut für Klassische Archäologie der Universität Wien, 2.-3. Mai 1998* (Wiener Forschungen zur Archäologie 3), Vienna: 83-88.

Otto, B. 2011. 'Das hohe und das erhöhte Thronen in der bronzezeitlichen Ikonographie der Ägäis', in F. Blakolmer, C. Reinholdt, J. Weilhartner and G. Nightingale (eds.), *Österreichische Forschungen zur Ägäischen Bronzezeit 2009. Akten der Tagung vom 6.*

bis 7. März 2009 am Fachbereich Altertumswissenschaften der Universität Salzburg, Vienna: 229-240.

Palaima, Th.G. 1981. 'On the painted Linear sign from a wall at Knossos', *Kadmos* 20: 79-82.

Palaima, Th.G. 1987. 'Comments on Mycenaean literacy', in J.T. Killen, J.L. Melena and J.-P. Olivier (eds.), *Studies in Mycenaean and Classical Greek Presented to John Chadwick* (= *Minos* 20-22), Salamanca: 499-510.

Palaima, Th.G. 1995. 'The nature of the Mycenaean Wanax: non-Indo-European origins and priestly functions', in P. Rehak (ed.), *The Role of the Ruler in the Prehistoric Aegean. Proceedings of a Panel Discussion Presented at the Annual Meeting of the Archaeological Institute of America, New Orleans, Louisiana, 28 December 1992* (Aegaeum 11), Liège – Austin: 119-139.

Palaima, Th.G. 2006. '*Wanaks* and related power terms in Mycenaean and later Greek', in S. Deger-Jalkotzy and I. Lemos (eds.), *Ancient Greece: From the Mycenaean Palaces to the Age of Homer* (Edinburgh Leventis Studies 3), Edinburgh: 53-71.

Palaima, Th.G. 2016. 'The ideology of the ruler in Mycenaean Prehistory: twenty years after the missing ruler', in R. Koehl (ed.), *Studies in Aegean Art and Culture. A New York Aegean Bronze Age Colloquium in Memory of Ellen N. Davis*, Philadelphia: 133-158.

Panagiotopoulos, D. 2010. 'A systemic approach to Mycenaean sealing practices', in W. Müller (ed.), *Die Bedeutung der minoischen und mykenischen Glyptik. VI. Internationales Siegel-Symposium aus Anlass des 50 jährigen Bestehens des CMS, Marburg, 9.-12. Oktober 2008* (CMS Beiheft 8), Mayence: 297-307.

Panagiotopoulos, D. 2014. *Mykenische Siegelpraxis. Funktion, Kontext und administrative Verwendung mykenischer Tonplomben auf dem griechischen Festland und Kreta* (Athenaia 5), Munich.

Pavúk, P. 2002. 'The city on the slope: some observations on two-dimensional representations of architecture in Aegean art', in R. Aslan, S. Blum, G. Kastl, F. Schweizer and D. Thumm (eds.), *Mauerschau. Festschrift für Manfred Korfmann, Vol. I*, Remshalden-Grunbach: 567-283.

Perna, M. 2014. 'The birth of administration and writing in Minoan Crete: thoughts on Hieroglyphics and Linear A', in D. Nakassis, J. Gulizio and S.A. James (eds.), *KE-RA-ME-JA. Studies Presented to Cynthia W. Shelmerdine* (Prehistory Monographs 46), Philadelphia: 251-259.

Peterson, S.E. 1981. *Wall Paintings in the Aegean Bronze Age: The Procession Frescoes* (Ph.D. thesis, University of Minnesota).

Petrakos, V. Ch. 2010. 'Άγιος Βασίλειος Λακωνίας', *Ergon* 57: 33-40.

Phillips, J. 2007. 'The Amenhotep III 'plaques' from Mycenae: Comparison, contrast and a question of chronology', in M. Bietak and E. Czerny (eds.), *The Synchronisation of Civilisations in the Eastern Mediterranean in the Second Millennium B.C. III. Proceedings of the SCIEM 2000 – 2nd EuroConference, Vienna, 28th of May – 1st of June 2003* (DenkschrWien Gesamtakademie 37), Vienna: 479-493.

Phillips, J. 2008. *Aegyptiaca on the Island of Crete in their Chronological Context: A Critical Review, Vol. II*, Vienna.

Phillips, J. and E. Cline. 2005. 'Amenhotep III and Mycenae: new evidence', in A. Dakouri-Hild and S. Sherratt (eds.), *Autochthon. Papers Presented to O.T.P.K. Dickinson on the Occasion of his Retirement, Institute of Classical Studies, University of London, 9 November 2005*, Oxford: 317-328.

Pini, I. 1997. *Die Tonplomben aus dem Nestorpalast von Pylos*, Mayence.

Pini, I. 1999. 'Minoische 'Porträts'?', in Ph.P. Betancourt, V. Karageorghis, R. Laffineur and W.-D. Niemeier (eds.), *MELETEMATA. Studies in Aegean Archaeology Presented to Malcolm H. Wiener as he enters his 65th Year, Vol. III* (Aegaeum 20), Liège – Austin: 661-670.

Pini, I. 2008. 'Are there any representations of feasting in the Aegean Bronze Age?', in L.A. Hitchcock, R. Laffineur and J. Crowley (eds.), *DAIS. The Aegean Feast, Proceedings of the 12th International Aegean Conference, University of Melbourne, Centre for Classics and Archaeology, 25-29 March 2008* (Aegaeum 29), Liège – Austin: 249-254.

Pliatsika, V. 2015. 'Tales of the unexpected. Identifying cult practice in the House M Quarter of the Mycenae citadel', in A.-L. Schallin and I. Tournavitou (eds.), *Mycenaeans up to date. The Archaeology of the North-Eastern Peloponnese – Current Concepts and New Directions*, Stockholm: 597-612.

Poursat, J.-C. 1977. *Les ivoires mycéniens. Essai sur la formation d'un art mycénien* (BÉFAR 230), Paris.

Preston, L. 2005. 'The Kephala Tholos at Knossos: a study in the reuse of the past', *British School at Athens Annual* 100: 61-123.

Protonotariou-Deilaki, E. 1990a. 'Burial customs and funerary rites in the prehistoric Argolid', in Hägg and G.C. Nordquist (eds.), *Celebrations of Death and Divinity in the Bronze Age Argolid. Proceedings of the Sixth International Symposium at the Swedish Institute at Athens, 11-13 June, 1988*, Stockholm: 69-83.

Protonotariou-Deilaki, E. 1990b. 'The tumuli of Mycenae and Dendra', in Hägg and G.C. Nordquist (eds.), *Celebrations of Death and Divinity in the Bronze Age Argolid. Proceedings of the Sixth International Symposium at the Swedish Institute at Athens, 11-13 June, 1988*, Stockholm: 85-106.

Puhvel, J. 1958. 'Helladic kingship and the god', in E. Grumach (ed.), *Minoica. Festschrift zum 80. Geburtstag von Johannes Sundwall*, Berlin: 327-333.

Rehak, P. 1984. 'New observations on the Mycenaean 'Warrior Goddess'', *Archäologischer Anzeiger* 99: 535-545.

Rehak, P. 1992. 'Tradition and innovation in the fresco from room 31 in the 'Cult Center' at Mycenae', in R. Laffineur and J.L. Crowley (eds.), *EIKΩN. Aegean Bronze Age Iconography: Shaping a Methodology. Proceedings of the 4th International Aegean Conference, University of Tasmania, Hobart, Australia, 6-9 April 1992* (Aegaeum 8), Liège: 39-62.

Rehak, P. 1995. 'Enthroned figures in Aegean art and the function of the Mycenaean megaron', in P. Rehak (ed.), *The Role of the Ruler in the Prehistoric Aegean. Proceedings of a Panel Discussion Presented at the Annual Meeting of the Archaeological Institute of America, New Orleans, Louisiana, 28 December 1992* (Aegaeum 11), Liège – Austin: 95-118.

Rehak, P. 1999. 'The Mycenaean "Warrior Goddess" revisited', in R. Laffineur (ed.), *POLEMOS. Le contexte guerrier en Égée à l'âge du Bronze, Actes de la 7e Rencontre égéenne internationale, Université de Liège, 14-17 avril 1998, Vol. I* (Aegaeum 19), Liège – Austin: 227-239.

Rehak, P. and J.G. Younger. 1998. 'International styles in ivory carving in the Bronze Age', in E.H. Cline and D. Harris-Cline (eds.), *The Aegean and the Orient in the Second Mil-*

lennium. Proceedings of the 50th Anniversary Symposium, Cincinnati, 18-20 April 1997 (Aegaeum 18), Liège – Austin: 229-256.

Rodenwaldt, G. 1911. 'Fragmente mykenischer Wandgemälde', *Mitteilungen des Deutschen Archäologischen Instituts, Athenische Abteilung* 36: 231-48.

Rodenwaldt, G. 1912. *Tiryns II. Die Fresken des Palastes*, Mayence.

Rodenwaldt, G. 1921. *Der Fries des Megarons von Mykenai*, Halle.

Rodenwaldt, G. 1933. *Griechische Reliefs in Lykien* (Sitzungsberichte der Berliner Akademie 27), Berlin.

Rystedt, E. 1999. 'No words, only pictures. Iconography in the transition between the Bronze Age and the Iron Age in Greece', *Opuscula Atheniensia* 24: 89-98.

Säflund, G. 1980. 'Sacrificial banquets in the 'Palace of Nestor'', *Opuscula Atheniensia* 13: 237-246.

Sakellariou, A. 1975. 'La scène du "siège" sur le rhyton d'argent de Mycènes d'après une nouvelle reconstitution', *Revue archéologique* 2: 195-208.

Schoep, I. 1999. 'Tablets and territories? Reconstructing Late Minoan IB political geography through undeciphered documents', *American Journal of Archaeology* 103.4: 201-221.

Schulz, R. 2002. 'Der Sturm auf die Festung. Gedanken zu einigen Aspekten des Kampfbildes im Alten Ägypten vor dem Neuen Reich', in M. Bietak and M. Schwarz (eds.), *Krieg und Sieg. Narrative Wanddarstellungen von Altägypten bis ins Mittelalter. Internationales Kolloquium 29.-30. Juli 1997 im Schloß Haindorf, Langenlois* (DenkschrWien Gesamtakademie 24), Vienna: 19-41.

Schulz, Th. 1988. 'Die Rekonstruktion des Thronpodestes im ersten großen Megaron von Tiryns', *Mitteilungen des Deutschen Archäologischen Instituts, Athenische Abteilung* 103: 11-23.

Shaw, M.C. 1986. 'The Lion Gate Relief of Mycenae reconsidered', in *Φίλια Έπη εις Γεώργιον Ε. Μυλωνάν, Vol. I*, Athens: 108-123.

Shaw, M.C. 1997. 'Aegean sponsors and artists: Reflections of their roles in the patterns of distribution of themes and representational conventions in the murals', in R. Laffineur and Ph.P. Betancourt (eds.), *TEXNH. Craftsmen, Craftswomen, and Craftmanship in the Aegean Bronze Age, Proceedings of the 6th International Aegean Conference, Philadelphia, Temple University, 18-21 April 1996, Vol. II* (Aegaeum 16), Liège – Austin: 481-504.

Shank, E.B. 2007. 'Throne room griffins from Pylos and Knossos', in Ph.P. Betancourt, M.C. Nelson and H. Williams (eds.), *Krinoi kai Limenai. Studies in Honor of Joseph and Maria Shaw* (Prehistory Monographs 22), Philadelphia: 159-165.

Shank, E. 2008. 'Decorated Dining Halls', in L.A. Hitchcock, R. Laffineur and J. Crowley (eds.), *DAIS. The Aegean Feast, Proceedings of the 12th International Aegean Conference, University of Melbourne, Centre for Classics and Archaeology, 25-29 March 2008* (Aegaeum 29), Liège – Austin: 97-104.

Shelmerdine, C.W. 1999. 'Administration in the Mycenaean palaces: Where's the chief?', in M.L. Galaty and W.A. Parkinson (eds.), *Rethinking Mycenaean Palaces. New Interpretations of an Old Idea. The Cotsen Institute of Archaeology, University of California* (Los Angeles Monograph 41), Los Angeles: 19-24.

Smith, W.S. 1965. *Interconnections in the Ancient Near East. A Study of the Relationship between the Arts of Egypt, the Aegean, and Western Asia*, New Haven.

Spartz, E. 1962. *Das Wappenbild des Herrn und der Herrin der Tiere in der minoisch-mykenischen und frühgriechischen Kunst* (Ph. D. thesis, Munich).

Spyropoulos, Th. 2015. 'Mural paintings from the Mycenaean palace of Boeotian Orchomenos', in H. Brecoulaki, J.L. Davis and Sh.R. Stocker (eds.), *Mycenaean Wall Painting in Context: New Discoveries, Old Finds Reconsidered* (Meletemata 72), Athens: 355-368.

Stais, V. 1915. 'Das silberne Rhyton des vierten Grabes der Burg von Mykenai', *Mitteilungen des Deutschen Archäologischen Instituts, Athenische Abteilung* 40. 1: 45-52.

Stocker, Sh.R. and J.L. Davis 2004. 'Animal sacrifice, archives and feasting at the Palace of Nestor', in J.C. Wright (ed.), *The Mycenaean Feast* (= *Hesperia* 73.2), Princeton – New Jersey: 59-76.

Thaler, U. 2015. 'Movement in between, into and inside Mycenaean palatial megara', in A.-L. Schallin and I. Tournavitou (eds.), *Mycenaeans up to date. The Archaeology of the North-Eastern Peloponnese – Current Concepts and New Directions*, Stockholm: 339-360.

Thomas, R, 1995. 'Written in stone? Liberty, equality, orality and the codification of law', *Bulletin of the Institute of Classical Studies of the University of London* 40: 59-74.

Tournavitou, I. 1995. 'The Mycenaean ivories from the Artemision at Delos', *Bulletin de correspondance hellénique* 119.2: 479-527.

Tournavitou, I. 2009. 'Η καθημερινή ζωή στην κάτω πόλη των Μυκηνών: αποσπάσματα από τις τοιχογραφίες της Δυτικής Οικίας', in D. Danielidou (ed.), *Δώρον. Τιμητικός τόμος για τον καθηγητή Σπύρο Ιακωβίδη*, Athens: 647-672.

Tournavitou, I. 2012. 'Fresco decoration and politics in a Mycenaean palatial centre: the case of the West House at Mycenae', in M.-L. Nosch and R. Laffineur (eds.), *KOSMOS. Jewellery, Adornment and Textiles in the Aegean Bronze Age. Proceedings of the 13th International Aegean Conference, University of Copenhagen, Danish National Research Foundation's Centre for Textile Research, 21-26 April 2010* (Aegaeum 33), Leuven – Liege: 723-729.

Tournavitou, I. 2015. 'Sport, prestige, and ritual outside the palaces: Pictorial frescoes from the West House at Mycenae', in H. Brecoulaki, J.L. Davis and Sh.R. Stocker (eds.), *Mycenaean Wall Painting in Context: New Discoveries, Old Finds Reconsidered* (Meletemata 72), Athens: 145-169.

Tournavitou, I. and H. Brecoulaki. 2015. 'The Mycenaean wall paintings from Argos: A preliminary presentation', in H. Brecoulaki, J.L. Davis and Sh.R. Stocker (eds.), *Mycenaean Wall Painting in Context: New Discoveries, Old Finds Reconsidered* (Meletemata 72), Athens: 212-245.

Valmin, N. 1953. 'Malthi-Epilog', *Opuscula Atheniensia* 1: 29-46.

Vermeule, E.T. 1964. *Greece in the Bronze Age*, Chicago.

Vermeule, E.T. 1975. *The Art of the Shaft Graves of Mycenae, Lectures in Memory of Louise Taft Semple, Delivered April 30 and May 1, 1973*, Cincinnati.

Vonhoff, Ch. 2008. *Darstellungen von Kampf und Krieg in der minoischen und mykenischen Kultur*, Rahden.

Vonhoff, Ch. 2011. 'Jagddarstellungen in der spätmykenischen Kunst der Palast- und Nachpalastzeit', *Mitteilungen des Deutschen Archäologischen Instituts, Athenische Abteilung* 126: 29-61.

Wace, A.J.B. 1921-23a. ‘Excavations at Mycenae. VII. The Lion Gate and Grave Circle area’, *British School at Athens Annual* 25: 9-146.
Wace, A.J.B. 1921-23b. ‘Excavations at Mycenae IX. The tholos tombs’, *British School at Athens Annual* 25, 1921-23: 283-402.
Wace, A.J.B.1949. *Mycenae. An Archaeological History and Guide*, Princeton.
Wardle, K.A. 2015. ‘Reshaping the past: Where was the “Cult Centre” at Mycenae?’, in A.-L. Schallin and I. Tournavitou (eds.), *Mycenaeans up to date. The Archaeology of the North-Eastern Peloponnese – Current Concepts and New Directions*, Stockholm: 577-596.
Weingarten, J. 2010. ‘Corridors of power: a social network analysis of the Minoan, ‘replica rings’, in W. Müller (ed.), *Die Bedeutung der minoischen und mykenischen Glyptik. VI. Internationales Siegel-Symposium aus Anlass des 50 jährigen Bestehens des CMS, Marburg, 9.-12. Oktober 2008* (CMS Beiheft 8), Berlin: 395-412.
Whittaker, H. 2001. ‘Reflections on the socio-political function of Mycenaean religion’, in R. Laffineur and R. Hägg (eds.), *POTNIA. Deities and Religion in the Aegean Bronze Age, Proceedings of the 8th International Aegean Conference, Göteborg, Göteborg University, 12-15 April 2000* (Aegaeum 22), Liège – Austin: 355-360.
Whittaker, H. 2002. ‘Religion and Power. The nature of Minoan influence on early Mycenaean religion’, *Opuscula Atheniensia* 27: 151-157.
Whittaker, H. 2005. ‘Social and symbolic aspects of Minoan writing’, *European Journal of Archaeology* 8.1: 29-41.
Whittaker, H. 2014. *Religion and Society in Middle Bronze Age Greece*, Cambridge.
Whittaker, H. 2015. ‘The hidden ruler: art and politics in Minoan Crete’, *Journal of Ancient Egyptian Interconnections* 7.3: 90-94.
Wiener, M.H. 2015. ‘The Mycenaean conquest of Minoan Crete’, in C.F. Macdonald, E. Hatzaki and S. Andreou (eds.), *The Great Islands. Studies of Crete and Cyprus presented to Gerald Cadogan*, Athens: 131-142.
Winter, I.J. 1981. ‘Royal rhetoric and the development of historical narrative in Neo-Assyrian reliefs’, *Studies in Visual Communication* 7: 2-38.
Winter, I. 1986. ‘The king and the cup: iconography of the royal representation scene on Ur III seals’, in M. Kelly-Buccellati (ed.), *Insights through Images. Studies in Honor of Edith Porada*, Malibu: 253-268.
Winter, I.J. 1996. ‘Sex, rhetoric, and the public monument’, in N. Boymel Kampen (ed.), *Sexuality in Ancient Art. Near East, Egypt, Greece, and Italy*, Cambridge: 11-26.
Winter, I.J. 1998. ‘The affective properties of styles: an inquiry into analytical process and the inscription of meaning in art history’, in C.A. Jones and P. Galison (eds.), *Picturing Science. Producing Art*, New York: 55-77.
Woodard, W.S. 1968. ‘The later history of Grave Circle A at Mycenae’, *American Journal of Archaeology* 72: 174-175.
Wright, J.C. 1994. ‘The spatial configuration of beliefs: The archaeology of Mycenaean religion’, in S.E. Alcock and R. Osborne (eds.), *Placing the Gods. Sanctuaries and Sacred Space in Ancient Greece*, Oxford: 37-78.
Wright, J.C. 2004. ‘A survey of evidence for feasting in Mycenaean society’, in J.C. Wright (ed.), *The Mycenaean Feast*, Princeton – New Jersey: 13-58.

Wright, J.C 2006. 'The formation of the Mycenaean palaces', in S. Deger-Jalkotzy and I. Lemos (eds.), *Ancient Greece: From the Mycenaean Palaces to the Age of Homer* (Edinburgh Leventis Studies 3), Edinburgh: 7-52.

Wyatt, W.F. 1994-1995. 'Homeric and Mycenaean Λαός', *Minos* 29-30: 159-170.

Yalouris, N. 1989. 'Ein Schlachtengemälde im Palast des Nestor', *Mitteilungen des Deutschen Archäologischen Instituts, Athenische Abteilung* 104: 41-48.

Younger, J.G. 1987. 'The Elgin plaques from the Treasury of Atreus: evidence for a new reconstruction of the façade', in *Kolloquium zur Ägäischen Vorgeschichte, Mannheim, 20.-22.2.1986* (Schriften des Deutschen Archäologen-Verbandes 9), Mannheim: 138-150.

Younger, J.G. 1995. 'The iconography of rulership: a conspectus', in P. Rehak (ed.), *The Role of the Ruler in the Prehistoric Aegean. Proceedings of a Panel Discussion Presented at the Annual Meeting of the Archaeological Institute of America, New Orleans, Louisiana, 28 December 1992* (Aegaeum 11), Liège – Austin: 151-211.

Younger, J.G. 1997. 'The stelai of Mycenae Grave Circles A and B', in R. Laffineur and Ph.P. Betancourt (eds.), *TEXNH. Craftsmen, Craftswomen and Craftsmanship in the Aegean Bronze Age. Proceedings of the 6th International Aegean Conference, Philadelphia, Temple University, 18-21 April 1996, Vol. I* (Aegaeum 16), Liège – Austin: 229-239.

A Great King of Alašiya? The archaeological and textual evidence

Eleni Mantzourani, Konstantinos Kopanias and Ioannis Voskos

Introduction

Alašiya's king is mentioned as an equal to the Egyptian king in the Amarna letters, despite the fact that this kingdom was no match to Egypt from a political and military point of view. It seems that Alašiya's significance as a trade partner, as well as the fact that it was beyond Egypt's reach, were sufficient reasons to pretend that its ruler(s) belonged to the 'big league'. In this paper, we offer a brief overview of various texts from Egypt, Ḫatti and Ugarit concerning the political status of the king of Alašiya, as well as a summary of the available archaeological evidence on Cyprus. It seems that there is no major site, which could be considered as the capital of a Great Kingdom. However, one of these sites was apparently viewed as such by Egypt for its own reasons. The same could apply also in the case of Aḫḫiyawa. Although we have no undeniable archaeological evidence to prove the 'supremacy' of a single Mycenaean centre over the whole of the Aegean, one of these centres seems to have been considered by the Hittites as the capital of a Great King.

1. The Identification of Alašiya as Cyprus

The evidence from the Hittite, Ugaritic and Egyptian texts (Kitchen 2009: 8-10), as well as the recent petrographic analysis of tablets originating from Cyprus (Goren et al. 2003; 2004: 57-70; 2011: 696) leaves no doubt about the identification of Alašiya with the latter island.[1] Previous attempts to locate Alašiya outside Cyprus, either in Cilicia or Syria, proved unrewarding.[2] If Alašiya is not to be identified with Cyprus, then we are confronted with two insurmountable problems: firstly, this would mean that Cyprus, a copper producing and trade centre with exports in all of the eastern Mediterranean, was never mentioned in any of the existing Bronze Age Near Eastern texts (Catling 1975: 205). Secondly, we would

1 Goren et al. 2003; 2004: 57-70; 2011: 696. Merrillees' (2011) insistence on his earlier position is inexplicable; on that, e.g., Cline 2005: 41. For a more detailed discussion, see Knapp 2008: 300-3.

2 See, e.g., Merrillees 1987; but see also the book review of Van den Hout 1994.

in: Kelder, J.M. and Waal, W.J.I. (eds) 2019: *From 'LUGAL.GAL' to 'Wanax'. Kingship and Political Organisation in the Late Bronze Age Aegean*, Sidestone Press (Leiden), pp. 95-130.

have to assume that a copper producing centre, with a king who at times was considered to be an equal to the Egyptian king and superior to the king of Ugarit, was based somewhere on the mainland, but somehow managed to escape the attention of the Hittite, the Mitanni and the Egyptian armies (Kitchen 2009: 6).

In the extant cuneiform texts Alašiya is always determined as either a land (KUR) or a land-city (KUR + URU). Merrillees understood the combination KUR + URU as city-state and proposed that Alašiya was nothing more than a minor centre like Ugarit (Merrillees 1987: 42). However, in the Hittite texts this combination of determinatives is not only used to describe minor states, but also, for example, the Hittite empire itself (KUR ^{URU}Ḫattuša, see Van den Hout 1994: 139.) Thus, the use of the combination KUR + URU in the case of Alašiya offers no indication for the size of the kingdom.

2. Textual evidence from the Middle Bronze Age Near East and Egypt (KK)

2.1. Mesopotamia and Syria

The earliest references to Alašiya come from Mari and Babylonia. Three are dated to the reign of Yaḫdun-Lim or Sûmû-Yamam of Mari[3] and three to the time of Zimri-Lim of Mari.[4] They all mention various quantities of Alašiyan copper imported to the city. Of particular interest is an additional fragmentary text from Mari dated to the 18th c. BCE which mentions URU^{KI} *a-la-ši-ia* (i.e. in the city-land of Alašiya) probably in connection to bronze.[5] The determinative URU^{KI} shows that Alašiya was also a city, which had the same name as the land.[6]

Most of these texts refer to significant quantities of Alašiyan copper that were imported to Mari. No further details are presented as to whether Alašiyan merchants reached the city or if the actual exchange took place somewhere else by the coast.[7] This

---

3 Dossin 1965: 402; Charpin 1990: 125 n. 2: 1) 14 GÚ 50 MA.NA URUDU KUR-*i* 50 MA.NA URUDU KUR-*i* ***a-la-si-um*** (T.361), 2) 1 MA.NA 14 SU URUDU LUḪ ***a-la-s[u-u]m*** [S]AG (T.370), 3) 50 MA.NA URUDU ***a-la-ši-ia*** (T.505).

4 Dossin 1939: 111; Charpin 1990: 125: 1) *erû misû* (LUḪ-ḪA) ***a-la-šu-ú***, 2) [x] *manû erê* ***a-la-ši-i***, 3) *siparru* ***a-la-šu-ú***.

5 M.5572 + M.14742: Charpin 1990: 127; Knapp 2008: 307.

6 Charpin 1990: 126; Marcus 2007: 148. Note that one of the texts differentiates between URUDU KUR-*i* and URUDU KUR-*i a-la-si-um*, i.e. 'mountain copper' and 'Alašiyan mountain copper' respectively (see n. 3 no. 1. Dossin 1965: 402). This has been interpreted as a direct reference to the copper ore deposits of the Troodos Mountains of Cyprus (Knapp 1996: 18; Knapp and Kassianidou 2008: 135). However, this could not have been the case. In the Mari texts two different qualities of copper are generally defined, namely 'copper of the mountains' (i.e. unrefined, unpurified) and 'washed copper' (i.e. refined, purified), see Limet 1985; Winter 2010: 353 n. 16. This implies that this particular quantity of Alašiyan copper was imported unrefined to Mari, which is quite puzzling; it would make more sense to assume that this copper was already refined somewhere in Alašiya, in order to reduce its size and thus facilitate its transportation. Taking into consideration the aforementioned assumption, it can be suggested that a second, finer purification of this particular shipment of Alašiyan copper would have been necessary upon its arrival at Mari (Muhly and Wertime 1973: 121-2; Limet 1985: 203).

7 Zimri-Lim reportedly sold tin to the chief merchant from Kaptara (i.e. Kaphtor/Keftiu/Crete: for the equation, see, e.g., Kitchen 2009: 9) and gave also 20 shekels of tin to a translator who assisted with the transaction (A.1270): Heimpel 2003: 12 n. 27; Podany 2010: 108. It is indeed implied that the merchants from Kaptara came to Mari, although the transaction could have taken place in a coastal site. The price of 20 shekels of tin paid to the translator seems unreasonably high, a fact probably meaning that additional service must have been offered.

place could have been the port of Ugarit from which then the copper may have been transported to Mari through the territory of the kingdom of Yamḫad.[8] A tablet from Tell Sianu (Bretschneider et al. 2004: 219 n. 12; Aruz 2008: cat. no. 17), near the Syrian coast, mentions objects imported from Alašiya and another 18th c. BCE tablet from Alalaḫ also mentions silver received from Alašiya, probably as payment for something else.[9]

Some of the Alašiyan copper seems to have been further exported to Babylonia. A tablet dated to ca. 1745/4 BCE from an unknown Babylonian site, mentions 12 minas of refined copper from Alašiya and Dilmun.[10] It seems that Ḫammurabi's diplomatic and military successes made it possible to also import goods from the Mediterranean. It has been suggested that Alašiya became the main copper supplier for Mesopotamia by the Old Babylonian Period, replacing its older trading partners from Oman/Bahrain (Heimpel 2003: 38). The copper quantities mentioned in the Mari texts are significant, even though the texts are indeed very restricted in number. It seems plausible that some Syrian and perhaps some Mesopotamian kings found a new copper supplier in Alašiya, allowing them not to rely exclusively on their previous suppliers.

2.2. Egypt

In Egyptian texts two terms are used which could be linked with Cyprus: *Irs*, i.e. Alas(i)a, and *Isy*, i.e. Asiya (Kitchen 2009: 1).[11] The oldest reference to Alas(i)a comes from an inscription of Amenemhat II at Memphis dating to ca. 1900 BCE (Altenmüller and Moussa 1991; Marcus 2007: 139-42; Kitchen 2009: 2). Military expeditions have been sent against Lebanon (M7) and Sinai (M13-4). A naval expedition was conducted against Asia (*Sṯt*), and in particular the foreign countries *ỉwꜣ* (M8, M16, M25) and *ỉꜣsi* (M16, M25).[12] According to this inscription '[the] fighting army, which was sent to cut up the fortifications of *ỉwꜣ* and of *ỉꜣsi* brought back a bounty: among other things, 1554 Asiatics, 646 deben (= 17.64 kg) of copper scrap, 125 deben (= 3.41 kg) of new copper, 1734 deben (= 47.34 kg) of malachite and 375 deben (= 5.1 kg) of lead (M16-8)'.[13]

The terms ỉꜣsi and *ỉwꜣ* can be identified with Alašiya and (possibly) Ura on the Cilician coast respectively (see also below §4.1).[14] Alašiya is here referred to as a land but it was probably also a fortified centre, since its name is written enclosed in a fortified oval (Kitchen 2009: 3), reminding us of the above mentioned Mari text with the reference to URI^{KI} *a-la-ši-ia*, i.e. the city-land of Alašiya.[15] The copper as well as the malachite[16] were

---

8 Zimri-Lim personally visited Yamḫad and also Ugarit (Podany 2010: 107-9), which means that he had excellent relations with them.

9 AT 385.2. Wiseman 1953: 8, 154; Catling 1975: 203; Knapp 2008: 307-8. For an overview of the archaeological evidence, see Yener 2012.

10 Birmingham City Museum inv. no. WHM 114046. Millard 1973: 12 MA.NA URUDU *mi-si* ***a-la-ši-im***; Knapp 2008: 308. Dilmun was probably located in Bahrain.

11 Kitchen 2009: 1. The identification of the *Irs* with Alašiya is secured through a docket in the Amarna letter EA 39 by the king of Alašiya, which mentions in Egyptian hieratic script 'Ruler of Alaš(i)a': Moran 1992: 112 n. 2.

12 Note that the ship determinative has been used: Marcus 2007: 144; Kitchen 2009: 2. The terms are written in the Middle Kingdom spelling.

13 For a detailed calculation of the weight of the transported objects, see Marcus 2007: 151.

14 Helck 1989; Marcus 2007: 144; Kitchen 2009: 2; contra Altenmüller and Moussa 1991: 35 n. 24.

15 See n. 5 and also Marcus 2007: 148.

16 Both Pliny and Theophrastus mention that copper malachite (chalcosmaragdus) was abundant in the copper mines of Cyprus. For a brief discussion, see Scott 2002: 105.

most probably been obtained from Alašiya, whereas the lead in all likelihood came either from Anatolia (through Ura) or the Aegean (Gill 2010; Kopanias 2015b; Kelder 2016).

The account of such a large number of prisoners (1554) implies that the size of the Egyptian flotilla must have been quite significant.[17] The text only refers to the expeditions against the above targets and not necessarily to their conquest.[18] It is possible that (at least) the last expedition was in fact a commercial one (Podany 2010: 111), or simply a raid to the Alašiyan coastline targeting the rural population. The city of Alašiya did not necessarily have to be located directly by the coast, as the similar case of Ugarit and its port Minet el-Beida indicates. If this hypothesis is correct, then the population of Alašiya would have enough time to prepare its defences against any attacks from the sea, like the one mounted by Amenemhat II. This attack resulted in a rather disappointing bounty, taking into consideration the size of the naval and military forces involved.

3. Prehistoric Bronze Age Cyprus from an archaeological perspective (EM, IV)

3.1. Late Chalcolithic to Early Bronze Age

Any research attempting to explain the socio-political situation in Bronze Age Cyprus should take into consideration a complex set of archaeological data, textual evidence and a number of long-debated subjects such as the Alašiya-Cyprus equation (see §1), the conditions that led to socio-economic complexity and social stratification, the development of interregional/international trade and the matters of settlement hierarchy, central administration and/or heterarchy on the island. Most of these issues have been analysed at length and will therefore not be addressed here.[19]

Cyprus apparently entered a period of major socio-economic transformations during the Late Chalcolithic (ca. 2700-2400 BCE), notably during the formative period of the so-called 'Philia phenomenon' (ca. 2400-2300 BCE). Alongside other developments, the various communities of the island also started to expel their insularity and isolation. In order to explain this change, Frankel and Webb have argued for a migration of Anatolian peoples (see, e.g., Webb and Frankel 1999, 2007, 2011; Frankel 2000, 2005), whereas other scholars (see, e.g., Peltenburg 1996, 2007; Bolger 2007; Knapp 2013: 260-77) have discussed the possibility of local evolution via intensified contacts between Cyprus and its neighbours.

Whichever of the two interpretations is accepted, the basic incentive for this change was the discovery of the Troodos sulphide copper ore bodies (see, e.g., Knapp 1990) and – after a period of internal metallurgical development (Manning 1993: 35) – the attempt of certain emerging power groups to control them. This process, possibly stemming from the increasing competition between households and the subsequent unequal access to wealth and power, led to a gradual break with the egalitarian past (Voskos 2018). The concomitant influx of 'foreign' elements and practices rapidly transformed the Cypriot material culture

17 For a calculation, see Marcus 2007: 157.

18 As proposed by, e.g., Schneider 2008: 61.

19 For recent discussions on sociopolitical organisation, settlement hierarchy, heterarchy, archaeological evidence and textual data on Cyprus, see, for example, Knapp 2008: 134-53, 298-341; 2013: 432-47. For the development of social complexity and stratified society on Cyprus, see, for example, Keswani 1993, Manning 1993 and various other papers in BASOR 292. For a recent brief review of available archaeological and textual data concerning the copper production industry and trade, see Kassianidou 2013.

and society. Similarly, while broadly discussing the issue of socio-economic transformation and the growth of political economy during the Bronze Age, Knapp (1985: 245) has pointed out that '...increased foreign demand for Cypriote copper most likely led to administrative formalization of internal copper production and in turn to the economic transformation of a village-based culture into an international urban-oriented complex society'.

Indeed, the few excavated Early Bronze Age settlements such as Marki *Alonia* (Frankel and Webb 1996, 2006), Sotira *Kaminoudhia* (Swiny et al. 2003) and notably the cemeteries of Cyprus[20] witness an explosion in the amount of copper artifacts, which is a clear contrast with the previous period. Alongside with the advances in metallurgical production there is an increasing presence of imported goods[21] such as pottery, bronze items and jewellery.[22] The most relevant examples of 'foreign' products are the abundant faience beads recovered at many sites, a few gypsum vessels from Vasilia *Kilistra* (Merrillees 2009) and also the Egyptian alabaster vessels from Vasilia *Kafkallia* (Hennesy et al. 1988: 25-39). It this seems that Cypriot social groups were already participating in the rising interregional trade networks of the eastern Mediterranean area.

However, the economic basis of Cypriot communities largely remained agropastoral and there are few signs of economic intensification, surplus manipulation and craft specialisation. Generally speaking, the social groups of the island managed to adapt to the new situation by continuing for the most part their traditional way of life within the sphere of simple socio-economic structures.

3.2. Middle Bronze Age

A quick look at the Middle Bronze Age architecture, topography, social and burial practices provides a view of increasing complexity, albeit with little if any differentiations from the previous period. The excavated sites of Alambra *Mouttes* (Coleman et al. 1996), Politiko *Troullia* (Falconer et al. 2005, 2010) and Episkopi *Phaneromeni* (Swiny 1986) with an estimated size between ca. 2-3 and 10-15 hectares (Manning 1993: 40, Fig. 3) are still far from being considered as urban centres.[23] Material culture, social practices and ritual also seem to resemble the EC data. Economic practices remained largely agropastoral, despite the increasing engagement with copper production. Likewise, other craft activities, such as pottery-making, seem to have remained within household-level production (see, e.g., Frankel and Webb 1996: 111; cf. Barlow in Coleman et al. 1996: 266).

Regarding mortuary architecture, the EC type of chamber tomb remained popular and most of the EC cemeteries were utilised in the Middle Bronze Age without any discontinuity. Only burial customs stand out as the basic field of social display and renegotiation of individual and collective identities. The growing numbers of mortuary goods including large quantities of copper artifacts, imported items and pottery with complex shapes and decoration, reflect a tendency towards social differentiation, extended copper production for internal/external consumption and increasing contacts with Anatolia, the Levant and Egypt. The latter is attested by the MC White Painted jugs found in the Levant (see, for example, Maguire 2009). What is more, a few grave offerings from north coast cemeteries

---

20 See, for example, Philia *Vasiliko*, Karmi *Palealona*, Vasilia *Kafkallia*, Lapithos *Vrysi tou Barba*, Bellapais *Vounoi* etc.

21 For a recent summary of imported goods during the Early-Middle Cypriot period, see Knapp 2013: 307-11.

22 Swiny (1989: 27) refers to Syro-Palestinian vessels and Minoan bronzes.

23 For the size estimation of several LC sites, see Knapp 2013: 355, Fig. 95.

provide sufficient proofs for sporadic direct or indirect contacts with Crete and the Aegean in general. The most famous among them are a Middle Minoan II Kamares ware cup, which was discovered in the so-called 'seafarer's tomb' at Karmi *Palealona* (Stewart 1963) and an Early Minoan III-Middle Minoan IA bridge-spouted jar coming from tomb 806A at Lapithos *Vrysi tou Barba* (Grace 1940: 24-7; Herscher 1978). Important as they may be, these exotic goods as well as the increasing numbers of metal artifacts are not enough to alter the picture of a village-based society.

3.3. Summary

It follows that, until at least the end of the Middle Cypriot period (i.e. 1700-1600 BCE) the available archaeological data are insufficient to support the view of a well-organised copper production and consumption industry, nor the appearance of élites that exclusively controlled the entrepreneurial activities. Concerning social complexity, Swiny (1989: 25) argued that 'no single prehistoric Bronze Age settlement, either excavated or surveyed, stands out by its size, complexity and lavishness of architectural fixtures or number of foreign imports. None shows signs of extensive trading connections', concluding that 'all the settlement data suggests that Cypriot society was unstratified'.

Indeed, the current archaeological record and the extended excavations at Marki *Alonia*, Sotira *Kaminoudhia*, Alambra *Mouttes*, Pyrgos *Mavrorachi* (see, e.g., Belgiorno 2004) and other EC-MC sites reveal a village-based society (Manning 1993: 40) lacking any sign of urban orientation and institutionalised social inequalities. Even though the Cypriot social groups seem to have realised the potential of long-distance trade, their participation on available exchange networks is characterised at best as opportunistic. Moreover, it is doubtful whether local Cypriotes acted directly as traders or there were foreign middlemen and private entrepreneurs for this task.[24]

3.4. An alternative reading of the Middle Cypriot and Late Cypriot I archaeological data

3.4.1. Contradicting textual and archaeological evidence

Taking for granted that Alašiya was the Bronze Age name for Cyprus or at least part of it, we are confronted with a major discrepancy between the archaeological and textual data.[25] On the one hand, from an archaeological perspective, the available material data reveal a village-based society with few albeit increasing signs of social complexity and a number of local copper ore deposits utilised by various settlements at the outskirts of

24 This might be true only for the early stages of the Cypriot copper industry and not for the late MC and LC period; see for example Kassianidou 2013: 144. Recent research suggests the existence of metal trade networks and interaction spheres already in the Early Bronze Age, highlighting, among others, the pioneer role of the Minoans. The leading role of the Minoans and other foreign merchants until 1600-1500 BCE and the indirect participation of Cypriotes is also suggested by the nearly complete absence of models depicting boats in Cyprus and the primarily agropastoral orientation of the Cypriot economy. Early contacts between Cyprus and Crete are also proved by the identification of Cypriot copper in Crete (Webb et al. 2006). This fact might explain why the Cypriotes chose to adopt a variation of Linear A (i.e. the Cypro-Minoan script) instead of a script originating from Syria, Egypt and Mesopotamia (hieroglyphic, cuneiform etc.).

25 This has also been noted by other scholars, see, e.g., Manning and DeMita 1997: 110; South 2002: 68. Knapp (2013: 441) also refers to a 'disjuncture' between textual and material evidence.

the Troodos Mountains. This fact led some researchers like Kassianidou to the conclusion that even though the foundations of Cypriot copper industry lie in the Middle Bronze Age (Kassianidou 2008), it was only in the LC I period (i.e. from 1650/1600 BCE onwards) that the copper producing and exporting industry was truly developed (Kassianidou 2013: 133). Similarly, Knapp sets MC III-LC I period (i.e. ProBA I) as the starting point of urban expansion and politico-economic development (see for example Knapp 2013: 432; also Negbi 2005: 4, Table 2).

On the other hand, given the existence of the early textual references on Alašiya, we know that, by the beginning of the Middle Bronze Age (ca. 1900 BCE), Cyprus was acknowledged as a major copper-producing area and that the island had already gained an important position in the intensifying trade transactions of the eastern Mediterranean and the Near East. Which scenario is closest to the truth? If we accept the view from the archaeological perspective, then it is difficult to explain the existence of considerable quantities of Alašiyan copper to Mesopotamia and Egypt during the 19th-18th c. BCE. By contrast, if we take the textual references at face value, this would mean that we have an extraordinary gap in our archaeological knowledge concerning the processes of urbanisation and socio-economic development between ca. 2000-1600 BCE.

3.4.2. Possible evidence for a rising elite

Unfortunately, the available explanations of socio-economic organisation are largely confined to LC IIC-LC III period (see, e.g., Peltenburg 1996: 28; Webb 1999: 305), due to the lack of sufficient archaeological data before ca. 1400 BCE. Nevertheless, a careful reconsideration of available Middle Cypriot data might offer a different view, providing a possible explanation for this discrepancy. Firstly, concerning metallurgical production in Cyprus, the appearance of tin, alloyed with native copper in order to produce bronze, dates to approximately 2000 BCE. This coincides with evidence for the existence of sites with an exclusively metallurgical orientation. More specifically, the MC I site of Ambelikou *Aletri* (Merrillees 1984) offers some of the earliest evidence for systematic copper extraction and mining on the island (Knapp 1985: 240, 2013: 302).

Regardless of whether sites such as *Aletri* appeared for reasons of internal consumption or increasing external demand – or both (see for example Knapp 1990: 159-60, 2013: 310), the fact that a number of people were consciously cut off from the productive force and turned into specialised miners and metal producers, suggests a major re-orientation of local economic programmes. In fact, this development implies that there was sufficient agricultural surplus to support the specialised workers and that a group of people was authorised to organise the process of import the necessary amounts of tin and possibly to redistribute and/or export the outcome. Ultimately, this could be one of the earliest evidence of a rising élite group.

3.4.3 Explanations for the paucity of MC material

If we now turn to the topography of MC period, it seems that there are several under-investigated areas on the island, as well as regions with continuous occupation between the prehistoric and protohistoric Bronze Age periods, a fact that in the long run might be possibly linked with the gradual creation of broader regional political entities.[26]

For instance, even though a settlement related to the wealthy EC-MC cemeteries of the north coast has yet to be discovered, many researchers suggest the possibility of a major site in the area actively involved in the metals trade[27] and probably participating in wider trade networks including south-southeast Aegean, coastal Anatolia and other regions (see, for example, Webb et al. 2006). There is a comparable dearth of data to support the existence of a large town that preceded *Ayios Dhimitrios* in the Kalavasos valley.[28] However, Cline (2005: 42) is right to point out the continuous activity in the area, whereas a large MC cemetery with chamber tombs (Todd 1986) indicates an important settlement in direct proximity to it. MC tombs and a settlement are also reported in the vicinity of Kouklia *Palaepaphos* (Maier and Karageorghis 1984: 46-7; Rupp et al. 1992: 290), another area with long and continuous history of occupation.

Similarly, the MC tombs and settlement of Episkopi *Phaneromeni* (see, e.g., Carpenter 1981; Swiny 1986; see also Mantzourani 2001: 158-9) precede and partly overlap with LC Kourion/Episkopi *Bamboula* (Weinberg 1983) and there is also evidence for PreBA activity in the area around the large LC harbour town of Kition *Kathari* (Karageorghis 1974).[29] If we add to the above data the initial settlement[30] of Morphou *Toumba tou Skourou* (Vermeule and Wolsky 1990), Enkomi *Ayios Iakovos* (Schaeffer 1952; Dikaios 1969-1971; Courtois et al. 1986), Hala Sultan Tekke *Vyzakia* (Åstrom 1989, 1996), Athienou *Bamboulari tis Koukounninas* (Dothan and Ben-Tor 1983), Kalopsidha[31] and other sites, then it becomes apparent that Cypriot society had undergone important socio economic realignments already before the Late Bronze Age. Possibly, several power groups resided in long-inhabited inland areas and the newly established coastal sites somehow managed to control the copper industry and participate in the metals trade.

Ultimately, it seems that the paucity of excavated MC sites is both an outcome of insufficient archaeological research as well as the result of LC layers overlying MC settlements. Especially the latter largely obscures the reality and complicates any attempt to approach socio-economic development and the exact mode of growth of the copper industry.

3.4.4. Additional evidence for socio-economic developments

There are some further facts that suggest a missing link of socio-economic development within the MC period and support this interpretation. Firstly, a series of inland fortified sites[32] appear late in the MC III and early in the LC I period, which point to a period of unrest. Peltenburg (1996) in particular links these forts with the rise of Enkomi and its attempt to secure a steady flow of copper from the Troodos sources to the harbour town of

26 Peltenburg (2012: 2), for instance, refers to 'territories' (i.e. 'an urban core that mobilised its resource-rich hinterland').

27 For example, Swiny (1989: 28) refers to this possibility while discussing the extraordinary wealth of Lapithos *Vrysi tou Barba*.

28 Except perhaps for Kalavasos *Laroumena* (see Todd 1993).

29 MC tombs are also reported at Larnaca *Ayios Prodromos* (Herscher 1988).

30 Seemingly not before MC III (i.e. around 1700-650 BCE).

31 Åstrom 1966. Kalopsidha might have existed since MC II period.

32 For a full catalogue of the fortified sites, see Fortin 1981; also Mantzourani 2001: 121.

Famagusta bay. This interesting argument takes for granted the leading role of Enkomi, but the explanation for the existence of several contemporary forts in the Karpass peninsula and the northwestern coast as part of Enkomi's hinterland strategy is not very convincing. Instead of attributing the control of more than 20 forts – many of which seem to be quite far away – to Enkomi's defensive and procurement strategy, we might alternatively assume that a similar regional infrastructure was also valid in the case of other coastal/near coastal centres such as Morphou *Toumba tou Skourou*. In any case, Peltenburg is right to connect the unprecedented phenomenon of defensive outposts with the attempt of local élite groups to control copper ore transportation and to secure the precious metal against any possible internal competitors and external opponents.[33]

Secondly, the copper industry and technology appear to have been 'full-blown' (Muhly 1989: 299) by the time Enkomi was established. The parallel appearance of copper extraction and primary smelting sites such as Politiko *Phorades* may also be linked with this phenomenon, since Enkomi provides ample evidence mainly for the final stages of copper refinement and casting copper into ingots. Consequently, as Manning has noted many years ago, the 'sophisticated and knowledgeable external demand' (Manning 1993: 35) would have been impossible without a preceding stage of internal socio-economic development and growth of the copper industry. The subsequent uninterrupted expansion of many MC III/LC I-II sites[34] reveals an apparent view of prosperity and economic growth, proving the successful integration of the island into the wider eastern Mediterranean trade networks. Interestingly, the formative era of the Cypriot copper industry coincides with a dramatic paucity of textual information, preceding the abrupt development after the beginning of the New Kingdom period.

4. Late Bronze Age textual evidence (KK)

In the period between the 17th and the 16th century BCE, an era of upheavals and military clashes throughout the Near East, Alašiya is not mentioned in any of the surviving texts. After the 15th c. BCE the political situation in the Near East seems to have gradually become more stable and Alašiya is again mentioned in the texts.[35]

4.1. Textual evidence from Egypt

The Annals of Tuthmosis III mention diplomatic gifts sent by the Ruler of *Isy* (Asiya) three times. Assyria, Ḫatti and Babylon also are said to have sent respective diplomatic presents. In another text of Tuthmosis III Asiya seems to have been placed in the west, grouped together with Keftiu/Crete.[36] The inclusion of *Isy* (Asiya) in this list shows that it entertained diplomatic relations with Egypt at that time, and that it was seen as an important agent in the international political stage. Unfortunately, however, it is uncertain whether Asiya is an abbreviated version of the term Alašiya and refers to Cyprus.[37]

---

33 Such as the Lukka raiders (Peltenburg 1996: 34) or other military expeditions like the one described in §2.2.

34 For a summary of the most important LC I-II remnants, see Knapp 2008: 147-51.

35 From the reign of Hatshepsut an official called 'the Alasian' is mentioned (Kitchen 2009: 3), but it is not clear if he was somehow connected with Alašiya. Neither diplomatic nor commercial endeavour is mentioned concerning Alašiya.

36 Kitchen 2009: 7: Year 34 = ca. 1445 BCE, Year 38 = ca. 1441 BCE, Year 39 = ca. 1440 BCE.

37 Quack 1996: 75-8; Kitchen 2009: 8; Gander 2015: 446. An important indication that the term *Isy* indeed referred to Cyprus, is offered by the Hellenistic decree of Kanopos (238 BCE): Osing 1980.

In several topographical lists both the term *Irs* (Alas(i)a), and *Isy* (Asiya) appear as if they referred to different countries, while the abbreviated form *Isy* resembles the term *j-s-y-w*, probably pointing to *Assuwa/Asia*, which was located in west Anatolia (Helck 1983). As Kitchen (2009: 7) argued the simultaneous occurrence of the terms Asiya and Alašiya does not prove that these are related to two different places. Some later sources suggest that the term *Isy* referred to a completely different country, perhaps *j-s-y-w* (= Assuwa/ Asia). This would explain the fact that in the *List of Mineral Regions* in Luxor (dated to the reign of Ramses II) we read about a 'Mount of Asiya' as well as another 'Mount of Alasia', which offered to the Egyptian king silver and copper respectively (Kitchen 2009: 7). Cyprus had no silver reserves (Karageorghis et al. 1983) while *j-s-y-w* in west Anatolia did.

A more certain reference to Alašiya in the New Kingdom appears in the corpus of the Amarna letters. The first letter (EA 33) was sent by the ruler of Alašiya to an Egyptian king recently ascended to the throne, probably Akhenaten.[38] Recent petrographic analysis of tablets has shown that their clay originates from the region near the southeastern coast of Cyprus (Goren et al. 2004: 48-75). All the letters mentioning Alašiya seem to be dated to a rather short period of time.

The king of the Land of Alašiya (LUGAL KUR *A-la-ši-ia*) bears the same title as the king of the Land of Egypt (LUGAL KUR *Mi-iṣ-ri*) and has the same status, since the king of Egypt calls him 'brother' (ŠEŠ).[39] However, the king of Alašiya never uses the title LUGAL.GAL (Great King) in his letters, neither for himself nor for his Egyptian counterpart. Should we thus conclude that he did not consider himself to be a Great King (Helft 2010: 99 n. 165; Podany 2010: 254) and that, accordingly, the term 'brother' was used in the sense of 'business partner'? (Artzi 1978: 29 n. 5).

Mynářová (2007: 130-1) pointed out that the Assyrian king in his first letter (EA 15) to the Egyptian king – in which he cautiously initiated diplomatic relations – also used the title LUGAL, while in the second one (EA 16), obviously after his recognition by his Egyptian counterpart, he used the title LUGAL.GAL. This is a valid argument and we would expect the royal scribes to adhere to very strict and well-defined rules concerning the terminology they used for their kings. Surprisingly, however, this is not the case. All the Great Kings (i.e. the king of Ḫatti, Karaduniaš (= Babylonia) and Mitanni) never used exclusively the term LUGAL.GAL for themselves. Instead, they often used in their correspondence with the Egyptian king the 'inferior' title LUGAL (Mynářová 2007: 126-30). It is as if sometimes they felt like Great Kings, while, in other instances, they preferred to present themselves like simple kings.

The only profound consistency is that they had always used the same title for themselves as well as for their counterparts. What is more, they never called themselves LUGAL when they called their colleague LUGAL.GAL or the other way around. What seems to be more important is the use of the terms 'brother' or 'father' in their correspondence. In his first, cautious, letter, the Assyrian king avoids addressing the Egyptian king 'brother', although he does so in his second letter, after the latter accepted him as his equal. The status of a 'brother' was not offered easily and could be revoked

38 For the identification of the recipient of the letter with Akhenaten, see Rainey and Schniedewind 2015: 17.

39 EA 33:1-2, EA 34:1-2, EA 37:1-, EA 39:1-2. In EA 35:1-2 the title of king of Egypt is written in Akkadian (*[š]àr-ri* KUR *Mi-iṣ-ri*), while for the title of the king of Alašiya with the corresponding Sumerogram (LUGAL KUR *A-la-ši-ia*). In EA 38: 1-2 both kings have the title šarru. In EA 36 the greeting formula is not preserved, but the king of Alašiya again calls the king of Egypt his brother (EA 36: 6, 8, 12).

at any time.[40] In Tušratta's first letter to the Pharaoh (EA 17), his agony regarding his acceptance as a 'brother' or not by the Pharaoh, is quite evident. His 'love' declarations in this as well as in some of his other letters reveal his weak position. Thus, when the king of Alašiya does not make any assertions of devotion or friendship to the Egyptian king, this was not due to the fact that he did not like him, as suggested by, for example, Podany (2010: 254). On the contrary, it may indicate that he had a firm grip of his own state, allowing him to adopt a self-confident attitude.

The Alašiya letters in the Amarna archive offer us some indications regarding the organisation of the court of the king of Alašiya. First, all letters are written in Akkadian, the diplomatic language of the time, which means that in his court resided scribes who could write in Akkadian.[41] Moreover, the various Alašiya letters seem to have been written by different scribes, which implies that a group of scribes was in the service of the king of Alašiya.[42] It should not be taken for granted that any king could afford such a service. The king of Arzawa, who wished to upgrade his position in the 'great league', did not have scribes who were able to speak and write in Akkadian or Egyptian in his court. Thus, he was obliged (quite embarrassingly) to request from the Egyptian king to communicate with him in the Hittite language (E A32: 24-5, see Hawkins 2015; Kopanias 2015a).

4.1.1. The relations between Alašiya and Egypt

As the following passage from EA 35 inform us, there existed long-standing diplomatic relations between Alašiya and Egypt: 'Furthermore, **which of your fathers did this thing to my fathers in the past**? So now, my brother, don't take it to heart (EA 35: 49-53). Additionally, a treaty was being prepared between the two kings with no further details recorded: 'So may a treaty [be ma]de between us and my ambassad[or] will go to you and your envoy will come to me. (EA 34: 42-6)'.

The confidence of the king of Alašiya was further based on the fact that he also entertained diplomatic relations with two more major powers of that time, namely the king of Ḫatti and the king of Mitanni (interestingly, not with Babylonia as far as we know): 'You have not been ranked with the king of Ḫatti or with the king of Shanhar. As for me, whatever greeting gift they send to me, then I send double the amount to you (EA 35: 49-53).' It is implied that not only the king of Egypt but also the kings of Ḫatti and Mitanni recognised the king of Alašiya as their equal.

The correspondence and the exchange of greeting gifts between the kings of Egypt and Alašiya must have been quite regular. When the king of Alašiya detained the Egyptian messenger for three years, he felt obliged to apologise by stating that, not only did the

40 Kopanias 2015a: 215. Even major kingdoms were in danger of losing this status; Ramses II, for instance, was apparently unconvinced of the right of the Babylonian king to be considered his brother, as he remarked: '[...] the king of Babylonia is not a great king [...]' (Edel 1994: no. 105 obv. 56). See also the contribution of Waal in this volume.

41 Rainey and Cochavi-Rainey 2015: 1376: 'EA 33, 34, 39, 40 are written in the hybrid dialect used by scribes from Canaan who wrote letters in the Amarna collection.'

42 Rainey and Schniedewind 2015: 11: 'The Amarna tablets from Alašiya include examples in Canaano-Akkadian besides Hurro-Akkadian though two of them (EA 36, 37) seem to come from a scribe trained in the true Middle Babylonian tradition.'

'hand of Nergal'[43] (= a plague) befell his land, but also that one of his young wives had died.[44] In another case the Egyptian king complained that the king of Alašiya missed one of his celebrations and did not send him an envoy (together with a greeting gift), a common complaint in the Amarna correspondence.[45] The detainment of a messenger, a very common practice, occurred in order to postpone the sending of a greeting gift and it did not necessarily mean that during that particular period of time there were no trade contacts between the lands.

The correspondence between Egypt and Alašiya also refers to the exchange of copper for silver and grain (Rainey and Cochavi-Rainey 2015: 1376). In these eight letters, it is mentioned that the king of Alašiya sent a total of 113 talents and 934 ingots of copper to the king of Egypt, an amount that approximately corresponds to 29 tons (Knapp and Kassianidou 2008: 135). From the Amarna corpus we know that all the other kings wished to present themselves as being able to send greetings gifts including a variety of exotic and luxury objects, showing off their ability to obtain whatever they wished from distant lands.

However, this was not the case with the king of Alašiya. His first greeting gift to the newly enthroned king of Egypt consisted solely of copper,[46] although on other occasions he also included several luxury goods (see, e.g., EA 34: 16-31). Since we know from other letters that the kings did not hesitate to ask for special gifts or to complain about the quality of the gifts received, we can assume that the king of Alašiya mainly sent copper, for this is what was expected of him. The king of Alašiya, however, did not ask the king of Egypt to send him gold in return, a commodity which everybody knew that in Egypt was 'plentiful like dirt', but silver, which was not mined in Egypt.[47]

He did not specify the amount and only speaks of a 'very great amount of silver' (EA 35: 19-22, 43-48; EA 37: 13-20). It seems that the equivalent proportion of silver to copper was standardised and taken for granted. Silver was used as a currency since the 3rd millennium BCE throughout the Near East, consequently this particular exchange of gifts resembles a commercial transaction (Kopanias 2015b). This is further illuminated by a request of the king of Alašiya to also receive 'grain [in ships from] the province of Canaan [send to me as in] former [days], [so that I] may [make] bread' (EA 36: 12-7), something that no other king in the Amarna correspondence has ever asked.[48] Maybe

43 The Mesopotamian god Nergal was equated with Resheph (Teixidor 1976: 65; Ulanowski 2013: 158; Rainey and Cochavi-Rainey 2015: 1380) and the latter with Apollo in later Greek texts (Hellbing 1979: 22). In the letter EA 35: 37 the Summerogram [d]MAŠ.MAŠ could also directly refer to Reshef (Lipiński 2009: 117-8). Both Reshef and Apollo are arrow shooting gods, who were thought to send plagues (Ulanowski 2013: 160). The requested expert in vulture divination, which the king of Alašiya requests from the Egyptian king in the same letter (EA 35: 26, most probably is needed in order to fight the plague (Hellbing 1979: 23; Ulanowski 2013: 160).

44 EA 35: 35-9. In another case, the king of Egypt detained the messenger of Alašiya for two years: EA 36: 18-9.

45 EA 34: 7-5. We find such complaints very often in the Amarna correspondence. Their aim was to increase the value of the greeting gift that they should receive (Kopanias 2015b).

46 EA 33: 16, 18: 200 talents of copper (URUDU.MEŠ) and 10 talents of fine copper (URUDU DÙG).

47 There is no reason to assume, that the word silver was used here to mean generally 'wealth', as Podany (2010: 255) proposed. All the kings in the Amarna correspondence always made it quite clear what they wanted to receive in return to their own gifts. Tušratta went even as far as to request solid cast gold statues of himself and his daughter (EA 27: 19-7) and he complained intensely when he received plated ones of wood (EA 27: 32-3). The king of Alašiya would not have been the sole exception to this rule. When he asked for silver, he meant exactly that.

48 Nevertheless, Egypt sent several shipments of grain to Ḫatti and other Syrian states: Singer 1999: 707.

this is indeed an indication for a three way channel of trade: copper went from Alašiya to Egypt in return for shipments of grain from Canaan and silver from Egypt (Rainey and Schniedewind 2015: 17-8).

The trade between Alašiya and Egypt was not only conducted in the form of greeting gifts. In another letter from the king of Alašiya we are informed that 'the men of my country are talking about my lumber which they delivered to the king of the land of Eg[ypt], so, my brother, [pay] the sums that are due.'[49] These men were not directly in the service of the king. That is why the payment was to be given directly to them. Moreover, the letters EA 39 and EA 40, sent by the king and the 'commissioner of the land of Alašiya' respectively, refer to merchants: 'These men are my merchants. My brother, send them safely (and) quick[l]y. As for my merchant(s) (and) my ship, may your customs' inspector not draw near to them' (EA 39: 14-20, Rainey and Schniedewind 2015: 355).

Apparently, an agreement was in effect enabling at least some of the Alašiyan merchants to conduct tax-free trade in the realm of Egypt (Moran 1992: 113 n. 1; Rainey and Cochavi-Rainey 2015: 1384). In the fragmentary letter regarding a transaction between Alašiya and Egypt which involved the exchange of copper and grain, the king of Alašiya mentions that one business agent participated from his side, while twenty business agents were involved from Egypt's side.[50] Unfortunately, we have no information concerning the role of those business agents.

From a letter sent by Rib-Ḫadda, the ruler of Byblos to the Egyptian king, we can deduce that ships could travel directly from Alašiya to Egypt and not necessarily along the Levantine coast (EA 114: Rainey and Schniedewind 2015: 307-9). In that particular letter, Rib-Ḫadda complained to the Egyptian king that the ships of Tyre, Beirut and Sidon blocked the direct route to Egypt, forcing him to return an Egyptian official via Alašiya (Knapp 2008: 316-7).

4.1.2. Topographical lists

Later references of Alašiya in the Egyptian texts mainly derive from topographical lists. Interestingly, Alašiya has never been included in the *Nine Bows*, i.e. the enemies of Egypt. In the topographical list from the reign of Sethos I at the Kanais temple Alašiya is mentioned after the *Nine Bows*, along with the kingdoms of Ḫatti and Naharin (= Mitanni). Then, the list continues with minor centres in Phoenicia and Canaan, where Asiya is also included (Kitchen 2009: 5, 11 n. 12 with further references). The place names of such topographical lists are often copied from older inscriptions and, consequently, they do not offer us a reliable picture of the political status of the mentioned kingdoms.

For instance, at that time Naharin (= Mitanni) was no longer a Great Kingdom. Another topographical list from the reign of Ramses II at Aksha (Serra West), possibly mentions Naharina, Ḫatti, Al[ašia?], Babylonia and then several Levantine places (Kitchen 2009: 11 n. 12), but the reading of Alašiya is not certain. Finally, a scribal training text of the late 13th/early 12th c. BCE mentioning oil and copper from Alašiya offered as a gift to the

---

49 EA 35: 27-9. This is indeed a private affair, because in the same section the case of an Alašiyan person who died in Egypt is presented, and the king of Alašiya asks for his possession to be returned to his wife in Alašiya (EA 35: 30-4).

50 EA34: 32-41: '[...] grain [...] So [...] my [ambassa]dor wi[th...] his [...] sen[d with haste] and as for [your] ambassa[dor, send to] my [lan]d and [may they come] with haste [to the land of A]lashia, my business agent [and tw]enty [busin]ess agents of yours and [...] with them' (Rainey and Schniedewind 2015: 339).

Egyptian king could have been a copy from an earlier inscription (Papyrus Anastasi IV: Caminos 1954: 200-1; Kitchen 2009: 5).

4.2. Hittite textual evidence

4.2.1. The Madduwatta text

The oldest reference to Alašiya in the Hittite texts is found in a tablet from the reign of Arnuwanda I, which partly refers to events that occurred during the reign of his predecessor Tudḫaliya I/II (early 14th c. BCE). The text, that is usually called 'Indictment of Madduwatta', mentions that both kings complained to the Hittite vassal king Madduwatta about his behaviour in Alašiya, which they considered to be Hittite territory. Apparently Madduwatta, in collaboration with Attariššiya of Aḫḫiya (= Achaia) and a certain Piggaya, often raided the land of Alašiya and captured civilians there.[51] We emphasise that this text does not mention an actual conquest of the island by Madduwatta and his allies. It only mentions that they conducted raids, captured some inhabitants of Alašiya and subsequently the Hittite king requested their release. Such raids were apparently not so rare. In one of his letters in the Amarna corpus the king of Alašiya mentions that 'men of the land of Lukka, year by year, are taking small towns in my land' (EA 38: 10-2, Rainey and Schniedewind 2015: 351). Men from Lukka, joined by men from Alašiya, also raided the realm of the Egyptian king, provoking the latter to issue a strict complaint.

The term used in the Hittite text is KUR ^{URU}*A-la-ši-ia*, i.e. Land-City Alašiya, which is equivalent to that used in the older Mari texts. The claim of the Hittite kings that Alašiya was under their control is not convincing, since Madduwatta's line of defence was simply that he was not aware of this. It is more probable that the Hittite king had diplomatic (and possibly also trade) relations with the Land of Alašiya and he did not wish to offend his partner. However, in the eyes of his subjects, this partnership was presented as a submission. To compare, all Egyptian kings presented their diplomatic partners as their tributaries and their 'greeting gifts' as tribute in their public texts and imagery (see, e.g., Gander 2015: 444 n. 2).

As already mentioned above (§4.1.1), in one of his Amarna Letters the king of Alašiya claims that he received gifts from the kings of Ḫatti and Mitanni, which strongly implies that he was recognised as their equal.[52]

4.2.2. Banishment to Alašiya

In two different cases the Hittite texts mention that two kings of Ḫatti banished some of their political adversaries to Alašiya. The earliest text is dated to the reign of Muršili II (1321-1295 BCE) although it describes an event that took place in the beginning of the

51 Beckman et al. 2011: 95 AhT3 §36: 'His Majesty said thus [...]: "Because [the land] of Alasiya belongs to My Majesty, [and the people of Alasiya] pay [me tribute–why have you continually raided it?"' But] Madduwatta said thus: "[When Attarissiya and] the ruler [of Piggaya] were raiding the land of Alasiya, I often raided it too. But the father of his Majesty [had never informed] me, [nor] had his Majesty ever informed [me] (thus): "The land of Alasiya is mine–recognize it as such!" if his Majesty is indeed now demanding back the civilian captives of Alasiya, I will give them back to him."" And given that Attarissiya and the ruler of Piggaya are rulers independent of My Majesty, while (you), Madduwatta, are a servant of My Majesty–why have you joined up with [them]?'. See for this text also the contribution of Waal in this volume.

52 De Martino (2008: 252) assumes that the term 'KUR ^{URU}*a-al-zi-ia*' in the incantation text of unknown date KUB XV 34 i 58 (CTH 483) also refers to Alašiya. Nevertheless, it is more probable that it refers to Alš/zi.

reign of his father Šuppiluliuma I (1350-1322 BCE).[53] The second text is dated to the reign of Ḫattušili III (1267-1237 BCE) and mentions that his predecessor Muwattalli II (1295-1272 BCE) banished the wife and son of one of his adversaries to Alašiya.[54] The initial impression from both texts is that Alašiya was at that time part of the Hittite realm and this is the reason why the Hittite king banished his opponents there (see, e.g., Edwards et al. 1973: 202). However, this was not necessarily the case. We know from an earlier text that Muwatalli II banished one of his wives to the Land of Aḫḫiyawa, not because this land belonged to him, but obviously because he considered it trustworthy enough for the task.[55] The fact that Alašiya was chosen as the place of exile for senior members of the Hittite society in the middle of the 14th c. BCE and again during the first quarter of the 13th c. BCE, shows that it entertained friendly diplomatic relations with Ḫatti and enjoyed a considerable political status (De Martino 2008: 251, 258).

4.2.3. Conflicts with Alašiya

A deterioration of the relations between Ḫatti and Alašiya probably took place during the reign of Ḫattušili III (1267-1237 BCE). A text from Ugarit mentions that several people from Alašiya fled to Ḫatti and then Ḫattušili III sent them to the king of Karkamiš.[56] It is not clear whether these persons were banished by the king of Alašiya (meaning that Ḫatti had the same obligation to host Alašiyans in exile) or if they were fugitives.

A tablet from the reign of the last Hittite king, Šuppiluliuma II, preserves two different texts which are copies or blueprints of stone inscriptions. The first one is an inscription on a statue of Tudḫaliya IV relating the latter's deeds and the second one is an inscription of his own.[57] Both texts refer to events related to Alašiya. According to this tablet, king Tudḫaliya IV attacked the land of Alašiya (KUR *A-la-ši-ia*), captured its king (LUGAL KUR *A-la-ši-ia*), his wives and children, seized his goods, silver, gold, as well as people from his land and transported all of them to Ḫattuša making the land a tributary.[58] Then, the text lists the tribute that the king of Alašiya and also a person bearing the title *pidduri* had to pay to Ḫatti. It consisted of gold, copper and *gayatum*.[59]

---

53 KUB XIV 14 obv. 16-22 (CTH 378.I), Singer 2002: 61-4; De Martino 2008: 250.

54 'Apology of Ḫattušili' [BI], col. i 3ff and iii 14ff; Klengel 1998: 209 n. 323; Heltzer 2001; De Martino 2008: 250. It was also proposed that Urḫi-Teššub was sent (or fled) to Alašiya and that Puduḫepa's letter was addressed to the king of Alašiya (Wouters 1989: 233), but the majority of scholars believe that it was sent to Ramses II and that Urḫi-Teššub fled to Egypt (KUB 21 38: 11-2, Klengel 1998: 383 n. 224; Beckman 1999: 125-6, see also the contribution of Waal in this volume).

55 CTH 214.12.A (= Beckman et al. 2011: 159 no. AhT 12 §2). De Martino 2008: 251; Kopanias 2015a: 212.

56 RS 18.114 (see also RS 17.28; PRU IV S. 109f.). See also Del Monte and Tischler 1978: 6; RS 17.352, 4-11.

57 KBo 12.38 (CTH 121). Güterbock 1967; Klengel 1998: 302; De Martino 2008: 248-9.

58 Güterbock 1967: 77: col. i §3: '[PN (or: The king of Alašiya] with his wives, his children, [and his.....] I seized; all the goods, [with silver, g]old, and all the captured people I [re]moved and [brought] them home to Ḫattuša. The country of Alašiya, however, I [enslaved] and made tributary on the spot.'

59 Güterbock 1967: 77: col. i §10: '...for the king of Alašiya and for the *pidduri*, this shall be the tribute...' Singer and Gestoso Singer (2014: 321-9) argued convincingly that *gayatum* is to be identified with the Cyperus grass, which was used for the production of a certain perfumed oil. The term is also attested also in the Linear B tablets as *kuparo* and possibly also in the attestation *ku-pi-ri-jo* (Singer and Gestoso Singer 2014: 325-6). If the Red Lustrous Wheelmade Ware indeed originates from Cyprus, then it could have been used for the transportation of this product, as proposed by Singer and Gestoso Singer 2014: 329.

The success of Tudḫaliya IV must have been short-lived, since his successor Šuppiluliuma II had to fight again in Alašiya.[60] In the same tablet he mentions that he crossed (or reached) the sea and fought successfully three times against the ships from the land of Alašiya (GIŠMÁ.ḪI.A *ŠA* KUR *Alašiya*). When he 'arrived on dry land(?), the enemies from Alašiya came in multitude against' him and fought him.[61] From the text it is not possible to conclude with certainty whether the mentioned ships were Alašiyan or simply came from Alašiya (Güterbock 1967: 80 n. 10) and if the land battle took place in Anatolia (Singer 2000: 27; Knapp 2008: 331) or in Alašiya, although the latter is more probable (De Martino 2008: 247-8). Interestingly, there is no reference to the king of Alašiya in connection to the ships from Alašiya, which gives the impression that they did not belong to a state (Otten 1963: 21).

4.2.4. A treaty between Alašiya and Ḫatti

The fragmentary draft of a vassal treaty between Alašiya and Ḫatti[62] is dated either to the reign of Tudḫaliya IV (Güterbock 1967: 80-1; Singer 1985: 121-2; Beckman 1996: 32) or Šuppiluliuma II (De Martino 2007; Vigo 2008). The text refers to the king of Alašiya (LUGAL) and the p*idduri*,[63] just like the above-mentioned tablet from the reign of Šuppiluliuma II. Interestingly, in this text some of the verbs that refer to the king of Alašiya are in the second plural person (Otten 1963: 12; De Martino 2007: 483), as in the case of treaties with polities with no central organisation, such as the Kaška (Fuscagni 2014). Moreover, since the text explicitly refers to the king and also to the *pidduri* (see also §4.4 below), I agree with Otten[64] that the plural form is used because the Hittites wanted the treaty to bind both officials. It seems that they have *de facto* shared the political power in the kingdom of Alašiya.

4.2.5. Goods and copper from Alašiya

In a letter of unknown date written in Akkadian, we come across a reference to the land of Alašiya (KUR *Alašiya*) and the request by the sender that the recipient of the letter should send gold objects, rhyta, belts, horses and gold.[65] Knapp (1980: 44) argued that this letter was sent from Ḫatti to Alašiya, but the petrographic analysis confirms the provenance of the clay from Cyprus (Goren et al. 2011: 686 no. 3; De Martino 2008: 250; Singer and Gestoso Singer 2014: 317 n. 1). The fact that the king of Alašiya requests various items and

60 Bryce 2005: 332. These events are most probably connected with Šuppilululiuma II's campaign against several lands to west Anatolia (Wiyanawanda, Tamina, Maša, Lukka and Ikuna), all in the wider area of Lukka (Bryce 2005: 329; 2016: 6) and possibly also Tarḫuntašša (De Martino 2008: 249). These are recorded in the SÜDBURG inscription in Ḫattuša: Hawkins 1995: 61 ff.; Melchert 2002; Yakubovich 2009: 6 ff.; Gander 2014: 375; contra Oreshko 2016: 351. The aim of the Hittites was either to secure sea transports (Bryce 2005: 356-8) and/or to repel the 'Sea People' (Singer 2000; Cline 2014: 128 no. 4).

61 Güterbock 1967: 78, col. iii §5: 'My father [...] I mobilized and I, Šuppiluliuma, the Great King, immediately [crossed reached?] the sea. The ships of Alašiya met me in the sea three times for battle, and I smote them; and I seized the ships and set fire to them in the sea. But when I arrived on dry land(?), the enemies from Alašiya came in multitude against me for battle. I f[ought] them, and [...] me[...].'

62 KBo 12.39 (CTH 141), see Otten 1963: 10-2; Klengel 1998: 301; De Martino 2007, 2008: 249; Vigo 2008.

63 LUGAL KUR URU*A-la-ši-ia*, LÚ*pí-id-du-ri-ia*.

64 Otten 1963: 12-5. As he points out, this would not have been a unicum; there is, for instance, a treaty of Muršili II with three noblemen of a foreign country.

65 KBo 1.26 (CTH 216). Klengel 1998: 302 no. 8; De Martino 2008: 250. For horses sent from Ugarit to Alašiya, see Singer 1999: 677.

gold from Ḫatti, obviously in return for copper, implies that this letter must be dated prior to the attack of Tudḫaliya IV against the island (see §4.2.3). If he was a Hittite vassal he could not have made such a request.

Remarkably, there are only two references to Alašiyan copper among the thousands of the surviving Hittite texts: the first is a ritual of unknown date including 'copper and bronze from Alašiya, from Mount Taggata.'[66] The second one concerns a text referring to the tribute that Alašiya had to pay to Tudḫaliya IV (see §4.2.3). In addition, very few Hittite objects have been so far found in Cyprus, a fact indicating that trade between Ḫatti and Alašiya must have been very limited.[67] Hittites had access to copper in the Taurus region (Yener 2012: 163) as well as in north Anatolia and thus, they apparently did not need copper from Alašiya. Nevertheless, the fact that so few Hittite objects have been unearthed in Cyprus should not be conceived as an indication for the absence of diplomatic relations between Ḫatti and Alašiya. At Ugarit, also a Hittite vassal, very few Hittite objects have been excavated so far. Consequently, if our assumptions were solely based on material finds and not on textual evidence, it would have been impossible to conclude that Ugarit had such close relations with Ḫatti.

4.3. Textual evidence from Ugarit

Several tablets have been found in Ugarit, which mention either Alašiya (*altyy*) or Alašiyans, dated to the period between the middle of 14th to the early 12th c. BCE. Unfortunately, these tablets do not have a clear archaeological context so they cannot be safely dated (Singer 1999: 705). Furthermore, several Cypro-Minoan inscriptions have been unearthed in Ugarit, all coming from private archives, and so far none from the royal ones.[68] It is possible that some texts were written in Ugarit by Alašiyans for Alašiyans (Catling 1975: 206; Ferrara 2012: 136). As this script still remains undeciphered, their content is unknown to us.

An obscure ritual from Ugarit contains a description of a sacrifice offered to the gods, in order to protect the people of Ugarit from various foreign enemies, amongst them the chiefs of the Hurrians, Hittites and Alašiyans.[69] The name of king Niqmaddu is mentioned in the text, referring probably to Niqmaddu II of the 14th c. BCE. Interestingly, Alašiya seems to have been considered by the king of Ugarit as an important neighbour of similar significance as Ḫatti and Mitanni as well as a potential threat (cf. Knapp 2008: 321).

Most tablets mentioning Alašiya seem to be dated between the reign of Ammittamru II (1260-1235 BCE) and Ammurapi II (1200-1190/85 BCE). Several Alašiyans are recorded

66 KBo 4.1 obv. 40. De Martino 2008: 251; Singer and Gestoso Singer 2014: 317-8. For a discussion about the comparison of this term with mount *Troodos* and further references, see Vigo 2010b: 160.

67 Singer 1999: 650; Kozal 2002; Knapp 2008: 314-6; De Martino 2008: 253-4; Helft 2010: 169-78; Genz 2011. Two inventories mention 'linen of Alašiya' (GAD [URU]***Alašiya***; IBoT 1. 31 obv. 2-4) and '5 shirts of linen of Alašiya' (5 GÚ GAD [URU]***Alašiya***; KBo 18.175 i 5): De Martino 2008: 251; Singer and Gestoso Singer 2014: 318. According to Vigo (2010a, 293) Alašiya imported linen from Egypt and crafted it into prestigious goods. Furthermore, a Hittite medical text mentions *maruwašḫa* from Alašiya (KUB 8.38 + KUB 44.63 iii 10-7), which probably is either azurite (Beckman 1996: 35; De Martino 2008: 252) or pulverised green malachite (Singer and Gestoso Singer 2014: 318-20).

68 Ferrara 2012: 132. Residence of Yabninu: two fragments from the same tablet (RS 19.01, 19.02) and an inscribed pithos rim (RS 27.237); Residence of Rašapabu: fragment of tablet (RS 17.06); Residence of Rap'anu: one tablet (RS 20.25); Residence of Urtenu: two labels (RS 94.2328, 99.2014). An inscribed silver bowl was also found in Ugarit (RS 3.389).

69 RS 1929.2: Knapp 1996: 39. Possibly also in RS 17.100: Knapp 1996: 39-40.

to reside in Ugarit and to participate in the activities of the palace as craftsmen, temple officials and royal personnel (Yon 1999: 114-6; Knapp 2008: 318-9). A tablet contains a list of the names of 29 men, their wives, children and servants (RS 11.857), who were somehow related to Alašiya, since the term URU*A-la-ši-ia* was written on the right edge of the tablet. However, it is uncertain if they were Alašiyans in Ugarit (Liverani 1962: 92-4; Ferrara 2012: 144-5) or Ugaritians in Alašiya (Knapp 2008: 319). In another tablet we read about an Alašiyan, who asked the king of Ugarit for permission to buy ships owned by some merchants in Ugarit (RS 18.113A: Knapp 1996: 36; Singer 1999: 677-8). In a tablet of unknown date (RS 18.119, Knapp 1996: 37; 2008: 311) we are informed about a ship from Alašiya which was docked in the Ugaritian port of ʿAtlg/Atalig carrying a cargo of 'fifteen talents of ...' and 'three talents of...' of an unknown commodity, probably copper (Singer 1999: 676; Knapp 2008: 311). The fact that copper from Alašiya was imported to Ugarit and was further distributed is attested on a tablet from Ugarit, mentioning that Alašiyan copper was sent to Emar, a site which played an important role for the inland trade.[70] Oil and wheat were also sent from Alašiya to Ugarit (Yon 2000: 192).

4.3.1. The Urtenu archive

Two tablets found in the Urtenu archive in Ugarit were sent by a 'Great Commissioner' (*rabisu rabû*) from an unnamed country. One of them is addressed to an unnamed king of Ugarit requesting the release of some Alašiyans detained for unknown reasons in Ugarit (RS 2177 + 2491, Ferrara 2012: 143). Consequently, it is reasonable to assume that the letter was sent from Alašiya. The second one, of uncertain provenance, is addressed to the king Niqmaddu III and refers to some horses (RS 94.2173, Ferrara 2012: 143). Another letter from the Urtenu archive mentions the case of the messenger Zu-Aštarti, who traveled with an Ugaritian ship to the territory of Ušnatu, where he was held up for unknown reasons.[71] This letter informs us that the king of Ugarit gave some horses to a messenger from Alašiya, although the context of this action is not clarified. If both letters refer to the same event, then it could be argued that the former letter was also sent from Alašiya (Peltenburg and Iacovou 2012: 346). This was probably no mere commercial transaction, since a letter from the Hittite king Tudḫaliya IV to king Ammištamru II of Ugarit (RS 17.450A; Monroe 2009: 188-9) informs us that the export of horses to Egypt – as well as to its vassals – was prohibited by the Hittites (Cline 2014: 108).

A letter from the king Kušmešuša of Alašiya to the king Niqmadu (III?) was unearthed in the Urtenu archive but unfortunately it still remains unpublished (RS 94.2475 + 94.2561). The king of Alašiya allegedly refers to his counterpart in Ugarit as 'his son', indicating that he considered himself as his superior.[72] In his letter, the Alašiyan king informs the king of Ugarit that he intends to send him 33 ingots of copper of total weight of 30 talents, i.e.

---

70 RS 34.153: Knapp 1996: 28. Such a role is also confirmed by another letter sent to the king of Ugarit from the commissioner of Kadeš, which mentions the shortfall in the delivery of bronze and tin (RS 20.016: Bell 2012: 182).

71 RS 34.153: Bordreuil 1991: 75-6. Monroe 2009: 188-9: 'On the sixth day I was at sea. As a wind took me, I reached the territory of Sidon. From Sidon to the territory of Ušnatu it bore me, and in Ušnatu I am held up. May my brother know this. . . Say to the king: If they have received the horses which the king gave to the messenger of the land of Alašiya, then a colleague of the messenger will come to you. May they give those horses into his hand.'

72 Kitchen 2009: 4. Kitchen also proposed the equation of the name *Kušmešuša* with Κοσμετος.

ca. 900 kgs (Kassianidou 2013: 143). On the reverse of the tablet, its scribe, apparently an Ugaritian working in the court of Alašiya, added a personal note requesting a fine table and five chairs (Knapp 2008: 319).

4.3.2. The Rap'anu archive

In a fragmentary letter in the Rap'anu archive sent from king Niqmaddu III (1210-1200 BCE) of Ugarit to the king of Alašiya, the payment of an oil shipment is discussed (RS 20.168 = Ug 5, no. 21). The king of Ugarit addresses his counterpart as 'his father', thus acknowledging his own inferior political position. Similarly, the king Ammurapi II (1200-1190/85 BCE) of Ugarit addressed the king of Alašiya as 'his father' (RS 20.238), a fact showing the political importance of the state of Alašiya (Peltenburg and Iacovou 2012: 346; Cline 2014: 105-6). As Singer noted, this 'should therefore reflect an acknowledged hierarchy between the two royal courts, based not only on the relative age of the correspondents' (Singer 1999: 720). We can observe similar cases in other letters from Ugarit. The king of Amurru, a kingdom mightier than Ugarit, addresses his counterpart in Ugarit as 'his son' (RS 17.152: Lackenbacher 2002: 183), while the latter refers to the former as 'his father' (RS 17.286: Lackenbacher 2002: 184). In another letter this relationship is reversed, probably reflecting a change in the correlation of power (RS 15.24 + 50, Lackenbacher 2002: 184). The king of the inferior kingdom of Ušnatu addressed the king of Ugarit as 'his father' (RS 17.83; RS 17.143, Lackenbacher 2002: 185-6). Kings, regarding themselves as equals referred to each other as 'brothers', as in the case of the king of Kadeš (RS 20.17: Lackenbacher 2002: 189-90), of Alalaḫ/Mukiš, RS 17.315, Lackenbacher 2002: 192) and of Beirut (Vidal 2005: 292). The fact that Ugarit and Alašiya had developed good diplomatic relations is also confirmed by a letter mentioning that two of the sons of a queen from Ugarit have been exiled there.[73]

From the Rap'anu archive come three very well-known letters which further illuminate the close relations between Alašiya and Ugarit.[74] They belong to the reign of the king Ammurapi II of Ugarit, although their precise date cannot be determined. In the first letter, king Ammurapi II not only addresses the unnamed king of Alašiya as 'his father' but also adds that he falls at his feet (RS 20.238. Nougayrol et al. 1968: 85-9 no. 24; Hoftijzer and Van Soldt 1998: 344; Huehnergard 1999: 376-7; Gander 2010: 47; Halayqa 2010: 321-2). This is generally something that a vassal king would write to his master. However, in this case, it seems that times were desperate for Ugarit and its king was ready to humiliate himself, in order to secure the much-needed support of Alašiya. The king of Ugarit informs his counterpart that, while his troops were in Ḫatti and all his ships in Lukka (i.e. Lycia), seven enemy ships appeared at his coastline and set fire to some towns of his kingdom. He also asks to be informed in case more enemy ships would appear, which indicates that the enemy was probably coming from

73 RS 24.274. These princes have also been compelled to swear their agreement before 'Ištar of the steppes', thus implying that this deity was worhsipped also in Alašiya; this is also indicated by the Hittite tablet KBo XII 39 dealing with Hittite exiles on Alašiya, which was also to be kept 'before Ištar' (Knapp 2008: 320-1). In a Hurrian text in Ugarit is also mentioned 'Alašiyaḫḫe, the father, god of Alašiya' (RS 24.274: Knapp 1996: 41; 2008: 320).

74 These have not been found in the 'baking oven' in Court V of the royal palace, as was erroneously claimed by the excavator, and do not necessarily refer to events that occurred to the very last days of Ugarit (Singer 1999: 705).

the west. Interestingly, he does not ask for any military assistance, showing that the king of Alašiya was either not willing or not able to offer it to him.

The second letter was sent by an unnamed king of Alašiya to Ammurapi.[75] It is possible that this was the response to the aforementioned letter (Halayqa 2010: 320 n. 67). The greeting formula is almost insultingly short, a detail further accentuating the higher position of Alašiya. In this letter, the king of Alašiya does not offer either help or new information regarding the enemy. He merely asks the king of Ugarit for the location of the Ugaritian troops and simply advises him to entrench himself in his fortified cities.

The third letter was sent by Ešuwara, the Great Commissioner (see also §4.4) of Alašiya to an unnamed king of Ugarit (RS 20.18. Nougayrol et al. 1968: 83-5 no. 22; Hoftijzer and Van Soldt 1998: 343; Lehmann 1996: 27; Halayqa 2010: 321). Ešuwara mentions that the men and ships from Ugarit committed some transgressions and the king of Ugarit should not be angry with him. The content of this letter could imply a naval defeat of the Ugaritian fleet somewhere in the coast of Anatolia or even in Cyprus (Vita 1999: 498; Watson and Wyatt 1999: 498) or perhaps that some Ugaritians surrendered their ships to the enemy (Astour 1965: 255-6; Catling 1975: 204). Then, Ešuwara warns the king of Ugarit that twenty enemy ships have been sighted in Alašiya and afterwards had departed to an unknown destination, possibly Ugarit.

4.4. Political structures and the role of the commissioner in Alašiya

From the Amarna Letters we are informed that the king of Alašiya had in his service a MAŠKIM. This Sumerogram corresponds to the Akkadian term *rābiṣu*, usually translated as commissioner/governor (Rainey and Cochavi-Rainey 2015: 1385), or *sākinu*, usually translated as prefect (Buccellati 1963; Rainey 1966; Van Soldt 2001; 2002; 2006). Interestingly, the commissioner of the land Alašiya (MÁŠKIM *š*]*a* KUR *A-la*[*-ši-ia*]) corresponded directly with his Egyptian counterpart (M]ÁŠKIM *ša* KUR *Mi*[*-iṣ-ri*) and on equal terms. Not only does he call him 'brother' (ŠEŠ) but they even exchanged greeting gifts just like their masters (EA 40: 1, 3). The same term MAŠKIM also occurs in the correspondence of Egypt's vassals in Canaan with the Egyptian king. In this case, the term refers to the Egyptian officials who represented the interests of the Egyptian king in that region (Mynářová 2015: 159-61). The official with the title M]ÁŠKIM *ša* KUR *Mi*[*-iṣ-ri* seems to have had a high position in the administration and probably resided in the royal court. He obviously had a similar status to the 'Great Scribe' in the Hittite court mentioned in the letters of Šuppiluliuma II.[76] In Ugarit, the *sākinu* of Ugarit also held an important position. As Vita (1999: 469) remarks:

75 RSL 1. Nougayrol et al. 1968: 85-6 no. 23. It was disputed whether its sender was the king of Alašiya (Nougayrol et al. 1968: 85-6; Wachsmann 1998: 343; Halayqa 2010: 322; Yasur-Landau 2010: 164; Van de Mieroop 2016: 206) or the king of Karkamiš (Yamada 1992: 437-9; Singer 1999: 720 n. 394), but the petrographic analysis of the tablet showed that its clay originates in Cyprus: Goren et al. 2003; 2004: 55-7; Knapp 2008: 302.

76 For this office, see Singer 2003. The case of RS 94.2523 (Beckman et al. 2011: 258-61 no. AhT 27B) shows that this Great Scribe was authorised to send letters to vassal kings.

> The 'prefect' (*sākinu*), at the head of a 'House of the prefect', complemented the king in every aspect of government, whether internal or external, political, commercial or juridical. He was also the king's deputy when he was outside the kingdom and acted as regent if the king was a minor.[77]

It is probable that the *sākinu* of Ugarit was *ex officio* also the *sākinu* of the palace MAŠKIM É.GAL (Van Soldt 2006: 685). Moreover, we know that there was also a *sākinu* of the queen's house (Van Soldt 2006: 682-6) as well as a *sākinu* in several towns within the realm of Ugarit (Van Soldt 2006: 675-82). The *sākinu* of Ugarit held the highest position.

The commissioner of Alašiya must have had a similar position to the *sākinu* of Ugarit. His letter in the Amarna archive shows that he held a significant position in the palatial hierarchy and was also authorised to manage administrative affairs in the name of the king of Alašiya. However, he was apparently not entirely independent from the king and this may be the reason why the archivists of the correspondence in Amarna wrote on the reverse of the tablet including this letter of the commissioner of Alašiya in hieratic script: 'Letter of the great one of Alašiya' (i.e. the king of Alašiya).[78] As already mentioned above, some of the MAŠKIM.GAL (i.e. Great Commissioner/Governor/Prefect) of Alašiya corresponded directly with the kings of Ugarit namely Šinama,[79] Šangiwa (RS 94.2447 +2588 +2590, Lackenbacher and Malbran-Labat 2005: 229; Peltenburg and Iacovou 2012: 346) and Ešuwara.[80] This office most probably corresponded to the office of the 'Commissioner of the Land of Alašiya' (MÁŠKIM *š*]*a* KUR *A-la*[*-ši-ia*]) of the Amarna letter as well as with the title *pidduri* mentioned in some Hittite texts (Otten 1963: 15; Helck 1971: 248; Moran 1992: 113 n. 1). The term 'Great Commissioner' indicates that junior commissioners also existed, a fact pointing at the presence of a structured bureaucratic hierarchy (Peltenburg and Iacovou 2012: 346).

In other cases, a commissioner was allowed to communicate directly with a foreign king, as shown for example by the letter sent by the commissioner of Kadeš to the king of Ugarit (RS 20.16, Lackenbacher 2002: 188, see also Bell 2012: 182). The kings of Ugarit and Kadeš considered each other as equals, i.e. brothers (RS 20.17, Lackenbacher 2002: 189-90). Therefore, the fact that the commissioner of the latter sent a letter directly to the king was definitely not understood as an insult. Moreover, the commissioner of Kadeš was extremely polite in his letter. In fact, such an attitude could be considered as servility. Quite on the contrary, the greeting of the commissioner of Alašiya to the king of Ugarit was very short ('may you and your country be well') and he does not even address him as his father. The letter leaves no doubt as to that Ugarit was more in need

---

77 See, e.g., in the letter RS 34.129, sent from the Hittite king to the prefect of Ugarit: 'Thus says His Majesty, the Great King. Speak to the prefect: Now, (there) with you, the king your lord is (still too) young. He knows nothing...' (Wachsmann 1998: 343).

78 The letter sent by the commissioner (EA 40) and the one sent by the king for the same purpose (EA 39) have been written by the same scribe (Rainey and Cochavi-Rainey 2015: 1384) and their content overlaps to a great extent (cf. EA 39: 14-20 with EA 40: 16-20, 24-8); the fact that only the commissioners and not the kings exchange greeting gifts shows that the actual communication was between them, not the kings. Maybe because the Alašiyan administrator could not contact his Egyptian counterpart directly, he needed an accompanying, formal letter by his king and that's why they did not have to exchange greeting gifts.

79 RS 94.2173, Ferrara 2012: 143.

80 RS 20.18. Nougayrol et al. 1968: 83-5 no. 22; Hoftijzer and Van Soldt 1998: 343; Lehmann 1996: 27; Halayqa 2010: 321.

of Alašiya than the other way around (Lambrou-Phillipson 1993: 169). The letter offers us also a hint that, maybe at the time, the Great Commissioner had a particularly strong position in Alašiya. For instance, the phrase 'so do not be angry with me!' implies that he himself and not the king of Alašiya, who is actually not even once mentioned in the letter, had the power. Could this be so because the king was a minor or because he was in some other way indisposed?

The elevated position of the Alašiyan Great Commissioner brings to mind the important role that the office of *pidduri* played within the framework of the treaty of Tudḫaliya IV or Šuppiluliuma II. However, this probably was a temporary situation. It is mentioned in the Hittite text that Tudḫaliya IV brought the king of Alašiya and his family to Ḫattuša after his victory.[81] It is unclear whether he reinstated the same person on the throne of Alašiya, after this person had taken an oath of loyalty or if he appointed a new king. The former is more probable, since otherwise, this event would have been mentioned in the text.

As stated above, the *sākinu* of Ugarit acted as the king's deputy when the latter was outside the kingdom. This situation may apply to Alašiya when its king was away from his country and detained in Ḫattuša. Either way, it seems the Hittite king did not trust the king of Alašiya and probably this is why he also made the *pidduri* responsible towards him. It is possible that the holder of this office kept his political power even after the aforementioned events. This may be why Ešuwara, the Great Commissioner of Alašiya, corresponded directly with the king of Ugarit and in such a confident manner.

5. The archaeological evidence: The Late Cypriot II period (EM, IV)

Even if we accept the problematic equation of Asiya with Cyprus (see above §4.1), the mighty king of Alašiya, seemingly equivalent in power with the great Pharaohs, is virtually absent from textual information before the 15th c. BCE. In fact, as it was previously noted, the Amarna letters and nearly all the Hittite/Ugarit diplomatic correspondence that prove the existence of an Alašiyan king, cover only a short time span within the 14th – 13th centuries BCE. This largely coincides with the LC II period (c. 1450-1200 BCE), an era characterised by intensive contacts between eastern Mediterranean 'states'/polities[82] and the notable expansion of international trade. Within the island of Cyprus there are clear signs of urbanisation, a process that peaked (Negbi 1986: 2005) during the LC IIC phase (c. 1300-1225/1200 BCE), along with the concomitant creation of social stratification and further expansion and restructuring of the copper industry. The large coastal/near coastal centres of Enkomi, Hala Sultan Tekke, Morphou, Kition and Maroni *Vournes/Tsaroukkas* served as gateway communities for the island's exporting goods and were the focus of administrative, and perhaps craft specialist activities (see, for example, Cadogan 1989; Manning and DeMita 1997: 115-36). A few equally important inland sites like Alassa *Paleotaverna/Ano Mandilares* (Hadjisavvas 1989, 1996) and Kalavasos *Ayios Dhimitrios* (see, e.g., South 1996, 1997), possibly functioned as administrative and redistributive/industrial centres, containing facilities for olive-oil processing,[83] metallurgical activities and large-scale agricultural surplus storage. There were also several sites of possible

81 See n. 58.

82 On different notions of the Archaic or early 'state', see Peltenburg 2012: 5-8.

83 For the issue of olive-oil processing and its importance on Cyprus, see Hadjisavvas 1992.

religious/ideological character, namely 'rural sanctuaries', showing signs of ceremonial activity[84] and, lastly, a number of mining/primary smelting sites, pottery producing sites and agricultural support settlements. Based on the above, many researchers discussed the matter of settlement hierarchy (see, e.g., Catling 1962; Keswani 1993; Manning and DeMita 1997) on the island, an issue with direct repercussions on socio-political organisation.[85]

The question that arises is whether Enkomi and its supposed 'ruler' had a prominent position in the settlement hierarchy of the island or it was just another large coastal centre with urban characteristics, possibly controlling a specific area of eastern and/or central Cyprus.[86] The former case, supported mainly by Muhly and Knapp[87] would mean that the king of Alašiya was actually residing there. As Manning and DeMita (1997: 110) note, there are indeed some characteristics that might ascribe to Enkomi a leading role. With the possible exception of Morphou *Toumba tou Skourou*, it is described as being the first site with extended metallurgical production already in the beginning of the Late Bronze Age (see, e.g., Muhly 1989: 299; Kassianidou 2013: 134). It also shows evidence for inter-élite contacts with other eastern Mediterranean areas, which would make Enkomi a logical candidate for the prime centre of international affairs on the island. Moreover, Enkomi provides ample evidence for foreign imports, the earliest attestation of the Cypro-Minoan script (Dikaios 1969-1971: 23) and the largest assemblage of cylinder seals. In addition, some of the most important ashlar buildings (Negbi 2005: 9-13, Tables 4-6), characterised either as public or official, lie within its architectural remnants. Lastly, Enkomi's life-span is considerably long, covering at least six centuries of habitation before its demise and the rise of nearby Salamis.

On the other hand, there are many researchers that promote a heterarchical (Keswani 1993) or decentralised model[88] of LBA Cypriot society, based on a few signs of regionalism[89] and also on geographical, topographical, ecological and other factors.[90] For instance, Manning and DeMita argued for '...at best nominal control over what seem to be largely independent élite groupings elsewhere on the island'. Similarly, Peltenburg refers to 'strong regional traditions' and 'topographic enclaves' that '...constrained efforts at provincial integration and effective sovereignty throughout the LBA' (Peltenburg and Iacovou 2012: 351). Iacovou in the same paper notes the evolution of '...a number of LC polities, which in the 13th century, if not earlier still, were in the process of establishing independent economic territories' (Peltenburg and Iacovou 2012: 354). Keswani (1993, 1996) also argued against a central administration, promoting a model of highly autonomous regional entities

---

84 Knapp (1986) has linked the manipulation of ideological symbols with the rise of élite groups and their attempt to control rural populations and the copper industry in order to maintain their status.

85 For a recent argument of a four-tiered settlement hierarchy, see Knapp 2013: 354-9. Keswani (1993), on the other hand, proposed a two-three tiered model of settlement hierarchy. For another three-tiered model, see also Peltenburg and Iacovou 2012: 357-8.

86 Goren et al. (2003), for example, suggested that either Alassa or Kalavasos *Ayios Dhimitrios* was the administrative centre of the kingdom of Alašiya.

87 Knapp 2008: 324-41; 2013: 443-7. Muhly (1989: 299) even suggested that Enkomi was actually the city-state of Alašiya, whereas Peltenburg (1996) argued for a secondary state formation during the MC III-LC I period with a prominent role for Enkomi (although he dismissed that claim later; see, e.g., Peltenburg and Iacovou 2012: 346, n. 4). See also Kassianidou 2013: 144.

88 Peltenburg and Iacovou 2012: 350. Also, the 'networked households' model; see Peltenburg 2012.

89 There are, e.g., distinct pottery traditions that possibly mirror regional identities (Steel 2004: 150-2).

90 Manning and DeMita (1997: 107), for example, suggest that it would be almost impossible for Enkomi or any other polity to control the large and resource-rich island of Cyprus.

competing with each other and maintaining their own economic programmes and trade relations.[91] More specifically, she supported a model of heterarchy in the eastern part and a simultaneous model of settlement hierarchy[92] in the southern part of the island. Keswani dismissed the idea of Enkomi's prominence (see also Crewe 2007) based on the notable absence of symbolic and iconographic evidence of subordination to a central authority (cf. Webb 1999: 307) and the fact that the town of Enkomi was far from the largest LC centre of the island.[93] What is more, she sees no stylistic/functional consistencies between the official buildings at Enkomi and equivalent buildings on other, seemingly subordinate, sites. Lastly, the élite burials and the included prized tomb offerings are evenly distributed in Cyprus and there are no signs of concentration at any site.

The same view of wide distribution is also clear for the metallurgical activities, ubiquitous among the excavated LC sites all over the island, and also for the luxury goods manufactured by specialised producers that seem to be scattered in all urban centres. Craft specialists were normally depended on centrally-controlled institutions based on palatial complexes. However, there are no palaces in Bronze Age Cyprus (Manning and DeMita 1997: 110; Peltenburg and Iacovou 2012: 345; Peltenburg 2012: 4) and the few objects with Cypro-Minoan symbols are largely insufficient to prove the existence of bureaucrats and a record-keeping system (see, e.g., Manning and DeMita 1997: 107), similar to contemporary states/polities of the eastern Mediterranean. It seems that the highly influential prestige goods that were used to shape local élite identities and to mark their superior status were not the exclusive privilege of a king and its court.[94]

6. Concluding remarks (EM, KK, IV)

In the cuneiform texts, there is not the slightest indication that Alašiya was in any way different from the rest of the kingdoms of the MBA and LBA Eastern Mediterranean. It had a king who entertained diplomatic and trade relations with the major powers of the time, Ḫatti, Mitanni and Egypt. He was considered to have a higher status than the king of Ugarit and was equal to the Egyptian king, and probably to those of Mitanni and Ḫatti. Alašiya also had trade and diplomatic contacts with the Aegean.[95] The 'court' of the king of Alašiya included scribes who were able to communicate in Akkadian, the *lingua franca* of the period, as well as in Ugaritic.

The administration was headed by a MAŠKIM (.GAL), as other major political entities of the time (Singer 1999: 721). The fact that the same office appears in the Amarna and in later Ugaritic correspondence is a strong indication that 'the Cypriot partner of, respectively, Egypt, Ḫatti and Ugarit was the same political entity, which existed between the second half of the 14th c. and the end of the 13th c.' (De Martino 2008: 256, also Peltenburg and Iacovou 2012: 347). We know that in the MBA and LBA Near East the palatial economy

91 This is very much alike the subsequent polities of Iron Age Cyprus.

92 Based on staple and wealth finance exchange models, see Keswani 1993: 76-9.

93 See, for example, the four points of argument in Keswani 1993: 74-5. For the site distribution, see Knapp 2013: 355 fig. 95.

94 On the manipulation of foreign luxury goods and symbols and also the limited access to them by élite groups, see for example Webb 1999: 307-8; 2005: 181.

95 The use of the terms *Ku-pi-ri-jo* and, *A-ra-si-jo* in the Linear B tablets (Knapp 2008: 303-7), and also the similarity of the shapes of the Cypro-Minoan signs with the ones of the Linear A (Smith 2012: 84) make this assumption very probable.

did not control all aspects of economic life. The texts from Ugarit clearly demonstrate the important role played by various merchant houses, which in fact seem to have controlled more or less the economic life (Monroe 2009: 275; Bell 2012). A similarly decentralised economic system may have existed also in Alašiya.

Based on both the archaeological and the textual evidence, we conclude that Cyprus/Alašiya was most probably politically fragmented (cf. Goren et al. 2003: 252) and that local powerful élite groups controlled specific territories, including at least one copper producing area and a coastal centre for their international transactions. In fact, the absence of palatial complexes and their infrastructure with the concomitant direct dependence on bureaucrats, craft specialists, miners and other subordinate people, could be the main reason why Cyprus was never faced with any 'dark ages' following the eastern Mediterranean-wide crisis and collapse of nearly all the contemporary 'states'/polities, i.e. Mycenaean Greece, Ḫatti, Ugarit etc. (see, for example, Peltenburg and Iacovou 2012: 354, 356).

Whether Enkomi once had the exclusive privilege of exporting copper via royal gifts or inter-island relations is not clear, but this was certainly not the case after about 1400 BCE. This view of political fragmentation created by the parallel presence of several competing entities is not necessarily incompatible with the existence of a king. As Peltenburg has argued, the title 'king' could be understood in quite different ways in various parts of Mesopotamia and Syria (Peltenburg 2012: 5-8, Peltenburg and Iacovou 2012: 347-9) and it should not be indispensably related with a person that controls all the political, ideological and entrepreneurial activity.[96] Even if Enkomi was indeed the prime centre of inter-island transactions (see, e.g., Keswani 1996: 222), or even if its rulers were able to control partly the metals trade,[97] it is still doubtful that any king of Alašiya could claim authority over the whole island and its scattered natural resources. From this point of view, Sherratt was right to note that the king (and the kingdom) of Alašiya is 'no more than a product of the need of Near Eastern powers to make Cypriot political structures conform, at least on paper, to their own norms of diplomatic perception and convention' (Sherratt 1998: 297). Conversely, we might assume that the 'king of Alašiya' was the local response to the international norms, apparently adopted in order to participate in the 'big league' and not necessarily mirroring the exact socio-political reality on Cyprus.

In our opinion, a model with a commonly accepted representative of Alašiya, a *primus inter pares*, possibly residing at Enkomi or another major site of Cyprus, such as Alassa or Kalavassos, would be the most probable according to current data. This person, apparently the head of the most powerful local household, having been acknowledged as an equal by the king of Egypt and even as a superior to the king of Ugarit, would be responsible for the island's diplomatic correspondence and the necessary international contacts, thus securing the importing/exporting activities. His historical privilege to communicate with other overseas powers would ensure the 'loyalty' of other local power groups, which sought to secure their social rank via the restricted access to luxury goods, foreign symbolic insignia and the uninterrupted expansion of long distance trade. It is suggested that in order to moderate internal reaction, the title of the 'king of Alašiya' might have been awarded from time to time to a commonly accepted representative, perhaps coming

96 For a more detailed discussion and further bibliography: Bell 2012; Kopanias 2015b.

97 I.e. the import-export of gold, silver, tin etc., see Kassianidou 2013: 252.

from different urban centres. Nevertheless, the possibility of conflict between powerful élite groups in order to promote their candidate should not be excluded.

In addition to this, it seems that different parts of the island followed different socio-political trajectories based on the logic of reciprocal benefit from international trade. Thus, regional élite groups cooperated with each other creating wider, albeit fragile, politico-economic entities maintaining trade relations with selected areas of the eastern Mediterranean. For example, Morphou *Toumba tou Skourou* and Enkomi *Ayios Iakovos* might show closer ties with the Aegean and Ugarit/Northern Syria respectively, whereas, if Goren et al. are right concerning the provenance of the Amarna letters (Goren et al. 2003), southern Cyprus would be the most suitable candidate for close trade transactions with Egypt and southern Levant. Even if some or all of these trade transactions were carried out under the aegis of the king of Alašiya, the parallel active participation of private entrepreneurs or cooperative élite groups, often competing with the state's formal policy, should not be excluded,[98] a fact that in the long term promoted regional identities and ultimately led to the Iron Age 'kingdoms' of Cyprus.

Bibliography

Altenmüller, H. and M.A. Moussa. 1991. 'Die Inschrift Amenemhets II. Aus dem Ptah-Tempel von Memphis. ein Vorbericht', *Studien zur Altägyptischen Kultur* 18: 1-48.

Artzi, P. 1978. 'The Rise of the Middle-Assyrian Kingdom, according to El-Amarna Letters 15 & 16', in P. Artzi (ed.), *Bar-Ilan Studies in History*, Ramat-Gan: 25-41.

Aruz, J. (ed.) 2008. *Beyond Babylon: Art, Trade, and Diplomacy in the Second Millennium B.C.*, New Haven – London.

Astour, M.C. 1965. 'New Evidence on the Last Days of Ugarit', *American Journal of Archaeology* 69.3: 253-258.

Åström, P. 1966. *Excavations at Kalopsidha and Ayios Iakovos in Cyprus* (Studies in Mediterranean Archaeology 2), Lund.

Åström, P. 1989. *Hala Sultan Tekke, Vol. 9: Trenches 1972-1987* (Studies in Mediterranean Archaeology 45), Göteborg.

Åström, P. 1996. 'Hala Sultan Tekke – A Late Cypriot harbour town', in P. Åström and E. Herscher (eds.), *Late Bronze Age Settlements in Cyprus: Function and Relationship* (Studies in Mediterranean Archaeology and Literature, Pocketbook 126), Jonsered: 9-14.

Beckman, G.M. 1996. 'Hittite Documents from Ḫattuša', in A.B. Knapp (ed.), *Sources for the history of Cyprus. Near Eastern and Aegean texts from the third to the first millennia BC* (Sources for the History of Cyprus 2), New York: 31-35.

Beckman, G.M. 1999. *Hittite Diplomatic Texts* [2nd edition] (Writings From the Ancient World 7), Atlanta.

Beckman, G.M., T.R. Bryce and E.H. Cline. 2011. *The Ahhiyawa Texts* (Writings From the Ancient World 28), Atlanta.

Belgiorno, M.R. 2004. *Pyrgos Mavrorachi: Advanced Technology in Bronze Age Cyprus*, Nicosia.

Bell, C. 2012. 'The Merchants of Ugarit: Oligarchs of the Late Bronze Age Trade in Metals?', in V. Kassianidou, G. Papasavvas and J.D. Muhly (eds.), *Eastern Mediterrane-*

98 On the 'mercantile perspective' and its possible consequences, see for example Voskos and Knapp 2008: 677.

an metallurgy and metalwork in the second millennium BC. A conference in honour of James D. Muhly: Nicosia, 10th-11th October 2009, Oxford: 180-187.

Bolger, D. 2007. 'Cultural interaction in 3rd millennium B.C. Cyprus: evidence of ceramics', in S. Antoniadou and A. Pace (eds.), *Mediterranean crossroads*, Athens: 162-186.

Bordreuil, P. (ed.) 1991. *Une bibliothèque au sud de la ville: Les textes de la 34e campagne (1973). Ras Shamra-Ougarit VII*, Paris.

Bretschneider, J., M. Al-Maqdassi, K. Vansteenhuyse, J. Driessen and K. van Lerberghe. 2004. 'Tell Tweini, Ancient Gabala, in the Bronze Age', *Ägypten und Levante* 14: 215-230.

Bryce, T.R. 2005. *The Kingdom of the Hittites*, Oxford – New York.

Bryce, T.R. 2016. 'The land of Hiyawa (Que) revisited', *Anatolian Studies* 66: 67-79.

Buccellati, G. 1963. 'Due note ai testi accadici di Ugarit', *Oriens Antiquus* 2: 223-228.

Cadogan, G. 1989. 'Maroni and the monuments', in E. Peltenburg (ed.), *Early society in Cyprus*, Edinburgh: 43-51.

Caminos, R.A. 1954. *Late-Egyptian miscellanies*, London.

Carpenter, J.R. 1981. 'Excavations at Phaneromeni, 1975-1978', in J.C. Biers and D. Soren (eds.), *Studies in Cypriot Archaeology*, Los Angeles: 59-78.

Catling, H.W. 1962. 'Patterns of settlement in Bronze Age Cyprus', *Opuscula Atheniensia* 4: 129-169.

Catling, H.W. 1975. 'Cyprus in the Late Bronze Age', in E.S. Edwards, C.J. Gadd, N.G.L. Hammond, J. Boardman, F.W. Walbank, A.K. Bowman, E. Champlin, A. Lintott, S.A. Cook, F.E. Adcock, M.P. Charlesworth, A. Cameron, P. Garnsey, D. Rathbone, B. Ward-Perkins and M. Whitby (eds.), *The Cambridge ancient history. History of the Middle East and the Aegean Region c. 1380-1000 B.C., Vol. II.2*, Cambridge: 188-216.

Charpin, D. 1990. 'Une mention d'Alašiya dans une lettre de Mari', *Revue d'assyriologie et d'archéologie orientale* 84.2: 125-127.

Cline, E.H. 2005. 'Cyprus and Alašiya. One and the same!', *Odyssey*: 41-44.

Cline, E.H. 2014. *1177 B.C. The year civilization collapsed*, Princeton.

Coleman, J.E., J.A. Barlow, M. Mogelonsky, and K.W. Scharr. 1996. *Alambra: A Middle Bronze Age Site in Cyprus. Investigations by Cornell University, 1975-1978* (Studies in Mediterranean Archaeology 118), Jonsered.

Courtois, J.-C., J. Lagarce and E. Lagarce. 1986. *Enkomi et le Bronze Récent à Chypre*, Nicosia.

Crewe, L. 2007. *Early Enkomi. Regionalism, Trade and Society at the Beginning of the Late Bronze Age on Cyprus* (British Archaeological Reports, International Series 1706), Oxford.

Del Monte G.F. and J. Tischler. 1978. *Die Orts- und Gewässernamen der hethitischen Texte* (Répertoire géographique des textes cunéiformes 6), Wiesbaden 1978.

De Martino, S. 2007. 'Il trattato tra Ḫatti e Alašiya, KBo XII 39', in M. Alparslan, M. Doğan-Alparslan and H. Peker (eds.), *Belkis Dinçol ve Ali Dinçol'a Armağan VITA. Festschrift in Honor of Belkis Dinçol and Ali Dinçol*, Istanbul: 483-492.

De Martino, S. 2008. 'Relations between Ḫatti and Alašiya According to Textual and Archaeological Evidence', in G. Wilhelm (ed.), *Ḫattuša-Boğazköy: Das Hethiterreich im Spannungsfeld des Altens Orients* (Colloquium der Deutschen Orient-Gesellschaft 6), Wiesbaden: 247-264.

Dikaios, P. 1969-1971. *Enkomi. Excavations 1948-1958. 3 Volumes*, Mainz-am-Rhein.

Dossin, G. 1939. 'Les archives économiques du palais de Mari', *Syria* 20.2: 97-113.

Dossin, G. 1965. 'Les découvertes épigraphiques de la XVe campagne de fouilles de Mari', *Comptes rendus des séances de l'Académie des Inscriptions et Belles-Lettres* 109.2: 400-406.

Dothan, T. and A. Ben-Tor. 1983. *Excavations at Athienou, Cyprus* (Qedem 16), Jerusalem.

Edel, E. 1994. *Die ägyptisch-hethitische Korrespondenz aus Boghazköy in babylonischer und hethitischer Sprache* (Abhandlungen der Rheinisch-Westfälischen Akademie der Wissenschaften), Opladen.

Edwards, I.E.S., C.J. Gadd, N.G.L. Hammond and E. Sollberger (eds.). 1973. *The Cambridge ancient history. History of the Middle East and the Aegean Region c. 1800-1380 B.C., Vol. II.1,* Cambridge.

Falconer, S.E., Fall, P.L., Davis, T.W., Horowitz, M. and J. Hunt. 2005. 'Initial archaeological investigations at Politiko-Troullia, 2004', *Report of the Department of Antiquities, Cyprus*: 69-85.

Falconer, S.E., P.L. Fall, J. Hunt and M.C. Metzger. 2010. 'Agrarian settlement at Politiko-Troullia, 2008', *Report of the Department of Antiquities, Cyprus*: 183-198.

Ferrara, S. 2012. *Cypro-Minoan inscriptions, Volume 1: Analysis* 1, Oxford – New York.

Fortin, M. 1981. *Military Architecture in Cyprus During the Second Millennium B.C.* (Ph.D. thesis, University of London).

Frankel, D. 2000. 'Migration and ethnicity in prehistoric Cyprus: technology as *habitus*', *European Journal of Archaeology* 3.2: 167-187.

Frankel, D. 2005. 'Becoming Bronze Age. Acculturation and enculturation in third millennium B.C. Cyprus', in J. Clarke (ed.), *Archaeological Perspectives on the Transmission and Transformation of Culture in the Eastern Mediterranean* (Levant Supplementary series 2), Oxford: 18-24.

Frankel, D. and J.M. Webb. 1996. *Marki Alonia: An Early and Middle Bronze Age Town in Cyprus. Excavations 1990-1994* (Studies in Mediterranean Archaeology 123.1), Jonsered.

Frankel, D. and J.M. Webb. 2006. *Marki Alonia: An Early and Middle Bronze Age Settlement in Cyprus. Excavations 1995-2000* (Studies in Mediterranean Archaeology 123.2), Sävedalen.

Fuscagni, F. 2014. *hethiter.net/: CTH 141 (INTR 2014-02-17).* http://www.hethport.uni-wuerzburg.de/txhet_svh/intro.php?xst=CTH%20141&prgr=&lg=DE&ed=F.%20Fuscagni (19/7/16).

Gander, M. 2010. *Die geographischen Beziehungen der Lukka-Länder* (Texte der Hethiter 27), Heidelberg.

Gander, M. 2014. 'Tlos, Oinoanda and the Hittite Invasion of the Lukka lands. Some Thoughts on the History of North-Western Lycia in the Late Bronze and Iron Ages', *Klio* 96.2: 369-415.

Gander, M. 2015. 'Asia, Ionia, Maeonia und Luwiya? Bemerkungen zu den neuen Toponymen aus Kom el-Hettan (Theben-West) mit Exkursen zu Westkleinasien in der Spätbronzezeit', *Klio* 97.2: 443-502.

Genz, H. 2011. 'Foreign Contacts of the Hittites', in H. Genz and D.P. Mielke (eds.), *Insights into the Hittite History and Archaeology*, Leuven – Paris – Walpole MA: 304-334.

Gill, D.W.J. 2010. 'Amenhotep III, Mycenae and the Laurion', in N. Sekunda (ed.), *ERGASTERIA: Works Presented to John Ellis Jones on his 80th Birthday*, Gdańsk: 21-34.

Goren, Y., H. Mommsen and J. Klinger. 2011. 'Non-destructive provenance study of cuneiform tablets using portable X-ray fluorescence (pXRF)', *Journal of Archaeological Science* 38: 684-696.

Goren, Y., I. Finkelstein and N. Na'aman. 2004. *Inscribed in clay: Provenance study of the Amarna Letters and other ancient Near Eastern texts* (Monographs Series of the Institute of Archaeology 23), Tel Aviv.

Goren, Y., S. Bunimovitz, I. Finkelstein and N. N'Aman. 2003. 'The Location of Alašiya: New Evidence from Petrographic Investigation of Alašiyan Tablets from El-Amarna and Ugarit', *American Journal of Archaeology* 107.2: 233-255.

Grace, V. 1940. 'A Cypriote tomb and Minoan evidence for its date', *American Journal of Archaeology* 44: 10-52.

Güterbock, H.G. 1967. 'The Hittite Conquest of Cyprus Reconsidered', *Journal of Near Eastern Studies* 26: 73-81.

Hadjisavvas, S. 1989. 'A Late Cypriot community at Alassa', in E. Peltenburg (ed.), *Early society in Cyprus*, Edinburgh: 32-42.

Hadjisavvas, S. 1992. *Olive-Oil Processing in Cyprus. From the Bronze Age to the Byzantine Period* (Studies in Mediterranean Archaeology 99), Jonsered.

Hadjisavvas, S. 1996. 'Alassa: a regional center of Alašiya?', in P. Åström and E. Herscher (eds.), *Late Bronze Age Settlements in Cyprus: Function and Relationship* (Studies in Mediterranean Archaeology and Literature, Pocketbook 126), Jonsered: 23-28.

Halayqa, I.K.H. 2010. 'The Demise of Ugarit in the Light of its Connections with Ḫatti', *Ugarit-Forschungen* 42: 297-332.

Hawkins, J.D. 1995. *The hieroglyphic inscription of the sacred pool complex at Hattusa (Südburg)* (Studien zu den Boğazköy-Texten Beiheft 3), Wiesbaden.

Hawkins, J.D. 2015. 'The Political Geography of Arzawa (Western Anatolia)', in N. Stampolides, C. Maner and K. Kopanias (eds.), *NOSTOI. Indigenous Culture, Migration and Integration in the Aegean Islands and Western Anatolia during the Late Bronze and Early Iron Age. Proceedings of the International Conference held in Istanbul 31/3/11-3/4/11*, Istanbul: 15-36.

Heimpel, W. 2003. *Letters to the king of Mari. A new translation, with historical introduction, notes, and commentary* (Mesopotamian Civilizations 12), Winona Lake.

Helck, W. 1971. *Die Beziehungen Ägyptens zu Vorderasien im 3. und 2. Jahrtausend v. Chr.* (Ägyptologische Abhandlungen), Wiesbaden.

Helck, W. 1983. 'Asija', *Zeitschrift für ägyptische Sprache und Altertumskunde* 110: 29-36.

Helck, W. 1989. 'Ein Ausgreifen des Mittleren Reiches in den zypriotischen Raum?', *Göttinger Miszellen* 109: 27-30.

Helft, S. 2010. *Patterns of Exchange/Patterns of Power: A New Archaeology of the Hittite Empire* (Ph.D. thesis, University of Pennsylvania).

Hellbing, L. 1979. *Alasia Problems,* Goteborg.

Heltzer, M. 2001. 'Asylum on Alašiya (Cyprus)', *Zeitschrift für altorientalische und biblische Rechtsgeschichte* 7: 368-373.

Hennessy, J.B., K.O. Eriksson and I.C. Kehrberg. 1988. *Ayia Paraskevi and Vasilia: Excavations by the Late J.R. Stewart* (Studies in Mediterranean Archaeology 82), Göteborg.

Herscher, E. 1978. *The Bronze Age Cemetery at Lapithos, Vrysi tou Barba, Cyprus. Results of the University of Pennsylvania Museum Excavation, 1931* (Ph.D. thesis, University of Pennsylvania).

Herscher, E 1988. 'Kition in the Middle Bronze Age: the tombs at Larnaca-Ayios Prodromos', *Report of the Department of Antiquities, Cyprus*: 141-165.
Hoftijzer, J. and W.H. Van Soldt. 1998. 'Texts from Ugarit Pertaining to Seafaring.', S. Wachsmann (ed.), *Seagoing Ships and Seamanship in the Bronze Age Levant*, Texas: 333-344.
Huehnergard, J. 1999. 'The Akkadian Letters', in W.G.E. Watson and N. Wyatt (eds.), *Handbook of Ugaritic studies* (Handbuch der Orientalistik 39), Boston: 375-389.
Karageorghis, V. 1974. *Excavations at Kition. 1. The Tombs*, Nicosia.
Karageorghis, V., N. Gale and Z. Stos-Gale. 1983. 'Two silver ingots from Cyprus', *Antiquity* 57: 211-214.
Kassianidou, V. 2008. 'The formative years of the Cypriot copper industry', in I. Tzachili (ed.), *Aegean Metallurgy in the Bronze Age*, Rethymnon: 249-267.
Kassianidou, V. 2013. 'The Production and Trade of Cypriot Copper in the Late Bronze Age. An Analysis of the Evidence', *PASIPHAE* 7: 133-145.
Kelder, J.M. 2016. 'Mycenae, Rich in Silver.' in K. Kleber and R. Pirngruber (eds.), *Silver, money and credit. Festschrift for Robartus J. van der Spek on occasion of his 65th birthday on 18 September 2014*, Leiden: 307-317.
Keswani, P.S. 1993. 'Models of local exchange in Late Bronze Age Cyprus', *Bulletin of the American Schools of Oriental Research* 292: 73-83.
Keswani, P.S. 1996. 'Hierarchies, heterarchies, and urbanization processes: the view from Bronze Age Cyprus', *Journal of Mediterranean Archaeology* 9: 211-249.
Kitchen, K.A. 2009. 'Alas(h)i(y)a (Irs) and Asiya (Isy) in Ancient Egyptian Sources', in D. Michaelides, V. Kassianidou and R.S. Merrillees (eds.), *Proceedings of the International Conference Egypt and Cyprus in Antiquity, Nicosia, 3-6 April 2003*, Oxford – Oakville CT: 1-12.
Klengel, H. 1998. *Geschichte des Hethitischen Reiches* (Handbuch der Orientalistik 34), Leiden.
Knapp, A.B. 1980. 'KBo 1 26: Alašiya and Ḫatti', *Journal of Cuneiform Studies* 32.1: 43-47.
Knapp, A.B. 1985. 'Alašiya, Capthor/Keftiu and eastern Mediterranean trade: recent studies in Cypriote archaeology and history', *Journal of Field Archaeology*: 231-250.
Knapp, A.B. 1986. *Copper Production and Divine Protection: Archaeology, Ideology and Social Complexity on Bronze Age Cyprus* (Studies in Mediterranean Archaeology and Literature, Pocket-book 42), Göteborg.
Knapp, A.B. 1990. 'Production, location and integration in Bronze Age Cyprus', *Current Anthropology* 31: 147-176.
Knapp, A.B. (ed.). 1996. *Sources for the history of Cyprus. Near Eastern and Aegean texts from the third to the first millennia BC.* (Sources for the History of Cyprus 2), New York.
Knapp, A.B. 2008. *Prehistoric and protohistoric Cyprus. Identity, insularity, and connectivity*, Oxford – New York.
Knapp, A.B. 2013. *The archaeology of Cyprus: from earliest prehistory through the Bronze Age*, Cambridge – New York.
Knapp, A.B. and V. Kassianidou. 2008. 'The Archaeology of Late Bronze Age Copper Production Politiko *Phorades* on Cyprus', in Ü. Yalçın (ed.), *Anatolian Metal IV* (Veröffentlichungen aus dem Deutschen Bergbau-Museum Bochum 157), Bochum: 135-147.

Kopanias, K. 2015a. ‘From the Mythical Atreus to the Ruler Attarissiya. Aegean Kingship in the Late Bronze Age through the Prism of Near Eastern Texts’, in I. Kaiser, O. Kouka and D. Panagiotopoulos (eds.), *Ein Minoer im Exil. Festschrift zum 65. Geburtstag von Wolf-Dietrich Niemeier* (Universitätsforschungen zur Prähistorischen Archäologie), Bonn: 211-222.

Kopanias, K. 2015b. ‘The King’s Household, Royal Gifts and the International Trade in the Amarna Age’, in N. Birgalias (ed.), *Kingship in Ancient Greece: from Agamemnon to Cleopatra. International Conference in honor of Pierre Carlier. Athens, 6 – 8 February 2014* (KTEMA. Civilisations de l’Orient, de la Grèce et de Rome antiques 40), Strasbourg.

Kozal, E. 2002. ‘Hethitische und hethitisch beeinflusste Objekte aus Zypern’, in M. Korfmann and R. Aslan (eds.), *Mauerschau: Festschrift für Manfred Korfmann*, Remshalden-Grunbach: 651-661.

Lackenbacher, S. 2002. *Textes akkadiens d’Ugarit: textes provenant des vingt-cinq premières campagnes*, Paris.

Lackenbacher, S. and F. Malbran-Labat. 2005. ‘Ugarit et les Hittites dans les archives de la Maison d’Urtenu’, *Studi micenei ed egeo-anatolici* 47: 227-240.

Lambrou-Phillipson, C. 1993. ‘Ugarit: A Late Bronze Age thalassocracy? The evidence of the textual sources’, *Orientalia NS* 62.3: 163-170.

Lehmann, G.A. 1996. *Untersuchungen zur späten Eisenzeit in Syrien und Libanon*, Münster.

Limet, H. 1985. ‘La technique du bronze dans les archives de Mari’, in J.-M. Durand and J.-R. Kupper (eds.), *Miscellanea Babylonica: Mélanges Birot*, Paris: 201-210.

Lipiński, E. 2009. *Reseph. A Syro-Canaanite Deity*, Leuven – Paris.

Liverani, M. 1962. *Storia di Ugarit nell’età degli archivi politici*, Rome.

Maguire, L.C. 2009. *The Cypriot Pottery and its Circulation in the Levant* (Tell el-Dab’a 21. Denkschriften der Gesamtakademie 51), Vienna.

Maier, F.-G. and V. Karageorghis. 1984. *Paphos: History and Archaeology*, Nicosia.

Manning, S.W. 1993. ‘Prestige, distinction and competition: the anatomy of socioeconomic complexity in Fourth to Second millennium B.C.E. Cyprus’, *Bulletin of the American Schools of Oriental Research* 292: 35-58.

Manning, S.W. and F.A. DeMita, Jr. 1997. ‘Cyprus, the Aegean and Maroni *Tsaroukkas*’, in D. Christou (ed.), *Cyprus and the Aegean in Antiquity*, Nicosia: 103-142.

Mantzourani, E. 2001. Η Αρχαιολογία της Προϊστορικής Κύπρου, Athens.

Marcus, E.S. 2007. ‘Amenemhet II and the Sea: maritime aspects of the Mit Rahina (Memphis) inscription’, *Ägypten und Levante* 17: 137-190.

Melchert, H.C. 2002. ‘Tarhuntassa in the SÜDBURG Hieroglyphic Inscription’, in H.G. Güterbock, K.A. Yener, H.A. Hoffner and S. Dhesi (eds.), *Recent developments in Hittite archaeology and history. Papers in memory of Hans G. Güterbock*, Winona Lake: 137-144.

Merrillees, R.S. 1984. ‘Ambelikou-*Aletri*: a preliminary report’, *Report of the Department of Antiquities, Cyprus*: 1-13.

Merrillees, R.S. 1987. *Alašiya Revisited* (Cahiers de la Revue biblique 22), Paris.

Merrillees, R.S. 2009. ‘The stone vases of the Philia culture from Vasilia: Cypriot, Egyptian or other?’, in D. Michaelides, V. Kassianidou and R. Merrillees (eds.), *Egypt and Cyprus in Antiquity*, Oxford: 23-28.

Merrillees, R.S. 2011. 'Alašiya: A Scientific Quest for its Location', in P. Betancourt and S. Ferrence (eds.), *Metallurgy: Understanding how, Learning why. Studies in Honor of James D. Muhly*, Philadelphia: 255-264.

Millard, A.R. 1973. 'Cypriot Copper in Babylonia, c.1745 B.C.', *Journal of Cuneiform Studies* 25.4: 211-214.

Monroe, C.M. 2009. *Scales of Fate: Trade, Tradition, and Transformation in the Eastern Mediterranean ca. 1350-1175 BCE* (Alter Orient und Altes Testament Band 357), Münster.

Moran, W.L. 1992. *The Amarna Letters*, Baltimore – London.

Muhly, J.D. 1985. 'Sources of tin and the beginnings of bronze metallurgy', *American Journal of Archaeology* 89: 275-291.

Muhly, J.D. 1989. 'The organisation of the copper industry in Late Bronze Age Cyprus', in E. Peltenburg (ed.), *Early society in Cyprus*, Edinburgh: 298-314.

Muhly, J.D. and T.A. Wertime. 1973. 'Evidence for the sources and use of tin during the Bronze Age of the Near East: a reply to J. E. Dayton', *World Archaeology* 5: 111-122.

Mynářová, J. 2007. *Language of Amarna, language of diplomacy: perspectives on the Amarna letters*, Prague.

Mynářová, J. 2015. 'Egypt among the Great Powers and Its Relations to the Neighboring Vassal Kingdoms in the Southern Levant According to the Written Evidence: Thutmose III and Amarna', in E. Birgitta and R. Pruzsinszky (eds.), *Policies of Exchange. Political Systems and Modes of Interaction in the Aegean and the Near East in the 2nd Millennium B.C.E.* (Oriental and European Archaeology 2), Vienna: 157-165.

Negbi, O. 1986. 'The climax of urban development in Bronze Age Cyprus', *Report of the Department of Antiquities, Cyprus*: 97-121.

Negbi, O. 2005. 'Urbanism on Late Bronze Age Cyprus: LC II in retrospect', *Bulletin of the American Schools of Oriental Research* 337: 1-45.

Nougayrol, J., E. Laroche, C. Virolleaud and C. Schaeffer. 1968. *Ugaritica 5. Nouveaux textes accadiens, hourrites et ugaritiques des archives et bibliothèques privées d'Ugarit. Commentaires des textes historiques (première partie)* (Mission de Ras Shamra), Paris.

Oreshko, R. 2016. *Studies in Hieroglyphic Luwian: Towards a Philological and Historical Reinterpretation of the SÜDBURG inscription* (Ph.D. thesis, Freie Universität Berlin).

Osing, J. 1980. 'Zum ägyptischen Namen für Zypern', *Göttinger Miszellen* 40: 45-51.

Otten, H. 1963. 'Neue Quellen zum Ausklang des Hethitischen Reiches', *Mitteilungen der Deutschen Orient-Gesellschaft zu Berlin* 94: 1-23.

Peltenburg, E.J. 1996. 'From isolation to state formation in Cyprus, *c.* 3500 – 1500 B.C.', in V. Karageorghis and D. Michaelides (eds.), *The development of the Cypriot economy from the Prehistoric period to the present day*, Nicosia: 17-44.

Peltenburg, E.J. 2007. 'East Mediterranean interactions in the 3rd millennium B.C.', in S. Antoniadou and A. Pace (eds.), *Mediterranean crossroads*, Athens: 141-161.

Peltenburg, E.J. 2012. 'Text meets material in Late Bronze Age Cyprus', in A. Georgiou (ed.), *Cyprus: an Island Culture. Society and Social Relations from the Bronze Age to the Venetian Period*, Oxford: 1-23.

Peltenburg, E.J. and M. Iacovou. 2012. 'Crete and Cyprus: contrasting political configurations', in G. Cadogan, M. Iacovou, K. Kopaka and J. Whitley (eds.), *Parallel Lives: Ancient Island Societies in Crete and Cyprus* (British School at Athens Studies 20), London: 345-363.

Podany, A.H. 2010. *Brotherhood of kings: how international relations shaped the ancient Near East*, Oxford – New York.

Quack, J.F. 1996. 'kftȝw und iȝsy', *Ägypten und Levante* 6: 75-81.

Rainey, A.F. 1966. 'LÚ MAŠKIM at Ugarit', *Orientalia* NS 35.4: 426-428.

Rainey, A.F. and W.M. Schniedewind. 2015. *The El-Amarna Correspondence. A New Edition of the Cuneiform Letters from the Site of El-Amarna based on Collations of all Extant Tablets, Vol. 1* (Handbook of Oriental Studies 110), Leiden – Boston.

Rainey, A.F. and Z. Cochavi-Rainey. 2015. *The El-Amarna Correspondence. A New Edition of the Cuneiform Letters from the Site of El-Amarna based on Collations of all Extant Tablets, Vol. 2* (Handbook of Oriental Studies 110), Leiden – Boston.

Rupp, D.W., J.T. Clarke, C. D'Annibale and S. Stewart. 1992. 'The Canadian Palaipaphos Survey Project: 1991 field season', *Report of the Department of Antiquities, Cyprus*: 285-317.

Schaeffer, C. F.-A. 1952. *Enkomi-Alasia*, Vol. I: *Nouvelles Missions en Chypre, 1946-1950*, Paris.

Schneider, T. 2008. 'Egypt and the Levant', in J. Aruz (ed.), *Beyond Babylon: Art, Trade, and Diplomacy in the Second Millennium B.C.*, New Haven – London: 61-69.

Scott, D.A. 2002. *Copper and bronze in art: corrosion, colorants, conservation*, Los Angeles.

Sherratt, S. 1998. 'Sea Peoples and the economic structure of the late second millennium in the eastern Mediterranean', in S. Gitin, A. Mazar and E. Stern (eds.), *Mediterranean Peoples in Transition: Thirteenth to Tenth Centuries B.C.E.*, Jerusalem: 292-313.

Singer, I. 1985. 'The Battle of Niḫriya and the End of the Hittite Empire', *Zeitschrift für Assyriologie und vorderasiatische Archäologie* 75: 100-123.

Singer, I. 1999. 'A Political History of Ugarit', in W.G.E. Watson and N. Wyatt (eds.), *Handbook of Ugaritic studies* (Handbuch der Orientalistik 39), Boston: 603-733.

Singer, I. 2000. 'New Evidence on the End of the Hittite Empire', in D.W. Jones (ed.), *External relations of early Iron Age Crete, 1100-600 B.C.* (Archaeological Institute of America Monographs. New Series no. 4), Dubuque: 21-33.

Singer, I. 2002. *Hittite prayers* (Writings from the Ancient World 11), Leiden – Boston.

Singer, I. 2003. 'The Great Scribe Taki-Šarruma', in G.M. Beckman, R.H. Beal and G. McMahon (eds.), *Hittite studies in Honor of Harry A. Hoffner, Jr. On the Occasion of his 65th Birthday*, Winona Lake: 341-348.

Singer, I. and G. Gestoso Singer. 2014. 'Alašian Products in Hittite Sources', in Z. Csabai (ed.), *Studies in Economic and Social History of the Ancient Near East in Memory of Péter Vargyas, Budapest* (Ancient Near Eastern and Mediterranean Studies 2), Budapest: 317-336.

Smith, J.S. 2012. 'Languages, scripts and administration', in D. Pilides and N. Papadimitriou (eds.), *Ancient Cyprus. Cultures in dialogue: exhibition catalogue*, Nicosia: 84-87.

South, A.K. 1996. 'Kalavasos-*Ayios Dhimitrios* and the organisation of Late Bronze Age Cyprus', in P. Åström and E. Herscher (eds.), *Late Bronze Age Settlements in Cyprus: Function and Relationship* (Studies in Mediterranean Archaeology and Literature, Pocketbook 126), Jonsered: 39-49.

South, A.K. 1997. 'Kalavasos-*Ayios Dhimitrios* 1992-1996', *Report of the Department of Antiquities, Cyprus*: 151-175.

South, A.K. 2002. 'Late Bronze Age settlement patterns in southern Cyprus: the first kingdoms?', *Cahier du Centre d'Etudes Chypriotes* 32: 59-72.

Steel, L. 2004. *Cyprus Before History: From the Earliest Settlers to the End of the Bronze Age*, London.

Stewart, J.R. 1963. 'The tomb of the seafarer at Karmi', *Opuscula Atheniensia* 4: 197-204.

Swiny, S. 1986. *The Kent State University Expedition to Episkopi Phaneromeni* (Studies in Mediterranean Archaeology 74.2), Göteborg.

Swiny, S. 1989. 'From round house to duplex: a re-assessment of prehistoric Cypriot Bronze Age society', in E. Peltenburg (ed.), *Early society in Cyprus*, Edinburgh: 14-31.

Swiny, S., G. Rapp and E. Herscher (eds.). 2003. *Sotira Kaminoudhia: An Early Bronze Age Site in Cyprus* (Archaeological Reports 8, Cyprus American Archaeological Research Institute Monograph 4,) Boston.

Teixidor, J. 1976. 'The Phoenician Inscriptions of the Cesnola Collection', *Metropolitan Museum Journal* 11: 55-70.

Todd, I.A. 1993. 'Kalavasos Laroumena: test excavation of a Middle Bronze Age settlement', *Report of the Department of Antiquities, Cyprus*: 81-96.

Todd, I.A. (ed.) 1986. *The Bronze Age Cemetery in Kalavasos Village, Vasilikos Valley Project I* (Studies in Mediterranean Archaeology 71.1), Göteborg.

Ulanowski, K. 2013. 'God Reshef in the Mediterranean', in L. Bombardieri, A. D'Agostino, G. Guarducci, V. Orsi and S. Valentini (eds.), *SOMA 2012. Identity and connectivity: proceedings of the 16th Symposium on Mediterranean Archaeology, Florence, Italy, 1-3 March 2012*, Oxford: 157-164.

Van de Mieroop, M. 2016. *A History of the Ancient Near East ca. 3000-323 BC.* [3rd edition], Oxford.

Van den Hout, T.P.J. 1994. Review of: R.S. Merillees, *Alashiya Revisited* (Paris 1987), *Journal of Near Eastern Studies* 53.2: 137-138.

Van Soldt, W.H. 2001. 'Studies on the sākinu-Official (1). The spelling and the office-holders at Ugarit', *Ugarit-Forschungen* 33: 579-599.

Van Soldt, W.H. 2002. 'Studies on the sākinu-Official (2). The functions of the *sākinu* of Ugarit', *Ugarit-Forschungen* 34: 805-828.

Van Soldt, W.H. 2006. 'Studies on the sākinu-Official (3). The *sākinu* of other Ugaritic towns and of the palace and the queen's house, and the findspots of the tablets', *Ugarit-Forschungen* 38: 675-97.

Vermeule, E.T. and F.Z. Wolsky. 1990. *Toumba tou Skourou: A Bronze Age Potter's Quarter on Morphou Bay in Cyprus*, Cambridge MA.

Vidal, J. 2005. 'Beirut and Ugarit in the 13th Century BCE', *Studi micenei ed egeo-anatolici* 47: 291-298.

Vigo, M. 2008. ''Trudurre e non tradire' il problema delle integrazioni. Il caso di KBo XII 39', in B. Bellucci, E. Jucci, A. Rizza and B.M. Tomassini Pieri (eds.), *Traduzioni di tradizioni e tradizioni di traduzione. Atti del quarto incontro «Orientalisti» (Pavia, 19-21 aprile 2007)*, Milano: 191-248.

Vigo, M. 2010a. 'Linen in Hittite Inventory Texts', in C. Michel and M.L. Nosch (eds.), *Textile Terminologies in the Ancient Near East and Mediterranean from the Third to the First millennia BC.*, Oxford: 290-322.

Vigo, M. 2010b. 'Tarḫuntaš-trġ(n)ds. Troodos?', in A.M. Jasink and L. Bombardieri (eds.), *Researches in Cypriote History and Archaeology Proceedings of the Meeting held in Florence April 29-30th 2009*, Firenze: 155-164.

Vita, J.-P. 1999. 'The Society of Ugarit', in W.G.E. Watson and N. Wyatt (eds.), *Handbook of Ugaritic studies* (Handbuch der Orientalistik 39), Boston: 455-498.

Voskos, I. 2018. 'Rethinking the 'Cypriot paradox': socio-economic change in Late Neolithic and Chalcolithic Cyprus', in S. Dietz, F. Mavridis, Ž. Tankosić and T. Takaoğlu (eds.), *Communities in Transition: The Circum-Aegean Area during the 5th and 4th millennia BC* (Monographs of the Danish Institute at Athens 20), Oxford: 466-475.

Voskos, I. and A.B. Knapp. 2008. 'Cyprus at the end of the Late Bronze Age: crisis and colonization or continuity and hybridization?', *American Journal of Archaeology* 112: 659-684.

Wachsmann, S. (ed.). 1998. *Seagoing Ships and Seamanship in the Bronze Age Levant*, Texas.

Watson, W.G.E. and N. Wyatt (eds.). 1999. *Handbook of Ugaritic studies* (Handbuch der Orientalistik 39), Boston.

Webb, J.M. 1999. *Ritual Architecture, Iconography and Practice in the Late Cypriot Bronze Age* (Studies in Mediterranean Archaeology and Literature, Pocketbook 75), Jonsered.

Webb, J.M. 2005. 'Ideology, iconography and identity: the role of foreign goods and images in the establishment of social hierarchy in Late Bronze Age Cyprus', in J. Clarke (ed.), *Archaeological Perspectives on the Transmission and Transformation of Culture in the Eastern Mediterranean* (Levant Supplementary Series 2), Oxford: 176-182.

Webb, J.M. and D. Frankel. 1999. 'Characterising the Philia facies: material culture, chronology and the origins of the Bronze Age in Cyprus', *American Journal of Archaeology* 103: 3-43.

Webb, J.M. and D. Frankel 2007. 'Identifying population movements by everyday practice: the case of 3rd millennium Cyprus', in S. Antoniadou and A. Pace (eds.), *Mediterranean Crossroads*, Athens: 189-216.

Webb, J.M. and D. Frankel. 2011. 'Hearth and home as identifiers of community in mid-third millennium Cyprus', in V. Karageorghis and O. Kouka (eds.), *On Cooking Pots, Drinking Cups, Loomweights and Ethnicity in Bronze Age Cyprus and Neighbouring Regions*, Nicosia: 29-42.

Webb, J.M., Frankel, D., Stos, Z.A. and N. Gale. 2006. 'Early Bronze Age metals trade in the eastern Mediterranean. New compositional and lead isotope evidence from Cyprus', *Oxford Journal of Archaeology* 25: 261-288.

Weinberg, S.S. 1983. *Bamboula at Kourion: The Architecture* (University Museum Monograph 42), Philadelphia.

Winter, I.J. 2010. *On the art in the ancient Near East, Vol. 1.* (Culture and history of the ancient Near East 1), Leiden – Boston.

Wiseman, D.J. 1953. *The Alalakh Tablets*, London.

Wouters, W. 1989. 'Urḫi-Tešub and the Ramses-Letters from Boghazköy', *Journal of Cuneiform Studies* 41.2: 226-234.

Yakubovich, I. 2009. 'The Luvian Enemy', *Kadmos* 47.1/2: 1-19.

Yamada, M. 1992. 'Reconsidering the Letters from the 'King' in the Ugarit Texts: Royal Correspondence of Carchemish?', *Ugarit-Forschungen* 24: 431-446.

Yasur-Landau, A. 2010. *The Philistines and Aegean migration at the end of the Late Bronze Age*, Cambridge.

Yener, K.A. 2012. 'Late Bronze Age Alalakh and Cyprus: a relationship of metals?', in V. Kassianidou, G. Papasavvas and J.D. Muhly (eds.), *Eastern Mediterranean metallurgy and metalwork in the second millennium BC. A conference in honour of James D. Muhly: Nicosia, 10th-11th October 2009*, Oxford: 162-168.

Yon, M. 1999. 'Chypre et Ougarit à la fin du Bronze Récent' *Report of the Department of Antiquities, Cyprus*: 113-119.

Yon, M. 2000. 'A trading city: Ugarit and the west', *Near Eastern Archaeology* 63: 192-193.

Die Mykenische Staatenwelt: Zwischen Mykene und Theben

Michael Bányai

1. Einleitung

Trotz des unleugbaren Erkenntnisgewinns der letzten Jahrzehnte bleibt eine definitive Antwort der Mykenologie auf die Frage nach dem politischen Wesen der mykenischen Staatenwelt immer noch aus. Wenn es darum geht, ob die hethitische Vorstellung von Aḫḫijawa als Großmacht, daher als Staat, akzeptiert werden kann, oder dies stattdessen bloß eine hethitische Vorstellung ist ohne ausreichende Deckung in der Wirklichkeit, und ob Aḫḫijawa mit dem Territorium der mykenischen Kultur ohne Abstriche identifiziert werden darf, alle diese Fragen bleiben zentral für die mykenologischen Debatte.

Unter anderen auch aufgrund der in den Linear B Archiven durchscheinenden Kleinteiligkeit der mykenischen Welt, wie auch wegen der traditionellen Zersplitterung der antiken griechischen Welt in historischer Zeit, die man gerne auf die Vergangenheit projiziert, regt sich heftiger Widerstand gegen die wortwörtliche Übernahme des Bilds der hethitischen Quellen. Trotz Kelders (2010, 2012) jüngsten Plädoyers für die Annahme eines tatsächlichen mykenischen Gesamtstaates besteht offenbar noch sehr viel Argumentationsbedarf ehe sich die Vorstellung von einem tatsächlichen mykenischen Reich endgültig durchsetzen dürfte.

Eine weitere Frage ebenso relevant zur politischen Organisation der mykenischen Staatenwelt, ist diejenige, wo man sich das Zentrum eines mykenischen 'Reiches' vorstellen dürfte. Traditionell schien die Antwort mit Mykene bereits festzustehen. Seit einiger Zeit gibt es jedoch auch Befürworter der Vorstellung eines von Theben her regierten Staates.

2. SH IIIA Keramikfunde an der östlichen Mittelmeerküste

Eine mögliche Antwort auf diese Probleme könnte unter Umständen aus einem unerwarteten Winkel kommen: nämlich aus einer Auswertung der mykenischen Exporte.

Es ist eine Tatsache, die dank zahlreicher Publikationen bereits bekannt ist, dass ein Hauptanteil der mykenischen Keramik der SH IIIA Periode, welcher bisher außerhalb Griechenlands gefunden wurde, in den wohl von Mykene abhängigen Töpferzentren in

in: Kelder, J.M. and Waal, W.J.I. (eds) 2019: *From 'LUGAL.GAL' to 'Wanax'. Kingship and Political Organisation in the Late Bronze Age Aegean*, Sidestone Press (Leiden), pp. 131-148.

der Argolis, Tiryns-Asine und Mykene-Berbati, produziert wurde. Ich füge an dieser Stelle eine Zusammenfassung der zugänglichen Literatur hinzu.

- Raymond et al. (2016: 63, 67): 'The Milesians of the First Mycenaeanising Phase imported LH HIA1-2 fine wares mostly from the Peloponnese and few (if any) from Cretan and southeastern Aegean sources. This may also be the case for the Second Mycenaeanising Phase given that NAA analyses confirm that at least a portion of the Miletus VI imported pottery is from the northeastern Peloponnese, most probably the Argolid (H. Mommsen, personal communication. NAA Bonn 2009. MILE 194.207. 208.209.211.218).'
- Mühlenbruch und Mommsen (2011: 285): SH IIIA2/B Scherbe aus Kamid el-Loz hat die Signatur von Mykene-Berbati. LH IIIB Scherbe aus dem Fayum hat die Signatur von Mykene-Berbati.
- Zuckerman et al. (2010): Untersuchung von 183 Keramik-Proben von 14 verschiedenen Küsten Fundorte in Nord-Israel zeigt das die große Mehrheit das Mykene-Berbati Profil (75%) hat. Lediglich für etwa 7% konnte eine andere Herkunft auf dem mykenischen Festland festgestellt werden. Seite 414: 'The results of all previous provenance studies of Mycenaean pottery from 14th to early 13th centuries southern Levantine contexts (Asaro and Perlman 1973; Hoffmann and Robinson 1993; Gunneweg and Michel 1999; Mommsen and Maran 2000-2001: 102; Mommsen et al. 2005; also for Tel Kazel, in the northern Levant, see Badre et al. 2005: 17), as well as those of the current study, indicate that a single chemical profile dominates most of these imports. Initially, this profile was assigned to a workshop near Mycenae (Berbati, the MYBE group), yet, as noted above, this profile may represent a general profile of the northeastern Peloponnese and may also represent other workshops in other regions of the Peloponnese, which have not yet been archaeologically recognized. Vessels provenanced to other workshops in the Argolid (most notably four sherds attributed to a Tiryns/Asine workshop), as well as in other regions in Greece are rare, and their appearance mainly at Tell Abu Hawam and Hazor is noteworthy.'
- Badre et al. (2005) untersuchen u.A. mykenische Keramik der Periode SH IIIA und IIIB ausgegraben bei Tell Kazel. Leider wird die einzige Scherbe, TK 109, die auf Seite 19 unter Fragezeichen Kreta oder stattdessen Boeotia geführt wird, nicht zeitlich zugewiesen. Sämtliche nicht lokalproduzierten untersuchten mykenischen Keramikscherben sind sonst von Mykene-Berbati, bzw. ein noch kleinerer Teil von Tyrins-Asine.
- French and Tomlinson (2004: 20): 'One of the sherds from the Uluburun shipwreck, together with the sherds from Tell el-Ajjul, Tell el-Amarna and Lebanon, however, can be assigned an Argolid provenance.'
- French (2004: 16): Untersuchung von 102 Proben mykenischer Waren in der Levante und Ägypten ergab eine Provenienz in der Argolis. Vielleicht 2 Scherben (Lachisch und Tell Abu Hawam) sollen von Kreta stammen und eine Scherbe (Lachisch) von Theben. Keine Periodisierung der Abweichungen vorhanden.
- Tomlinson (2004: 1442): 'It seems that the Lachish cluster is comprised of pottery imported from the Argolid.'
- Mommsen und Maran (2000-1: 102, 104): 'A sample of a krater from Tell Dan dated to thc LH IIIA2/B 1 period 24 was measured also in Berkeley and is a good member of the Myc/Ber group. It can be considered as a probable import from the Argolid

to the Levant.' *Ibidem* 'For the pieces of Tell Abu Hawam again the pattern Myc/Ber prevails, 14 of the 15 vessels can be regarded as imports from the workshop in the Argolid using this paste.' *Ibidem* 104: 'All other pictorial pieces analysed from the eastern Mediterranean (Cyprus, Tell Dan, Tell Abu Hawarn) belong to two chemical groups and are very probable importations from the Argolid. The group Myc/Ber by far outweighs the second group Tir/As in this far-ranging trade.'

- Karantzali und Ponting (2000): Mehrheit der mykenischen Importe bei Pylona (Rhodos) hat eine Herkunft in der Argolis.
- Mommsen et al. (1992): Sämtliche untersuchten mykenischen Scherben gefunden bei el Amarna sind auf Mykene-Berbati zurückzuführen.
- Yellin und Maeir (1992): Ein in Tell Dan gefundener LH IIIA Krater ist auf Mykene-Berbati zurückzuführen.
- Hoffmann and Robinson (1993: 77): Proben mykenischer Keramik führen auf die Argolis zurück.
- Mommsen at al. (1990): Eine mykenische Scherbe ausgegraben in Spanien wird auf Mykene Berbati zurückgeführt.
- Jones und Mee (1978: 461): 'During the LB IIIA2 period the large majority of the cemetery pottery at Ialysos was imported from the Argolid. The same situation pertains in the IIIB period, but there are examples of imported pottery from centres other than the Argolid...'.

Diese Disproportion kann am ehesten mit der Annahme einer zentralen Ökonomie erklärt werden – an deren Spitze Mykene stand – erklärt werden.[1] Einsammeln von Tribut und Umverpackung der erzielten Überschüsse für den Export in der Zentrale in handelsgerechten Mengen wären die Ursache für die beobachtete Herkunft der Ausfuhrkeramik. Die von der Zentrale gesteuerte Redistribution, konnte dann den Zusammenhalt und die Loyalität der 'beschenkten' Regionen sichern. Wiener (2009: 711-2) benutzt ausgerechnet diesen einseitigen Bezug von Keramik aus einer Werkstatt in der Argolis als Argument gegen die These eines von Theben angeführten Aḫḫijawa. Leider verzichtet er auf dasselbe Argument, welches er in negativem Sinne gegen Theben verwendete, als positiven Beleg für die Existenz eines von Mykene aus gesteuerten Aḫḫijawa auszuwerten.

Die von Zuckerman, Ben-Shlomo, Mountjoy, Mommsen (2009: 414) vorgeschlagenen alternativen Erklärungen, ohne die Möglichkeit einer staatlichen Lenkung einzubeziehen, scheinen mir hingegen etwas unrealistisch:

---

1 Man muss die Bilanz vorsorglich von solchen Fundstellen, wo keramisch offene Formen häufiger vorkommen bereinigen. Solche Formen können nicht ausschließlich als Gegenstand einer Handelstätigkeit betrachtet werden. Sie können durchaus Gebrauchsgegenstände sein, die einen Mykener durchaus auch ins Ausland begleitet haben können. Es wird z.B. berichtet (Jones, Vagnetti, 1991), dass unter der SH IIIB – IIIC Keramik bei Scoglio del Tonno, bei Taranto offene Formen überwiegen. Tatsächlich schließt Yasur-Landau (2010, 52) mit Hinweis auf zahlreiche Studien, dass man in Italien während der SH IIIB – C Periode, von einer tatsächlichen Anwesenheit kleiner Gruppen von Mykener ausgehen kann, die gelegentlich sogar ihre eigene Keramik lokal töpferten. Ich schließe ebenfalls von der Beurteilung die Ergebnisse der Untersuchung der Funde in Enkomi, von Asaro, Perlman, 1973, die zwar für einen Viertel der untersuchten Funde eine Werkstatt in der Argolis identifizierte. Für den Rest der Keramik wurde allerdings ein anderer Produktionsort in Festland Griechenland postuliert. Professor Perlman suggerierte eine mögliche Herkunft wie Messenien, allerdings wurde diese Herkunft, laut Van Wijngaarden (2002, 13, N. 221) nie konkret bestätigt.

The phenomenon of a single chemical source for most of the Mycenaean pottery in the southern Levant can be interpreted in several ways:

1. All these Mycenaean vessels were produced in one workshop and exported from one major Argive center, probably Mycenae, to the southern Levant. Such a monopoly of a specific workshop dominating a system of directional trade was previously suggested by Podzuweit and embraced by Badre et al. for the imported Mycenaean pottery found at Tel Kazel on the Syrian coast (Badre et al. 2005: 15, 36). This assumption might lend support to Balensi's suggestion of a system of Mycenaean 'proto-marketing' to the southern Levant during the 14th and early 13th centuries BC, where Tel Abu Hawam served as 'port of trade' with particular relations to its suppliers in the Argolid (Balensi: 2004).
2. All these Mycenaean vessels were produced in one workshop, but then exported under the supervision of several Mycenaean centers in the Argolid, all acquiring pottery for this purpose from the same industrial workshop.
3. Alternatively, there is an option of several workshops providing for the needs of several Mycenaean centers in the Argolid (or even a larger region). The similarity of the geology of the Argolid sub-areas (Whitbread 1995: 355-359; Higgins and Higgins 1996: 40-42, fig. 5.1), as well as the limitations of the chemical grouping mostly due to the lack of sufficient reference material, prevents the distinction of these assumed workshops in the north-eastern Peloponnese (with the exception of the paste with pattern TIR).

Im Grunde stellen die ausgebreiteten Erklärungsmöglichkeiten einen Versuch dar, die Konsequenzen eines zentralen Staates durch die Hintertür einzuführen, ohne sich auf denselben zu berufen. Angesichts der vermutlich geringen sozialen Stellung der Töpfer ist der Ausbau einer Monopolstellung durch eine bestimmte Werkstatt gar nicht ohne eine starke Tempel- oder Palaststruktur dahinter, die das favorisiert, denkbar. Die Betrachtung der Keramik als bloßes added-value ohne Aussagekraft zu den eigentlichen Handelsflüssen stellt eine zwar heute gebräuchliche Vorstellung dar, führt jedoch in eine der Bronzezeit vollkommen fremde Betrachtungsweise herein, wonach die Belieferung der Naturalien-Produzenten durch einen fernen Verpackungslieferanten als durchaus wirtschaftlich betrachtet werden dürfte.

3. SH IIIB Keramikfunde an der östlichen Mittelmeerküste; ein Bild das sich wandelt

3.1. Troja

Wie ich betont habe, beschränkt sich die Alleinstellung der Domäne von Mykene, die sich anhand der Exporttätigkeit dieser Region erkennen lässt, lediglich auf die Zeit von SH IIIA. Während des SH IIIB wandelt sich das Bild der mykenischen Exporte und verlangt eine wesentlich differenziertere Betrachtung. Während dieser Periode scheinen die Exporte von Aḫḫijawa eine Zeitlang von Theben statt von Mykene gekommen zu sein. Denn es gibt, wenn auch einen in Verhältnis zu Mykene geringeren aber dennoch signifikanten Anteil von Exporten, der auf Theben zurückgeführt werden müsse. Die bisherigen Argumente, die für die Betrachtung Thebens als Mittelpunkt der mykenischen Welt vorgebracht wurden, dürften hinlänglich bekannt sein; man muss daher nicht in Detail auf diese eingehen (Aravantinos, Godart, Sacconi 2001; Niemeier 2005: 203, 2008: 304ff; Latacz 2004. Contra: Palaima 2011; Kelder 2010; Wiener 2009). Das Problem dieser These ist das gleiche wie dasjenige der gegensätzlichen These, die in Mykene *den* Mittelpunkt identifizieren möchte, dass sie eine Aussage mit Absolutheitsanspruch machen möchte, die so nicht von den mykenischen Keramiken-Exporten während der gesamten Zeit von SH IIIA und SH IIIB unterstützt wird.

Die NAA Untersuchung der in Troja gefundenen mykenischen Keramik in der Schliemann Sammlung Berlin durch Mommsen, Hertel, Mountjoy (2001) bestätigte das bereits für andere SH IIIA Fundorte bekannte Muster, wonach mykenische Exportwaren auf Mykene und die Argolis zurückzuführen sind. Der Untersuchungsbefund für die darauffolgende SH IIIB Periode sieht allerdings vollkommen anders aus. Die in Troia gefundene mykenisch SH IIIB Keramik stammt ausschließlich aus Böotien. Der Rest besteht aus einer lokalen trojanischen Produktion in Nachahmung derselben mykenischen Keramik.

Wenn man es sich erlauben dürfte Troja mit Wiluša gleichzusetzen,[2] so ließe sich die Periode des mykenischen Einflusses, welcher sich in den Keramikimporten erkennen lässt, besser als nur durch die zeitliche Vorgabe des SH IIIB Stils eingrenzen. Einen mykenischen Einfluss, der offenbar stark genug dafür war die Trojaner zu überzeugen auch eigene Nachahmungen mykenischer Keramik herzustellen (die überwiegende Mehrzahl der SH IIIB dekorierten Scherben ist in Troja lokale Nachahmung), kann man sich nur zu einem Moment vorstellen, als die Hethiter die Kontrolle über Troja beziehungsweise Wiluša verloren haben.

---

2 Obwohl die Zahl der Anhänger einer Identifikation Trojas mit Wiluša überwiegt, muss man vorsorglich erwähnen, dass es auch namhafte Forscher gibt, welche eine solche ablehnen, ohne zugleich eine glaubhaftere Alternative bieten zu können. Z.B. Heinhold-Krahmer 2002, 2014; Kolb: 2010. Das vorgeschlagene Ilouza (das zur byzantinischen Zeit erstmals attestiert ist) bietet keine optimale linguistische Entsprechung Jablonka 2008 [2011]: 544-5). Währenddessen sind die linguistischen Hürden im Wege einer Gleichsetzung Hom. *Ἴλιος*= Wiluša überwindbar (Hajnal 2004: 169-171). Gleichzeitig ist die mutmaßliche Lage von Ilouza im Inneren Anatoliens, in Phrygien, ein absolutes Disqualifikationskriterium (zumal laut dem Tawagalawa-Brief Wiluša Streitobjekt zwischen Hethitern und Aḫḫijawa gewesen sein sollte). Um es soweit kommen zu lassen, dass Aḫḫijawa Ansprüche auf Wiluša gegen den hethitischen König melden kann, müsste – bei einer Gleichung Ilouza = Wiluša – Aḫḫijawa zumindest einen Staat wie z.B. Arzawa, welches an Phrygien gegrenzt habe, kontrolliert haben. CTH 181, §12: 'O, my brother, write to him this one thing, if nothing (else):... The King of Ḫatti has persuaded me about the matter of the land of ⌜Wilusa⌝ concerning which he and I were hostile to one another, and we have made peace. Now(?) hostility is not appropriate between us.' (Beckman et al. 2011: 115-6). Dies ist auch anhand desselben Dokuments, des Tawagalawa-Briefes, auszuschließen.
In Wirklichkeit dürfte die Diskussion längst beendet sein, zumal man in Troja hergestellte Keramik bis soweit südlich wie Tell Miqne/Ekron verstreut feststellen kann (Allen 1994; Mommsen und Pavuk 2007; Badre et al 2005). Sollte Troja einen Konkurrenten namens Wiluša im gleichen geographischen Raum erfahren haben, in dem die Anatolische Grauware vorgeherrscht habe, wäre es erklärungsbedürftig, wieso keine sonstigen nordanatolischen Keramikproduzenten, außer Troja, in der Levante nachweisbar sind. Wiluša dürfte sich als wichtiger Staat der Region nicht minder als Troja selbst am internationalen Handel beteiligt haben. Die Ergebnisse der Neutron Aktivierungsanalysen von Anatolischer Grauware, gefunden in der Levante, führen solche Funde regelmäßig auf Troja als einzige anatolische Produktionsstätte zurück (Allen 1994; Mommsen und Pavuk, 2007, Badre et al. 2005: 17). Wiluša muss zwangsläufig eine küstennahe Lage gehabt haben, weil Aḫḫijawa nie fähig war politische Macht tiefer ins anatolische Inland zu projizieren. Dies kann man auch an der Verteilung mykenischer keramischer Funde in Anatolien erkennen, welche Region deswegen von Mountjoy 'East Aegean – West Anatolian Interface' genannt wurde.

Cline (1991) denkt über ein eventuell auf dem Handel mit den Mykener lastendes hethitisches Embargo nach. Auch wenn ein solches nicht direkt anhand der historischen Quellen unmittelbar zu beweisen ist, ist der gegenseitige Ausschluss von Produkten des jeweiligen Nachbars augenfällig. Mykenische Kontakte mit Troja während der ersten Hälfte des 13ten Jahrhunderts, also mit der Zeit des SH IIIB1, als die hethitische Kontrolle über Troja auf ihrem Höhepunkt war (der Alakšandu-Vertrag), sollte man daher eher nicht annehmen. Die absolute Nicht-Erwähnung von Aḫḫijawa in dem genannten Vertrag, obwohl Aḫḫijawa einer der Nachbarn von Wiluša gewesen sein dürfte, könnte das Fehlen irgendwelcher für Alakšandu bindenden Embargo Klausel erklären. Zu diesem Zeitpunkt befand sich Aḫḫijawa gerade auf dem politischen Rückzug, warum auch seine Erwähnung nicht nötig war. Es ist ja auch schwer vorstellbar, dass die lokal trojanischen mykenischen Keramikimitate auf dem Höhepunkt der mykenischen Irrelevanz produziert wurden. Man könnte u.U. suggerieren, dass gerade dieser politische Rückzug Aḫḫijawas aus der Region der bis dahin präzedenzlosen politischen Ausweitung von Ḫatti – welche nun ohne militärische Konfrontation möglich wurde – in nördlicher Richtung Vorschub gab.

Allerdings scheint Troja-Wiluša zu einem späteren Zeitpunkt, dokumentiert u.A. im Tawagalawa-Brief, entsprechend des ebenfalls von Cline (2008) eingeführten Begriffs, zu einer 'contested periphery' zwischen Hethitern und Aḫḫijawa geworden zu sein.[3]

3.2. Ialysos und Tell Abu Hawam

In Ialysos auf Rhodos, das anders als Troia während der ganzen Zeit des 13. Jahrhunderts, also während der gesamten SH IIIB Periode, ungebrochen unter mykenischer Kontrolle blieb, sieht der archäologische Befund wiederum etwas anders aus. Die Quellen der SH IIIB Importe in Ialysos sind: Mykene und Theben.[4] Der Unterschied zwischen dem jeweiligen Befund in Troja und Rhodos scheint von der wesentlich längeren Periode, während der Rhodos mykenischen Importen ausgesetzt war, ab zu hängen. Da die Betrachtung der

3 Leider ist das Datum des Tawagalawa-Briefs unsicher, aber es wird allgemein angenommen, dass der Autor aller Wahrscheinlichkeit nach Ḫattušili III war (Beckman et al. 2011). Das Ergebnis der Popko Untersuchung (1984), wonach sowohl der Manapa-Tarḫunta-, wie auch der Tawgalawa-Brief, paläographisch spät sind (Tudḫalija IV. und seine Nachfolger) wurde lange Zeit mit der Annahme wegerklärt, dass die Texte spätere archivale Kopien seien. Goren et al. (2011) haben jedoch nachgewiesen, dass der Tonmaterial der Keilschrifttafel von Tawagalawa (CTH 181) aus der Ephesus Region stammt, also das Dokument nicht später als Archivkopie in Ḫattušša entstanden sein könnte. Dies Bedarf einer erneuten chronologischen Diskussion, mit der potentiellen Folge, dass damit ein späteres Datum dieser Korrespondenz plötzlich plausibel wird.

4 Jones und Mee 1978: 461: 'During the LB IIIA2 period the large majority of the cemetery pottery at Ialysos was imported from the Argolid. The same situation pertains in the IIIB period, but there are examples of imported pottery from centres other than the Argolid, such as Crete.' *Ibidem* 467ff.: 'The inability of researchers to distinguish between Knossian and Theban pottery compositions has been recognized since the initial studies of Catling et al. and those of Catling and Millett on the inscribed stirrup jars from Thebes... The better match with Thebes rather than Knossos may simply be the result of the wider ranges at the former site' and 'Only two of the 17 IIIB pots analysed are local but the imports are no longer exclusively from the Argolid. FS37 piriform jars are more or less unknown outside the Dodecanese but both Samples 9 and 47 are imported. Their composition matches Thebes/Knossos but neither looks remotely Minoan so that Boeotia seems the more likely centre of production. The two kraters, samples 11 and 40, also have Thebes/Knossos compositions and should likewise be imported from Boeotia. It must be stressed that there are no FS37 piriform jars or FS11 kraters from Boeotia, although FS281 kraters do occur. A much better perspective on the Mycenaean of Boeotia, however, should soon be possible as the mass of pottery from recent excavations is published.'

mykenischen SHIIIB Keramik Importe auf Rhodos diachronisch ist und diese Funde innerhalb dieser Periode nicht akkurat datiert werden können, dürfte der Eindruck einer gleichzeitigen Belieferung Rhodos durch Mykene und Theben nicht abzuwehren sein. Lediglich dank der mykenischen SH IIIB Funde in Troja, welche während einer zeitlich sehr begrenzten Periode den Weg dahin gefunden haben, können wir vermuten, dass es auch auf Rhodos zeitlich getrennte Perioden eines Zustroms von Importen aus Theben und Mykene gegeben haben könnte.

Dasselbe gilt für die SH IIIB Keramik in Tell Abu Hawam, die ebenfalls eine Mischung mykenischer Importe aus der Argolis (Tiryns, Midea, usw.) und Theben darstellt (Mommsen und Maran 2000-1: 102). Diese Erscheinung ist dadurch erklärlich, dass im späteren Teil der LH IIIB Periode Mykene eine Zeitlang durch Theben als Machtzentrum von Aḫḫijawa abgelöst worden sein durfte. Die Beschränkung der Exporte aus Griechenland in der Periode LH IIIA und IIIB auf allein ein paar Keramik Produktionszentren ist unkompliziert durch eine teilweise zentralgesteuerte Redistributions-Ökonomie zu erklären.[5] Man kann sich die Welt der mykenischen Paläste sowohl politisch-hierarchisch und in Spiegelung dessen auch ökonomisch in Form einer pyramidalen Struktur vorstellen, in der die einzelnen Paläste zwar autarke Produktionszentren sind, dennoch einen Teil ihrer Produktion an die Zentrale abzutreten haben.

3.3. *Schlussfolgerung*

Das, was man archäologisch in Form von Keramikscherben feststellt, ist das Ergebnis der ökonomischen Aktivität der mykenischen Paläste. Das statistisch aus deren Auswertung resultierende Bild ist das absolute Gegenteil dessen, was man erwarten würde, sollten sich die mykenischen Produzenten/Paläste gleichermaßen an dem Außenhandel beteiligt haben.

Es gibt eine weitere wichtige Folge der beobachteten mykenischen Keramikimporte im östlichen Mittelmeer. Da sich diese Keramikimporte praktisch auf solche aus Mykene (bzw. der Argolis) und Theben beschränken und sie parallel mit der Bezeugung der Aktivität des Staates Aḫḫijawa hauptsächlich entlang der anatolischen Küste ablaufen, bleibt kein Platz für einen von Mykene, später Theben, unterschiedlichen Staat als Anwärter für die Betrachtung als mykenische Zentrale übrig. Sollte es eine von Mykene, später Theben, verschiedenen Zentrale gegeben haben, dann dürfte dieser Staat gar keine Spuren ihrer unabhängigen Handelstätigkeit hinterlassen haben. Dies ist ein ernsthafter Grund Aḫḫijawa als den eigentlichen Namen des dank seiner Handelstätigkeit erfassten mykenischen Staates zu betrachten. Deswegen kann ich keinen guten Grund erkennen die verschiedene vorhandenen Alternativen zur Identifikation von Aḫḫijawa im Detail zu diskutieren.[6]

---

5 Man dürfte aufgrund der stark gemischten Herkunft der Importe der Periode SHIIIC auf einen Zusammenbruch der zentralisierten Palastökonomie von Aḫḫijawa schließen. So z.B. identifiziert dieselbe Untersuchung von Mommsen et al. in Troia ebenso die Tonsignatur Thessaliens (pyra), Böotiens (thec), von Dimini (dimi) und der Attika. Nach den wesentlich zusammengeschrumpften Importen allein aus dem allernächsten mykenischen Umkreis, nämlich Kreta, zu beurteilen, wird Rhodos während derselben Zeit (SH IIIC) von den Handelswegen abgehängt (Jones und Mee 1978).

6 So hat man mehrmals in der Vergangenheit als Identifikation für Aḫḫijawa Rhodos vorgeschlagen (Hrozný 1929; Page 1959: 15-18; Furumark 1965: 109; Mountjoy 1998) oder bloß eines der mykenischen Palatial-Staaten auf dem griechischen Festland.

4. Die überregionale Aktivität von Kollektoren im Spiegel der Keramikfunde in der Argolis und in Theben

Unter Umständen könnte ein winziger Beweis für die Aktivität von Kollektoren, welche die regionalen Überschüsse an die Zentrale in Theben weiterleiten, in Form eines im Westhaus in Mykene gefundenen Linear B Textes X 508 a vorliegen: X 508] *te-qa-de ta-*[...] *ze-ta, / pu-ka-ta-ri-ja ma-ri-ne*[. Der Text attestiert vermutlich die Gabe von Gewändern an den Tempel des Marineu in Theben.[7] Der Göttername Marineu wird durch eine Glosse des Stephanus Byzantios für den Namen des in Gaza angebeteten Marnas als Zeus Kretagenes erklärt.[8] Das Haus der Schilder wurde während der Periode SH IIIB1 (vor 1230 v.u.Z.) zerstört, also innerhalb der Periode, in der ich eine beginnende thebanische Vorherrschaft in Aḫḫijawa vermute. Verteidigungsmaßnahmen in Mykene wie die Ausweitung der Burganlage und der Bau des Löwentors, datiert ca. 1250, können mit

7 *Te-qa-de* wird als */Thēgʷansde/*, also "für Theben" gelesen (Rougemont 2014: 357). *pu-ka-ta-ri-ja* in Linear B wird von Ventris und Chadwick (1956: 321) als eine Form von Gewand gedeutet. *ma-ri-ne[u]/ ma-ri-ne-we, ma-ri-ne-wo,* attestiert in Mykene, Theben und Knossos wird von Hägg (1997: 163-168) aber auch von Palaima (2004: 443) als ein Göttername betrachtet.

8 Stephanos Byzantios (*Ethnica*: i 149), Markos Diakonos (*Vita Porphyrii episcopi Gazaensis*: 19 ff.) und Epiphanios (*Ancoratus* 106) in Cook 1940: 551ff. und Tubach 1986: 284. Der Gott Marnas erscheint bereits sehr früh in Form seines Symbols (der Buchstabe Mem) in der Münzprägung von Gaza (SNGANS 15), 4tes Jahrhundert v.u.Z. Ebenfalls bemerkenswert ist z.B. die Rekurrenz des Minos in der lokalen Münzprägung, z.B. MEINWC auf SNGCop 913 aus der Zeit Hadrians oder auch als MEINΩ (Macalister 1911: 15). Gaza trug in der Spätantiken Zeit übrigens den Beinamen *Minoa*. Die Erklärung des Stephanus scheint daher durchaus in einer lokalen Tradition verwurzelt zu sein und plausibel. Übrigens ist die Bezeichnung der Region bekannt als Kharu in ägyptischen Texten beginnend mit der frühen 18. Dynastie durch die Textfassungen des ptolemäischen Kanopus Dekrets ausreichend erklärt: hieroglyphisch – *Kftjw,* demotisch – *3rw* griechisch – φοινίκη. Das Alexandria Dekret gleicht miteinander: hieroglyphisch – *2Arw,* demotisch – *3rw* (Altenmüller 2010: 36.) Damit ist klar, dass Kharu (nach griechischer geographischer Vorstellung in etwa mit der phönizischen Küste südlich bis etwa Pelusium gleichgesetzt), mit dem hier eher ethnischen Begriff *Kftjw* = Kreta (akkadisch Kaptara, bibl. Kaphtor) zu assoziieren ist. Umgekehrt findet das ägyptische Kharu seine direkte biblische Entsprechung in den ethnischen Bezeichnungen, welche man regelmäßig mit der philistäischen Pentapolis assoziiert: Keret, beziehungsweise Kari/Kre häufig in fester Verbindung mit Plethi (1 Sam. 30:14, Zeph. 2:5, Hes. 25:16, 2 Sam. 8;18, 2 Sam. 15:18, 2 Sam. 20;7, 2 Sam. 20:23, 1 Kö. 1:38, 1. Kö. 1:44, 1 Chr. 18:17) . Hebräisch *kaf* entspricht sowohl den Lauten *k*, wie auch *kh*, hat sich jedoch im modernen hebräisch als *kh* nur innerhalb und nicht auch am Anfang von Wörtern als solches halten können. Die Septuaginta vokalisiert das *kaf* in diesem Namen immer als *kh-*, also z.B. χερεθθι. Es gibt zahlreiche archäologische Spuren von Beziehungen der Region, die Kharu genannt wird, hauptsächlich während des MB IIB-C mit Kreta: Tell Kabri, Awaris, oder u.U. auch die Tel Haror Linear A ex-voto Inschrift etc. Dies fügt sich gut ein in die Reihe der Zeugnisse, für die frühe Aufnahme direkter Beziehungen in der Zeit Zimri-Lims zwischen Kreta und der Levante (u.A. Jahresname in Mari 'als die [KI]Kaptariyu ein Schiff gebaut haben'). Interessanterweise zeigen die ägyptischen Darstellungen tributbringender Kreter, wie sie sich im Laufe der Regierungen Tuthmosis III. und seines Nachfolgers Amenophis II. vielleicht, anstatt eines Darstellungsfehlers des ägyptischen Künstlers anzunehmen, im Zuge der Akkulturation zunehmend den anderen levantinischen Völker ikonographisch anglichen (Lexikon der Ägyptologie I 75, N.37). Wachsmann (1987) nennt diese widersprüchliche Darstellungsweise von Ägäer, manchmal Seite an Seite auftretend im gleichen ägyptischen Grab und aus gleicher Künstlerhand Hybridism. Es stellt sich natürlich die Frage, ob diese Hybridisierung der Typologie des Ägäers/Kreters erst in der Vorstellung des Künstlers stattfand, oder stattdessen ein Teil der zeitgenössischen Realität darstellte. Rehak (1998: 47): 'In her 1993 talk, Davis went as far as to suggest that some of the Keftiu might have belonged to an Aegean enclave or colony actually located in the eastern Mediterranean, a suggestion that was originally made back in the early 1950s by G. Wainwright, and made much more plausible by the current excavations at Tell el-Dab'a.'

der gewachsenen Bedrohungslage, die in der Brandzerstörung der Häuser außerhalb der Mauer resultierte,[9] in der Stadt zusammenhängen.

Kelder (2010: 20, N. 45) weist mit Berufung auf Killen (1979: 179; 1999: 81) auf die identischen Namen und Funktion von Kollektoren in Knossos und Theben hin. Sollte, wie er hinweist, die Überzeugung an Boden gewinnen, dass die Knossos Linear B Archive statt ins späte 15. Jahrhundert um 1200 v.u.Z. datiert werden müssten, würde auch eine zeitliche Überlappung dieser Kollektoren vorliegen, die nur durch deren personelle Identität erklärt werden könne.[10] Geht man von der Identität der Kollektoren, nachgewiesen in Theben und Knossos aus, was noch keineswegs gesichert ist, so darf man nach der Richtung, in welche die Aktivität der Kollektoren die Produktion der Paläste zu diesem Zeitpunkt (kurz vor der Zerstörung von Theben) kanalisiert wurde, fragen.

Die Ausgrabungen in Theben haben Keramik aus verschiedenen Teilen Griechenlands zu Tage gefördert. Es ist leider so gut wie unmöglich darüber eine Aussage zu treffen, wie diese Keramik Theben erreicht hat: als Gegenstand einer Handelstätigkeit oder im Zuge der Redistribution/Umverteilung nach oben. Die Untersuchung von Mommsen, Andrikou, Aravantinos, Maran, (2002) weist als Herkunftsort dieser fremden Keramik auf Mykene Berbati, bzw. auch auf Aegina hin. Anders verhält es sich jedoch im Fall der ebenfalls in der zitierten Untersuchung diskutierten Keramiken aus Chania (Kreta), die zur Kategorie der Linear B beschrifteten mykenischen 'Steigbügel-Gefäße' gehören.

Judson (2013: 83-5) hat in ihrer Untersuchung sämtlicher Linear B beschrifteten mykenischen Steigbügel-Gefäße (Inscribed Stirrup Jars =ISJ), zu denen auch die vorhin erwähnten gehören, darauf hingewiesen, dass die Inschriften auf diesen Keramiken in der Regel den Namen des Kollektors nennen und unter Umständen auch die Namen der Produzenten.[11] Man kann anhand der darauf vorkommenden Namen feststellen, dass mit Ausnahme eines einzigen Exemplars, keine thebanisch ISJ Kollektoren-Namen zeigt, die außerhalb der Theben-Gruppe vorkommen.[12] Das könnte angesichts der archäologischen Fundlage bedeuten, dass keine zeitliche Überschneidung zwischen den Perioden, als jeweils Mykene (und Umland) und Theben mit ISJ versorgt wurden, besteht. Der Zeitabstand zwischen den thebanischen und mykenischen ISJ dürfte ca. eine Generation betragen haben, entsprechend dem vermutlichen Zeitabstand zwischen der Zerstörung Thebens und Mykenes. Die Erklärung von Duhoux (2010: 58), wonach diese Gefäße als *ksenwijon* (Gastgeschenke) gemeint gewesen seien, scheitert an ihrer ungewöhnlichen Ausbreitung auf dem Festland. Es sei denn, man nimmt an (abgesehen

---

9 French (1963: 50) lehnt (auch im ursprünglichen Sinne von Wace) ab eine Zerstörungsursache in Form eines Erdbebens anstelle eines menschlich verursachten Brandes, und bindet die Zerstörung dieser Häuser chronologisch zusammen. Mylonas (1987: 50, N.26) insistiert hingegen auf ein Erdbeben als Ursache. Bis auf Weiteres muss ein Urteil darüber noch abgewartet werden.

10 Killen (1979: 179 und 1999: 81): 'several names [...] appear in more than one archive, suggesting at least the possibility that all these persons were members of a single ruling dynasty'.

11 Judson 2013: 85: 'This strongly implies that the ISJs were, likewise, administrative objects, whose production and use is to be understood within an administrative system monitoring the production/ delivery of goods.'

12 Judson 2013: 103-4. a-re-(ị-)me-ne Gruppe: TH Z 849, 851, 852, 882. ḳụ-jạ-ni Gruppe: TH Z 844, 848, 881, [971]. ku-ru-zo Gruppe: TH Z 840, 841, 8̣4̣3̣, 845, 856, 879, 9̣5̣9̣, 9̣6̣0̣. pi-pi Gruppe: TH Z 846, 854, 878. Die von Mommsen nicht untersuchte Gruppe, die mit ta-(*22-)de-so assoziiert ist, kommt auch auf Chania vor: ta-(*22-)de-so Gruppe: TH Z 869, 870, 871, 872, 876; KH Z 5, 39.

von den irrelevanten statistischen Ausreißern), dass Chania lediglich Theben oder Mykene (Argolis) auf dem Festland 'beschenkte'.

Meiner Meinung nach, muss man, um zu einer Lösung der ISJ zu kommen, die Liste der Fundorte statistisch von einzelnen erratischen Fund Ausreißern bereinigt betrachten.[13] Demnach wurden außer in Chania selbst, woher wohl die meisten offensichtlich stammen, nur in Theben, Mykene und Tiryns und vielleicht Midea diskussionsrelevante Mengen entdeckt. Ich klammere einige ISJ Funde auf Kreta von der Diskussion aus, da sie u.U. bloß die Existenz weiterer Produzenten von ISJ auf Kreta belegen können. Zieht man in Betracht, dass Tiryns wie auch Midea als administratives/ wirtschaftliches Nebenzentrum an der Seite von Mykene fungiert haben dürften, könnte man von einer abnormalen ausschließlichen Konzentration solcher Steigbügel-Gefäße in den zwei vermuteten Zentren von Aḫḫijawa: Theben und Mykene, sprechen. Dies dürfte die Ansicht erschüttern, dass diese Ware in erster Linie zum Zwecke einer Erfassung durch die lokale kretische Verwaltung beschriftet wurde. Wegen der ausschließlichen Verteilung der ISJ auf dem Festland, ist es berechtigt anzunehmen, dass die ISJ kein normaler Handelsgegenstand waren. Da die Streuung der ISJ-Funde auf dem griechischen Festland nicht im Geringsten der Gauß'schen Normalverteilung entspricht – die im Falle ihrer Verbreitung durch Handel oder als Geschenke zu erwarten wäre – sollte man den Faktor Zufall in der Diskussion ausschließen.

Die Verteilung der ISJs ist derart verschieden von derjenigen anderer kretischer SJ Funde, dass man auch einen vollkommen anderen Grund für ihr Vorkommen erwägen muss.[14]

13 Vergleiche damit die vollkommene Abwesenheit von solchen Funden in Pylos, oder die einzige ISJ Scherbe, EL Z1, die man in Eleusis gefunden hat, welche laut Judson mindestens 3-Generationen lang vor ihrer Ablage herumgetragen wurde. Die Scherbe ist SH IIIB, während die Fundlage SH IIIC. Lediglich aus Midea ist eine Zahl von ISJ Scherben berichtet, wenn auch nicht mit dem Rest der Fundstätten vergleichbar, dennoch unter Umständen erwähnenswert. Allerdings liegt, wie auch im Falle von Tiryns eine mythische Assoziation von Midea mit Mykene, vor. Ob diese Überlieferung einen tatsächlichen historischen Hintergrund hat oder nicht, lässt sich nicht prüfen. Unabhängig von der historischen Überlieferung, lässt auch die äußerst geringe Distanz von Midea (11 km) und Tiryns (15 km) zu Mykene anzunehmen, dass diese befestigten Städte alle tatsächlich zum Herrschaftsbereich von Mykene gehörten. Bennets (1990, 2007: 188) Einschätzung des Einzugsgebiets des Palastes von Knossos auf seinem Höhepunkt mit ca. 3.000-4.000 km^2, lässt diese Annahme mehr als plausibel erscheinen. Selbst vor dem Höhepunkt der Expansion von Knossos schätzt Bennet (1990: 195) die mittlere Größe einer palatialen Domäne auf Kreta mit einem Durchschnittswert von 1.050 km^2 ein. Eine auch nur annähernd ähnliche Durchschnittgröße der Domäne von Mykene, zum selben Zeitpunkt als Knossos expandierte, setzt ihre Kontrolle von Midea und Tiryns voraus. Die von Bennet (1998) entworfene Domäne des Königreichs von Pylos, bietet eine ähnliche Größe von ca. 800-1.000 km^2 auf. Wie Bennet (2011: 157) feststellt: 'The density of major sites in the Argolid makes defining plausible, independent territories for them all extremely difficult.' Bennett akzeptiert deswegen die Möglichkeit, dass sich das Gebiet der Argolis auf lediglich zwei Staaten verteilte, allerdings mit der Einschränkung, dass er Tiryns anstatt Mykene Argos zuschlägt. Gemäß der Tradition, auf welche Bennet ebenfalls zurückgreift, soll Tiryns allerdings zwischen der Domäne von Argos und Mykene gewechselt haben.

14 Judson, 2013, 86: 'Most strikingly, no certain ISJ has yet been found outside of Crete and the Greek mainland: this contrasts sharply with the wide distribution of LM III Cretan SJs, which have been found across the central and eastern Mediterranean (including the Dodecanese, the southern coast of Asia Minor, Cyprus, the Levant, Sicily, and Sardinia).'

5. Politische Macht als Widerspiegelung demographischer Entwicklungen

Beide Regionen, die Argolis (Mykene, Tiryns, Midea, Argos, Asine, Nauplion(?)) wie auch Böotien (Gla, Eutresis, Haliartos und andere Stätten um das Bassin des Kopais), sondern sich von dem Rest von Griechenland ab, unter anderen durch die außergewöhnliche Dichte bedeutender befestigter Städte. Man muss jedoch im Falle Thebens selbst anmerken, dass bis jetzt noch kein Nachweis einer solchen monumentalen Fortifikation gelungen ist – sei es denn, weil es nie eine solche gab, oder weil sie von der modernen Stadt überlagert ist.

Ich bin daher überzeugt, dass die Sonderentwicklung in Böotien und der Argolis in erster Linie einen demographischen Hintergrund hatte. Die kritische demographische Dichte, die solche monumentalen Befestigungen erst ermöglichte, dürfte auf dem Festland als erste in der Argolis und Böotien erreicht worden sein. Schon die von der Argolis und Böotien bezeugte Leistungsfähigkeit in Form von Großbauprojekten wie z.B. der Damm und Kanal von Tyrins oder die Drainage des Kopais Beckens oder die enorme Befestigung von Gla, sondert diese Regionen vom Rest mykenischen Griechenlands ab. Demnach sind die Positionen in dem Streit um einen möglichen Regierungssitz von Aḫḫijawa, wegen ihres Absolutheitsanspruchs zu revidieren, gleichgültig ob sie diesen ausschließlich in Theben oder in Mykene identifizieren wollten.[15]

6. Ausländische königliche Geschenke in Theben und Mykene

Man könnte in Zusammenhang mit der These betreffend Theben als Schwerpunkt des mykenischen Reiches während der letzten Hälfte des 13. Jahrhunderts die Erklärung, die Porada (1981/82) für die im so genannten 'Arsenal-Areal' der Kadmea im böotischen Theben 1964 gefundenen Rollsiegelsammlung gegeben hat, in Betracht ziehen. Sie stellte die Frage, ob diese Lapislazuli Sammlung nicht eventuell aus der Plünderung Babylons durch Tukultī-Ninurta I herrühren könnte. Eine neuere Diskussion des Fundes von Theben durch Aruz (1998: 303) scheint der Hypothese von Porada zusätzliche Unterstützung zu geben. Die kassitischen Siegel in Theben sollen demnach von Anfang an ein in sich geschlossenes Corpus gebildet haben. Denn das Gewicht aller kassitischen Zylinder (sowie der unbearbeiteten Lapislazuli-Zylinder gleicher Größe), ausgenommen der mykenischen und zypriotischen Siegel, beträgt insgesamt genau eine *mina*, wie sie dem Gegenstand eines zusammenhängenden königlichen Geschenks während der Bronzezeit im Orient entspräche.

Das jüngste Siegel dieser Sammlung (Kudur-Enlil, 1238-1226[16]) erlaubt für die Ankunft der babylonischen Siegel in Theben kaum die Annahme eines früheren Zeitpunkts als die Eroberung Babylons, 1219. Babylon hat bis zu seiner Eroberung durch Tukultī-Ninurta I. politische Stabilität genossen und die wertvollen Objekte können die Stadt bis zu diesem Zeitpunkt nicht verlassen haben. Diese Erklärung ist naheliegend, zumal auch für ein weiteres königliches babylonisches Lapislazuli Siegel, dasjenige des Šagarakti-Šuriaš, dasselbe Schicksal nach der Eroberung Babylons, die Abschleppung nach Assyrien durch Tukultī-Ninurta I., attestiert ist[17].

15 Eine gute Zusammenfassung und einen vorläufigen Stand der Diskussion bietet Wiener (2009).

16 Chronologie nach Banyai 2015.

17 Faist 2001: 222. RIMA 1, A.0.78.28.

Ein Zeitpunkt während des SH IIIB2, der sich für die endgültige Zerstörung des Palastes in Theben durchzusetzen scheint,[18] ist bestens in Einklang mit dem Szenario von Porada und Aruz, wonach das Geschenk etwa kurz nach der Eroberung Babylons seinen Weg nach Theben gefunden hätte, in Einklang zu bringen. Während es dank dieses Funds evident ist, dass Theben zumindest gegen Ende der SH IIIB Periode so wichtig war u.U. diplomatische Geschenke aus dem fernen Assyrien zu empfangen, zeigt die überwältigende Menge der Aegyptiaca,[19] die ihren Weg nach Mykene gefunden haben, dass Mykene für die längste Zeit der mykenischen Geschichte das von außen her wahrnehmbare Zentrum dieser Kulturregion gewesen sein dürfte.

7. Anhaltspunkte zur Datierung einer möglichen thebanischen Vorherrschaft

Die kurze Episode in der Geschichte von Aḫḫijawa, als Theben das Zentrum dieses Reiches gewesen sein sollte, dürfte zeitlich durch die Zerstörungen, zu beobachten in Orchomenos (der lokale Konkurrent Thebens um die Macht in Boötien), und die vollständige Zerstörung von Gla (dem vorgeschobenen Posten von Orchomenos im Kopais-Becken) gegen Ende des SH IIIB1 eingeläutet worden sein. Damit dürfte sich Theben, nach dem Ausgang des Konflikts zu beurteilen, des wichtigsten regionalen Konkurrenten in Böotien entledigt haben. Wahrscheinlich sind etwa gleichzeitige Zerstörungen in Mykene gegen Ende des SH IIIB1 an den 'houses outside the walls' Zeugen eines Konflikts, welches die damalige Machtzentrale in Aḫḫijawa erreicht habe und zur Verschiebung des Zentrums nach Theben beigetragen haben kann. Die Frage wer und wie und genau wann, kann leider nicht anhand der archäologischen Funde beantwortet werden.

18 Contra, bzw. für ein SH IIIB 1 Datum: Symeonoglou 1985: 60. Kelder 2010 schließt sich der letzteren Auffassung ohne zusätzliche eigene Argumente. Ein Datum am Ende des SH IIIB2 wird vorgeschlagen von Snodgrass 1975: 314. Rutter 2017: 'The bulk of the so-called 'New Palace' in Thebes was probably destroyed by fire late in LH IIIB'. Dakouri-Hild 2001: 106-7: 'A LH III A2-BI fire is attested at the Tzortzi plot workshop. But, following the individual excavators' reports, the evidence from other 'palatial' sites points to either a destruction towards the middle of the thirteenth century BC (end of LH III B1), or its end (end of LH III B2 or transitional LH III B2 – C). The pottery from the Arsenal and the nearby Loukou plot is reportedly of LH III B1 date and the destruction of the latter at least has been provisionally placed at the end of the period. However, the new evidence from Pelopidou Street, which runs right between these plots, raises questions, as it points to a destruction at the very end of LH III B2 or the transitional LH III B2 – C period. The fire at the Soteriou-Dougekou building, as well as phase B in the Lianga-Christodoulou complex on the east extremity of the citadel, almost certainly occurred in the transitional LH IIIB2–C period. The new excavations at Pelopidou may indicate that the dating of the Arsenal and the Loukou workshop should be revised but need not mean that a destruction at the end of LH IIIB1 as attested in other plots is fictitious: the older phase in the Lianga-Christodoulou complex was destroyed at the end of LH III B1. Kordatzi phase B seems to have been abandoned in LH III B1, though no fire or earthquake is attested there. The conflagration at the Koropouli workshop further uphill to the south has also been dated to LH IIIB1. It is difficult to assess the extent to which the dating of certain sites has been influenced by others without going back to the material, but this diversity may suggest that the reconstruction of two architecturally and temporally separate palaces, one of which is the HK, reduces the complexity of the Theban townscape in the Late Helladic period.'

19 So gibt es z.B. laut Cline 1994: 29 in Mykene gefundene ägyptische Objekte, gegenüber nur 1 in Theben. Andererseits sollte man nicht allein nur diese Zahlen in Isolation betrachten, denn im Vergleich zu Mykene weist, z.B. Kreta während des SH IIIA aus weit mehr ägyptische Importe in Vergleich mit dem gesamten griechischen Festland. Das kann erstens an der geographischen Nähe Kretas zu Ägypten gelegen haben und an der höheren Intensität der archäologischen Ausgrabungstätigkeit auf Kreta im Vergleich mit dem Festland.

Das Abdanken Thebens als *das* Herrschaftszentrum im mykenischen Raum erfolgte wohl gegen Ende (aber nicht unbedingt gleich am Ende) der Periode SH IIIB2 (archäologisches Zerstörungsdatum). Damit bliebe aus meiner Sicht durchaus noch Zeit vor dem endgültigen Niedergang der Paläste für einen Machtwechsel in Aḫḫijawa, der danach stattgefunden haben könnte. Die Zerstörung Thebens wird meiner Meinung nach im Šauškamuwa-Vertrag (CTH 105) durch die Streichung von Aḫḫijawa von der Liste der Großmächte reflektiert. Die zurzeit mehrheitliche Sichtweise betrachtet darin allerdings das Signal der Zerstörung der mykenischen Paläste im Allgemeinen während der Periode SH IIIC. Je nach Datum, welches dem Šauškamuwa-Vertrag innerhalb der Regierungsperiode Tudḫalijaš IV. zugewiesen wird, beziehungsweise je nach Datum des Übergangs vom SH IIIB zur IIIC Phase, kann dieser Text jedoch mit dem SH IIIB2 oder SH IIIC synchronisiert werden und vollkommen unterschiedliche Deutungen zulassen. Eine Diskussion des Übergangs vom SH IIIB zu SH IIIC wird deswegen in einem Folgeartikel versprochen.

Bibliographie

Allen, S.H. 1994. 'Trojan Grey Ware at Tel Miqne-Ekron', *Bulletin of the American Schools of Oriental Research* 293 39-51.

Altenmüller, H. 2010. 'Bemerkungen zum Ostfeldzug Ptolemaios' III. nach Babylon und in die Susiana im Jahre 246/245', in J. Fincke (ed.), *Festschrift für Gernot Wilhelm anlässlich seines 65. Geburtstages am 28 .Januar 2010,* Dresden: 27-44.

Aravantinos, V. L., L. Godart und A. Sacconi. 2001. *Les tablettes en linéaire B de la Odos Pelopidou, Édition et Commentaire* (Thèbes Fouilles de la Cadmée 1), Pisa – Rome.

Artzy, M., H. Mommsen und F. Asaro. 2004. 'Neutron Activation Analysis of EA 32', in Y. Goren, I. Finkelstein und N. Na'aman (eds.), *Inscribed in Clay. Provenance Study of the Amarna-Tablets and Other Ancient Near Eastern Texts* (Monograph Series 23), Tel Aviv: 45-47.

Aruz, J. 1998. 'The Aegean and the orient: the evidence of stamp and cylinder seals', in E.H. Cline und D. Harris-Cline (eds.), *The Aegean and the Orient in the Second Millennium. Proceedings of the 50th Anniversary Symposium, Cincinnati, 18-20 April 1997* (Aegaeum 18), Liège – Austin: 301-310.

Bányai, M. 2013. 'Das Interregnum von Tukultī-Ninurta I in Babylonien', *Nouvelles Assyriologiques Brèves et Utilitaires* 2013.4: 140-146.

Bányai, M. 2014. 'Chronologie und Eponymen der späten Zeit Tukultī-Ninurta', *Nouvelles Assyriologiques Brèves et Utilitaires* 2014.2: 79-81.

Bányai, M. 2015. 'Die Chronologie der Zeit von Adad-šuma-uṣur', *Journal Asiatique* 303.1: 9-23.

Bányai, M. 2016. 'Zwei Mittelassyrische Träger des Namens Šulmānu-Mušabši', *Journal Asiatique* 304.1: 1-8.

Badre, L., M.-L. Boileau, R. Jung und H. Mommsen (with an appendix by M. Kerschner). 2005. 'The Provenance of Aegean- and Syrian-Type Pottery found at Tell Kazel (Syria)', Ägypten und Levante 15: 15-47.

Beckman, G.H., T.R. Bryce und E.H. Cline. 2011. *The Ahhiyawa Texts* (Writings from the Ancient World 28), Atlanta.

Bennet, J. 1990. 'Knossos in Context: Comparative Perspectives on the Linear B Administration of LM II-III Crete', *American Journal of Archaeology* 94: 193-211.

Bennet, J. 1998. 'The Linear B archives and the kingdom of Nestor', in J.L. Davis (ed.), *Sandy Pylos: An Archaeological History from Nestor to Navarino*, Princeton, NJ: 111-133.

Bennet, J. 2007. 'The Aegean Bronze Age', in W. Schiedel, I. Morris und R.P. Saller (eds.), *Cambridge Economic History of the Greco-Roman World*, New York: 175-210.

Bennet, J. 2011. 'The Geography of the Mycenaean Kingdoms' in Y. Duhoux und A. Morpurgo Davies (eds), *A Companion to Linear B Mycenaean Greek Texts and their World, Band 2*, Louvain-la-Neuve: 137-168.

Bridges jr., R. A. 1974. 'The Mycenaean Tholos Tomb at Kolophon', *Hesperia* 43: 264-266.

Carruba, O. 1996. 'Neues zur Frühgeschichte Lykiens', in F. Blakolmer, K. R. Krierer und F. Krinzinger (eds.), *Fremde Zeiten. Festschrift für Jürgen Borchardt*, Wien: 25-39.

Cline, E.H. 1991. 'A Possible Hittite Embargo against the Mycenaeans', *Historia* 40.1: 1-9.

Cline, E.H. 1994. *Sailing the Wine-Dark Sea: International Trade and the Late Bronze Age Aegean*, Oxford.

Cline, E.H. 2008. 'Troy as a 'Contested Periphery': Archaeological Perspectives on Cross-Cultural and Cross-Disciplinary Interactions Concerning Bronze Age Anatolia', in B.J. Collins, M.R. Bachvarova, und I.C. Rutherford (eds.), *Anatolian Interfaces: Hittites, Greeks and their Neighbours*, Oxford.

Cook, A.B. 1940. *Zeus: a Study in Ancient Religion, Vol. III*, Cambridge.

Crouwel, J.H. 1991. 'Mycenaean Pictorial Pottery from Cyprus in Oxford', *Oxford Journal of Archaeology* 10: 45-55.

Dakouri-Hild, A. 2001. 'The House of Kadmos in Mycenaean Thebes Reconsidered. Architecture, Chronology, and Context', *British School at Athens Annual* 96: 81-122.

Dickinson, O. 2004. *The Aegean Bronze Age*, Cambridge.

Duhoux, Y. 2010. 'La fonction des vases à étrier inscrits en linéaire B', *Kadmos* 49: 47-92.

French, E. 1963 . 'Pottery Groups from Mycenae: A Summary', *British School at Athens Annual* 58: 44-52.

French, E. 2004. '*The Contribution of Chemical Analysis to Provenance Studies*', in J. Balensi, J.-Y. Monchambert und S. Müller Celka (eds.), *La Céramique mycénienne de l'Égée au Levant. Hommage à Vronwy Hankey. Table ronde internationale, Maison de l'Orient et de la Méditerranée, 20 mars 1999* (Travaux de la Maison de l'Orient et de la Méditerranée 41), Lyon : 15-17.

French, E. und J. Tomlinson. 2004. '*Investigating the Provenance of Some Aegean-Type Potsherds Found in The Near East: Results from Neutron Activation Analysis*', in J. Balensi, J.-Y. Monchambert und S. Müller Celka (eds.), *La Céramique mycénienne de l'Égée au Levant. Hommage à Vronwy Hankey. Table ronde internationale, Maison de l'Orient et de la Méditerranée, 20 mars 1999* (Travaux de la Maison de l'Orient et de la Méditerranée 41), Lyon: 18-25.

Furtwängler, A und G. Loeschke. 1886. *Mykenische Vasen*, Berlin.

Gilmour, G. 1995. 'Aegean Influence in Late Bronze Age Funerary Practices in the Southern Levant' in S. Campbell und A. Green (eds.), *The Archaeology of Death in the Ancient Near East*, Oxford: 155-170.

Goren, Y., H. Mommsen und J. Klinger. 2011. 'Non-destructive provenance study of cuneiform tablets using portable X-ray fluorescence (pXRF)', *Journal of Archaeological Science* 38: 684-696.

Hajnal, I. 2004. *'Uiluša – Taruiša'*, in Chr. Ulf (ed.), *Der neue Streit um Troia: Eine Bilanz*, Munich: 169-172.
Heinhold-Krahmer, S. 2002. 'Ist die Identität von Ilios mit Wiluša endgültig erwiesen?', *Studi micenei ed egeo-anatolici* 46.1: 29-57.
Heinhold-Krahmer, S. 2013. 'Zur Lage des hethitischen Vasallenstaat Wiluša im südwesten Kleiasiens', in M. Mazoyer und S.H. Aufrére (eds.), *De Hattuša à Memphis. J. Freu in honorem*, Paris: 59-74.
Hoffmann, S.M.A. und V.J. Robinson. 1993, 'Neutron Activation Groupings of Imported Material from Tell Abu Hawam', in C. Zerner, P. Zerner und J. Winder (eds.), *Proceedings of the International Conference: 'Wace and Blegen–Pottery as Evidence for Trade in the Aegean Bronze Age, 1939-1989,* Amsterdam: 7-10.
Hrozný, B. 1929. 'Hethiter und Griechen', *Archiv Orientalni* 1: 323-343.
Jablonka, P. 2008 [2011]. Rezension von: F. Kolb, *Tatort 'Troia'* (Paderborn et al. 2010), *Jahresschrift für mitteldeutsche Vorgeschichte* 92: 527-555.
Jones, R.E. und Chr. Mee. 1978. 'Spectrographic Analyses of Mycenaean Pottery from Ialysos on Rhodes: Results and Implications', *Journal of Field Archaeology* 5.4: 461-470.
Jones, R.E. und L. Vagnetti. 1991. 'Traders and craftsmen in the central Mediterranean: archaeological evidence and archaeometric research', in N. Gale, (eds.), *Bronze Age trade in the Mediterranean* (Studies in Mediterranean Archaeology 90), Göteborg: 127-147.
Judson, A.P. 2013. 'The Linear B Inscribed Stirrup Jars', *Kadmos* 52.1: 69-110.
Karantzali, E. und M.J. Ponting. 2000. 'ICP-AES analysis of Some Mycenaean Vases from the Cemetery of Pylona, Rhodes', *Bulletin de Correspondence Hellénique* 95: 219-238.
Kelder, J. 2006. 'Mycenaeans in Western Anatolia', *Talanta* 36/37: 49-88.
Kelder, J. 2010. *The Kingdom of Mycenae,* Bethesda.
Kelder, J. 2012. 'Ahhiyawa and the World of the Great Kings. A Re-evaluation of Mycenaean Political Structures', in A. Papadopoulos (ed.), *Recent Research and Perspectives in the Late Bronze Age Eastern Mediterranean* (= *Talanta* 44): 41-52.
Killen, J.T. 1979. 'The Cnossos Ld (1) Tablets' in E. Risch und H. Mühlstein (eds.), *International Colloquium on Mycenaean Studies,* Neuchâtel: 151-181.
Killen, J.T. 1999. 'Critique: A View from the Tablets' in M.L. Galaty und W.A. Parkinson (eds.), *Rethinking Mycenaean Palaces,* Los Angeles: 87-90.
Kolb, F. 2010. *Tatort 'Troia',* Paderborn -München – Wien – Zürich.
Macalister, R.A.S. 1911. *The Philistines: Their History and Civilization,* London.
Mee, Chr. 1978. 'Aegean Trade and Settlement in Anatolia in the Second Millennium B.C.', *Anatolian Studies* 28: 121-126.
Mee, Chr. 1988. 'Anatolia and the Aegean in the Late Bronze Age', in E.H. Cline und D. Harris-Cline (eds.), *The Aegean and the Orient in the Second Millennium. Proceedings of the 50th Anniversary Symposium, Cincinnati, 18-20 April 1997* (Aegaeum 18), Liège – Austin: 137-148.
Merrilees, R.S. 1973. 'Egypt and the Aegean', *Aegeum* 14: 149-155.
Mommsen, H., E. Andrikou, V. Aravantinos und J. Maran. 2002. 'Neutron Activation Analysis Results of Bronze Age Pottery from Boeotia Including Ten Linear B Inscribed Stirrup Jars of Thebes' in E. Jerem und K. Biró (eds.), *Proceedings of the 31st Intemational Symposium on Archaeometry, Vol. II,* Oxford: 607-612.

Mommsen, H., T. Beier, U. Diehl und C. Podzuweit. 1992. 'Provenance determination of Mycenaean sherds found in Tell el Amarna by Neutron Activation Analysis', *Journal of Archaeological Science* 19.3: 295-302.

Mommsen, H., U. Diehl, D. Lambrecht, F.H. Pantenburg und J. Weber. 1990. 'Eine mykenische Scherbe in Spanien – Bestätigung ihrer Herkunft mit der Neutronenaktivierungsanalyse (NAA)', *Praehistorische Zeitschrift* 65.1: 59-61.

Mommsen, H., D. Hertel und P. A. Mountjoy. 2001. 'Neutron activation analysis of the pottery from Troy in the Berlin Schliemann collection', *Archäologischer Anzeiger* 2: 169-211.

Mommsen, H. und J. Maran. 2001-2002. 'Production Places of Some Mycenaean Pictorial Vessels. The Contribution of Chemical Pottery Analysis', *Opuscula Atheniensia* 25/26: 95-106.

Mommsen, H. und P. Pavúk 2007. 'Provenance of the Grey and Tan Wares from Troia, Cyprus and the Levant', *Studia Troica* 17: 25-41.

Mountjoy, P.A. 1998. 'The East Aegean-West Anatolian Interface in the Late Bronze Age: Mycenaeans and the Kingdom of Ahhiyawa', *Anatolian Studies* 48: 33-68.

Mountjoy, P.A. 2000. 'The Destruction of Troia VIh', *Studia Troica* 9: 253-295.

Mühlenbruch, T. und H. Mommsen. 2011. 'Neutronenaktivierungsanalysen an mykenischer Keramik aus Kuşakli-Sarissa und Sirkeli (Türkei), Kāmid El-Lōz-Kumidi (Libanon) und dem Fayum (Ägypten)', *Ägypten und Levante* 21: 281-290.

Mylonas Shear, I. 1987. *The Panagia Houses at Mycenae*, Philadelphia.

Nicolaou K. 1973. 'The First Mycenaeans in Cyprus' in V. Karageorghis (ed.), *Acts of the International Archaeological Symposium, The Myceneans in the Eastern Mediterranean*, Nicosia: 51-61.

Niemeier, W.-D. 2005. 'The Minoans and Mycenaeans in Western Asia Minor: Settlement, Emporia or Acculturation?' in R. Laffineur und E. Greco (eds.), *Emporia: Aegeans in the Central and Eastern Mediterranean* (Aegaeum 25), Liège – Austin: 199-204.

Niemeier, W.-D. 2008. 'Hattusas Beziehungen zum westlichen Kleinasien und dem mykenischen Griechenland nach den neuesten Forschungen', in G. Wilhelm (ed.), *Ḫattuša-Boğazköy- Das Hethiterreich im Spannungsfeld des Alten Orients* (Colloquien der Deutschen Orient-Gesellschaft 6), Wiesbaden: 291-349.

Olsen, B. 2014. *Women in Mycenaean Greece: The Linear B Tablets from Pylos and Knossos*, New York.

Otten, H. 1963. 'Neue Quellen zum Ausklang des Hethitischen Reiches', *Mitteilungen der Deutschen Orient-Gesellschaft zu Berlin* 94: 1-23.

Page, D. 1959. *History and the Homeric Iliad*, Berkeley.

Palaima, T. 2004. 'Linear B Sources', in S.M. Trzaskoma, R.S. Smith und S. Brunet (eds.), *Anthology of Classical Myth*, Indianapolis – Cambridge: 439-454.

Palaima, T. 2007. 'Ilios, Tros and Tlos. Continuing Problems with to-ro, to-ro-o, to-ro-wo, to-ro-ja, wi-ro and a-si-wi-ja/a-si-wi-jo', in F. Lang, C. Reinholdt und J. Weilhartner (eds.), ΣΤΕΦΑΝΟΣ ΑΡΙΣΤΕΙΟΣ, *Archäologische Forschungen zwischen Nil und Istros*, Wien: 197-204.

Palaima, T. 2011. 'Euboea, Athens, Thebes and Kadmos: The Implications of the Linear B References', in D. Rupp und J. E. Thomlinson (eds.), *Euboea and Athens – Proceedings of a Colloquium in Memory of Malcolm B. Wallace*, Athens: 53-75.

Porada E. 1981-1982. 'The Cylinder Seals Found at Thebes in Boeotia', *Archiv für Orientforschung* 28: 1-78.

Popko, M. 1984. 'Zur Datierung des Tawagalawa-Briefes', *Altorientalische Forschungen* 11, Berlin: 199-203.

Raymond, A., I. Kaiser, L.-C. Rizzotto und J. Zurbach. 2016. 'Discerning Acculturation at Miletus: Minoanisation and Mycenaeanisation', in E. Gorogianni, P. Pavúk und L. Girella (eds.), *Beyond Thalassocracies – Understanding Processes of Minoanisation and Mycenaeanisation in the Aegean*, Oxford: 58-75.

Rehak, P. 1998. 'Aegean Natives in the Theban Tomb Paintings: The Keftiu Revisited', in E.H. Cline und D. Harris-Cline (eds.), *The Aegean and the Orient in the Second Millennium* (Aegaeum 18), Liège – Austin: 39-50.

Rougemont, F. 2014. 'Sheep Rearing, Wool Production and Management in Mycenaean Written Documents', in C. Breniquet und C. Michel (eds.). *Wool Economy in the Ancient Near East and the Aegean*, Oxford: 340-371.

Rutter, J.B. 2017. http://www.dartmouth.edu/~prehistory/aegean/?page_id=615.

Singer, I. 1999. *A Political History of Ugarit* (Handbuch der Orientalistik 39), Leiden – Boston – Köln.

Singer, I. 2006. 'Ships Bound for Lukka. A New Interpretation of the Companion Letters RS 94.2530 and RS 94.2523', *Altorientalische Forschungen* 33: 242-262.

Snodgrass, A. 1975. Rezension von: S. Symenoglou, *Kadmeia I. Mycenaean finds from Thebes, Greece. Excavation 14 Oedipus str* (Göteborg 1973), *Gnomon* 47: 313-316.

Symenoglou, S. 1973. '*Kadmeia I: Mycenaean Finds from Thebes, Greece*' (Studies in Mediterranean Archaeology 35), Göteborg.

Tomlinson, J.E. 2004. 'Statistical Evaluation of Neutron Activation Data on Mycenaean Pottery found at Lachish', in D. Ussishkin (ed.), *The Renewed Archaeological Excavations at Lachish 1973-1994*, Tel Aviv: 1437-1445.

Tubach, J. 1986. *Im Schatten des Sonnengottes*, Wiesbaden.

Van Wijngaarden, G.J. 2002. *Use and Appreciation of Mycenaean Pottery in the Levant, Cyprus and Italy (1600-1200 BC)*, Amsterdam.

Ventris, M. und J. Chadwick. 1956. *Documents in Mycenaean Greek*, Cambridge.

Yasur-Landau, A. 2003. 'The Absolute Chronology of the Late Helladic III C Period', in S. Deger-Jalkotzy (ed.), *LH III C chronology and synchronisms*, Wien: 235-244.

Yellin, J. und A. Maeir. 1992. 'The origin of the pictorial krater from the 'Mycenaean' tomb at Tel Dan', *Archaeometry* 34: 31-36.

Wachsmann, Sh. 1987. *Aegeans in Egyptian Tombs*, Leuven.

Wiener, M. 2009. 'Locating Ahhiyawa', in S. Iakōvidēs und D. Danielidou (eds.), 'ΔΩΡΟΝ: Τιμητικοσ Τομοσ για τον Καθηγητη Σπυρο Ιακωβιδη', Athens: 701-715.

Zuckerman, S., D. Ben-Shlomo, P.A. Mountjoy und H. Mommsen. 2010. 'A provenance study of Mycenaean pottery from Northern Israel', *Journal of Archaeological Science* 37: 409-416.

Epilogue: Kings and Great Kings in the Aegean and beyond

Jorrit Kelder and Willemijn Waal

1. Introduction

This volume set out to address the role of the ruler in Mycenaean Greece by contextualising it with contemporary Near Eastern forms of kingship. In view of its proximity to the Aegean, and the textual indications for close connections with Mycenaean (Aḫḫiyawan) nobility, the Hittite world provides a natural point of reference, as has been demonstrated by Waal (this volume). But other regions in the Near East, especially Cyprus, are of interest, too, when it comes to assessing forms of kingship in Late Bronze Age Greece – if only because academic debate regarding the political state of Cyprus at that time (whether it was politically fragmented or, in fact, unified under a single king), so closely mimics current debate on the Mycenaean world. As may be clear from the contributions in this volume, we are probably no closer to reaching a consensus on the question as to how we tally the Hittite references to an Aḫḫiyawan 'Great King' to the *wanax* known from Linear B texts, and there remain fundamental differences in interpreting the relevant archaeological record (see now also Kelder 2018). Nevertheless, it seems that, on a number of major points, there is more agreement between proponents of different academic 'schools' than has hitherto been realised, while various bones of contention appear to be more a matter of semantics than of real disagreement. This concluding chapter aims to review the main arguments of the papers in this volume and will highlight points of disagreement and common ground between the various authors, whilst advancing some ideas of our own.

2. Archaeological evidence

2.1. Cultural uniformity

One of the editors of this volume (Kelder 2005, 2010, 2012; also Eder 2007) pointed out that the striking uniformity of Mycenaean material culture throughout the Aegean, generally referred to as the 'Mycenaean *koine*', is most easily explained as the result of a certain degree of political unification. This argument has not gone unchallenged,

in: Kelder, J.M. and Waal, W.J.I. (eds) 2019: *From 'LUGAL.GAL' to 'Wanax'. Kingship and Political Organisation in the Late Bronze Age Aegean*, Sidestone Press (Leiden), pp. 149-162.

with some arguing (quite rightly) that cultural uniformity does not necessarily equate to political unification. Against this, one could however counter that (as Eder and Jung 2015: 113 pointed out) homogeneity is by no means self-evident and it did not exist in the preceding and succeeding periods.

As our knowledge of 'Mycenaean material culture' increases, even the concept of a Mycenaean *koine* itself is now questioned. Thus, Dickinson (this volume) notes that the apparent cultural uniformity was not absolute and that regional differences in material culture existed throughout the palace era. In addition, he points out that Mycenaean culture did not emerge overnight, but rather was the result of a long and complex process of acculturation, experimentation and borrowing. These observations, valid though they are, do not change the overall picture of a remarkable degree of cultural homogeneity (cf. Kelder 2012; Petrakis 2009: 18). In our view, it is difficult to see how local differences should necessarily be an argument against political unity. Indeed, as Kelder (2010, 2012) has argued, it could well be viewed as supporting exactly the opposite view, for one would expect precisely the 'intrusive' cultural elements -the 'imperial veneer' – to affect only those parts of day-to-day life that were directly related (subordinate) to the central administration. This, of course, could (and almost certainly did) vary through time and space, and one should expect regional differences in the pervasiveness of such an 'imperial' culture.

Dickinson argues that there is no necessary link between cultural uniformity and political unity. It is certainly true that many ancient empires did not result in cultural homogeneity, as the lack of Egyptianisation of Syria and Palestine when they were under Egyptian control, as well as the absence of Hittite culture outside the Anatolian heartland eloquently show. Dickinson concludes that a Mycenaean Empire would not have automatically resulted in cultural homogeneity and therefore the argument backwards from supposed cultural uniformity to political union is illegitimate. These are mostly valid reflections – although Egyptian overlordship in the Levant is, in our view, quite notable in the archaeological record, too – but it may be more interesting to reverse the question: do we have examples of cultural uniformity without political unity? An ancient Near Eastern example that comes to mind are the Sumerian city states of the 3rd millennium BCE, which show clear cultural, religious and artistic links. Unfortunately, our information about their political organisation is limited. The city states were each led by a king, but there seems to have been one ruler, bearing the title 'King of Kiš', who had hegemony over the other political centres (Kuhrt 1995: 41-2). Though the precise nature of this control is uncertain, some form of overarching authority did exist.

The fact that the cultural uniformity is not absolute is hardly surprising. As we noted above, any supra-regional power would not have pervaded society deeply, affecting only those parts of society that were of direct interest to the central administration. In reality, it may only have been a thin veneer of imperial control, as, e.g., in the Hittite empire (see also below). For a large part, older traditions would have continued to exist. The case of the clay figurines may serve as a good case in point. They have been found throughout the Aegean, though more in some locations than others. This uneven distribution leads Dickinson to suggest that this might reflect differences in belief, which is quite possible. This does, however, not contradict the notion of political union. Local traditions were not completely abandoned and people retained many of their traditional beliefs and customs, which could co-exist with a newly introduced state religion. The omnipresence of the

Mycenaean figurines, even if at times less prominent in remote areas, can thus also be interpreted as evidence of superregional dominance in the religious sphere, however superficial this may have been.

2.2. Predominance of Argive pottery

Apart from the cultural homogeneity, the predominance of pottery from the Argolid is of interest. Bányai draws attention to the fact that Mycenaean pottery during the LH IIIA period on the east Mediterranean coast stems almost exclusively from Mycenae and surrounding areas. In the LH IIIB period this picture changes: now, the exported pottery mainly stems from Thebes (see also below). As he observes, this monopoly does not concur with the idea that all palaces had an equal share in export, but rather implies a centrally organised economy (compare also Dickinson who points out that the predominance of pottery of Argive origin could be seen as a sign that Mycenae was extending its influence and control to make itself the centre of Aḫḫiyawa).

Bányai further points to the concentration of inscribed stirrup jars in Mycenae and Thebes. This skewed distribution excludes the possibility of gift exchange, as this would not explain why Thebes and Mycenae were the only recipients. Note in this respect that for Eder and Jung (2015), the stirrup jars are also evidence for the existence of a unified Mycenaean kingdom, as they are representative of a closed interregional system, and not of a free market in which the different city-states competed.

2.3. Architecture

Despite some differences, there is ample evidence to suggest that the Mycenaean palaces followed a common 'master plan', with a prototype stemming from the Greek mainland (as argued by Blakolmer, this volume). There is no agreement as to how the adoption of this masterplan should be interpreted, and whilst Kelder and others have suggested that this may reflect changing political allegiances, it may perhaps also be interpreted in terms of peer polity interaction and the adoption, across political boundaries, of a way to show royal power. The same might perhaps apply to other architectural features, such as the remarkable similarity between a number of royal tholos-tombs. Dickinson in his paper rightly points out that the first tholoi on the Greek mainland, as far as we know, appeared in Messenia, and that tholoi only emerged in the Argolid during LH IIA. It thus seems highly likely that building royal tombs in this way was not, originally, a properly Mycenaean way of dealing with the dead. Then again, Mycenaean 'palace culture' – that is, the culture of the 14th and first half of the 13th century BCE – was always something of a hybrid, with major cultural influences from Minoan Crete and elsewhere (including, perhaps, Messenia) reworked and reshaped in a manner that, apparently, worked for the elites in the Argolid – from whence it spread (or, if one argues for a greater Mycenaean state, was exported) to other parts of Greece. Here we should highlight the similarities between the magnificent tholos at Orchomenos in Boeotia and the famous 'Treasury of Atreus' at Mycenae: virtually all specialists (cf. Dickinson this volume; Kelder 2010; Wood 1998: 71) agree that these splendid monuments are likely to have been planned and built by the same team, but explanations for the apparent mobility and ability of such a building team to operate in different regions of Greece are markedly different. Dickinson notes that it 'is hard to understand, if, as the advocates of a single major Mycenaean state might want to contend, Orchomenos was subordinate to Mycenae: why should it alone have such magnificent tombs, when other supposedly subordinate but major centres like Pylos and Thebes did not? But it might make sense if Mycenae and Orchomenos were separate powers, allied in their opposition to Thebes'. Here, however, one might point to the well-known practice in the contemporary Near East of establishing junior branches of the 'imperial family' at important centres in the provinces, from whence these kings could govern the region on behalf of the central 'Great King'. It is entirely plausible that Orchomenos, which likely controlled – as Dickinson himself notes – the vast agricultural expanse of the Kopais basin, was perceived as such an important asset that it warranted more or less 'direct' control by the central administration. And with that, it would have been fitted with the trappings of that central power, including a magnificent tomb for its scions of the Royal family. Possibly, close personal ties may also have played a part – but this must remain conjecture. It is impossible to know why the rulers of other centres, such as nearby Thebes and Pylos in Messenia, were not interred in similarly magnificent tombs – though it seems quite possible that Thebes, which seems 'different' from other Mycenaean centres in a number of ways and certainly appears to have been the major power in Boeotia, may have been a rather unstable and unreliable vassal (see also below), and indeed may occasionally have slipped away from Mycenaean control (all the more reason to have the Kopais basin controlled by a reliable ruler!). More importantly, *if* Thebes and Pylos and other Mycenaean palaces had been politically independent, would one not have expected similarly magnificent tombs at, at least, some of these centres, too? All of this, of course, remains impossible to prove or disprove and, as Kelder (2018) has noted, it is essentially a question of weighing probabilities, and thus inherently subjective. What may be pointed out, however, is that if Orchomenos and Mycenae were united in opposition against Thebes, the size and monumentality of Mycenae (as well as a number of other features) seem to suggest that Mycenae would have been the senior partner in this alliance. The step to a more formal relation, with Mycenae as overlord, would have been easily made, as indeed Dickinson himself seems to admit when suggesting that Mycenae may have had 'a circle of allies, some perhaps more like vassals but still technically independent' (see also below §6).

2.4. The supposed capital of Aḫḫiyawa: Mycenae or Thebes?

Whilst there is no consensus amongst the various contributors to this volume as to whether or not Mycenaean Greece was at some point politically unified, it is now generally accepted that there were, at least during the palatial era, two centres on the Greek mainland that stood out in terms of size, monumentality, and presumably political, economic and military might: Thebes in Boeotia and Mycenae in the Argolid. Dickinson has pointed out that the number of tholoi at Mycenae, its impressive fortifications, and a string of other features, indicate its pre-eminence amongst the Mycenaean palaces. Kelder (2010) also points to Mycenae's unique status in that it has a clearly designated 'sanctuary' within its citadel walls, although it remains unclear whom was the object of veneration at that place[1] and appears to have been the hub in an extensive network of roads. The real extent of this network requires further study, and whilst Dickinson certainly has a point

1 In view of the proximity to Grave Circle A and the Lion Gate with its monumental 'dynastic crest' – if one is correct in interpreting the two lionesses and the central column as such – it seems plausible to assume an ancestor cult.

in questioning the validity of Kelder's statement that a network of roads connected the various regions of Mycenaean Greece (for which the evidence is, admittedly, sparse), the point remains that the region around later-day Corinth is nowadays considered to have been the hinterland of Mycenae primarily because of a (reconstructed) road connecting that palace to it.[2] Regardless of such details, the sheer quality and the great effort that was invested in the construction of the Mycenaean roads and bridges are such that they can only be reasonably be compared to the roadworks of later, Roman-era Greece; again a time when Greece was politically unified – albeit under the aegis of a foreign power.

As has been noted above, there is a general consensus that power-relations in Mycenaean Greece, whether they were in the context of a Great Kingdom including various vassal states or within a framework of numerous more or less equal, independent polities, must have shifted over the course of time. The relation between Mycenae and Thebes, especially, must have been volatile, as both are likely to have controlled large territories and both seem to have engaged in foreign trade (and perhaps diplomatic exchange). Based on, e.g., the distribution of pottery and the presence of *orientalia* at the two centres (including the remarkable lapis lazuli Babylonian cylinder seals at Thebes) Bányai suggests that whilst Mycenae may have initially acted as some sort of a hegemon over (most of) Greece, its position may have been challenged and even taken over by Thebes at some point in the 13th century BCE. Whilst this is not inconceivable, there seems to be ample evidence for the continued prominence of Mycenae during LH IIIB – indeed, the Lion Gate was constructed during this period, apparently by means of Anatolian (type) tools and perhaps people (cf. Blackwell 2014). In addition, it must be significant that only in the Argolid, though notably not at Mycenae itself, but at its principle harbour, Tiryns, there appears to have been an attempt to resurrect some sort of palace-life following the destructions at the end of LH IIIB2/early LH IIIC. The observations of Bányai might thus be better explained by assuming that Thebes was temporarily (semi)independent from Mycenae, perhaps as a break-away vassal kingdom intent on taking over hegemony over Central Greece (see also below §6).

3. Iconographic evidence

The contribution of Blakolmer shows that the iconography in the Bronze Age Aegean differed from that of rulers in Mesopotamia and Egypt. Power was symbolised in a very general abstract and anonymous manner, making use of a limited spectrum of 'cultural rhetorics'. As a rule, the ruler is not depicted as an individual. This non-personal collective image of power can be traced back to Minoan Crete, and Blakolmer argues no adjustments were made to conform to the Mycenaean *wanax*-ideology. The apparently 'missing ruler' in Mycenaean Crete may, Blakolmer argues, thus partly be explained by the lack of models in Minoan imagery. In addition, the *wanax* kingship probably contained a strong theocratic component, which could be a further reason for the iconographic indistinctiveness. The representation of the *wanax* may not have been allowed or deemed unnecessary.

With respect to Mycenae, though it may have taken on a leading role in the formation and development of an 'iconography of power' during the LBA, there are no unique pictorial subjects which could point to an exceptional position of its rulers. All in all, the

2 Note that the absence of a really major centre in the Korinthia further strengthens the notion of Mycenae's lordship over the region.

lack of more explicit ruler ideology cannot be used as a conclusive argument for or against a political union. The fact that it differs from other contemporary iconographic traditions is neither troubling nor unique; the ruler iconography of the Hittite Empire is also quite distinct from that of Mesopotamia and Egypt.

4. Textual evidence

4.1. The Linear B tablets

As has often been pointed out (e.g. Postgate 2001; Palaima 2003: 159-62; Shelmerdine and Bennet 2008: 292), the Linear B tablets are strikingly uniform with respect to their script, language, scribal conventions and diplomatic features (shape, size, layout etc.), as well as their content. This is not to say, there was absolutely no room for variation. The texts are after all, produced by people, not by robots, and minor variations and local differences are only to be expected. The overall uniformity in script and language makes it likely that the scribes were trained in a particular tradition, as Dickinson notes. This observation has important consequences. Not only does it imply a very rigid training, it also suggests that we are dealing with centrally organised scribal schools. This is difficult to reconcile with the idea of various independent palatial states. What is more, uniformity of script and language may in fact be seen as an important indication of a centrally organised state (Postgate 2001). The fact that such scribal homogeny is by no means self-evident is eloquently demonstrated by the Greek Archaic period; here, there was no standardisation of the script, but within the different city-states numerous different alphabetic traditions developed – no less than 33 altogether.[3]

Not only the Linear B texts, but virtually all other aspects of administration are remarkably similar throughout the Aegean. They include the weighing and measuring system, taxation procedures and administrative practices, such as the use of seals and sealings (on which, cf. Eder 2009; Eder and Jung 2015; Bányai this volume). Following Eder and Jung, we feel that these common features imply some form of supra-regional control. Content-wise, the Linear B tablets offer little information about the political structures of Greece. Considering their strictly economic nature and limited regional scope, this is not to be expected. The texts make mention of a *wanax* and *lawagetas*, and although these titles have often been interpreted in the context of local, palace-specific officials, Kelder (2008; now followed, albeit without references, by Eder and Jung 2015) has argued that the *wanax* can be more plausibly be considered as a single, peripatetic Great King, whilst the *lawagetas* may have been a title for subordinate local (palace-specific) kings. In a similar vein, the presence of 'collectors' – a designation that is used to refer to a group of individuals that appear to have been active in several economic activities in the various Linear B archives – may lend further strength to such a scenario (Bányai this volume; Eder and Jung 2015; Kelder and Poelwijk 2016), although the argument that recurring names in various palace administrations may reflect supra-regional activity of the same persons has not ubiquitously been accepted. Regardless of all this, and whilst one could perhaps state that there is no unequivocal proof in the Linear B texts for a united Mycenaean state, it should be stressed that there is *no* evidence whatsoever in these same texts that

3 For these different Greek epichoric scripts, see Jeffery and Johnston 1990.

argues against such a notion -there are no indications that suggest that the palaces were independent polities.

4.2. The Hittite texts

The above observations are all the more relevant, because there is in fact unequivocal evidence for the notion of a Mycenaean 'Great King'. This evidence stems from a number of Hittite texts; two of which specifically refer to a 'Great King' of Aḫḫiyawa, who is the 'brother' (=equal) of the king of Ḫatti. At one point, Aḫḫiyawa is listed among the Great Powers of that time in a treaty text. The status of the king of Aḫḫiyawa as Great King is confirmed by the fact that Hittite dealings with the king of Aḫḫiyawa are the same as those with other Great Kings in other respects, such as the manner of communication, gift exchange and extradition of fugitives (Waal this volume). The suggestion that the Hittite king calling the king of Aḫḫiyawa a 'Great King' was merely a case of *ad hoc* diplomacy is unfounded, and seems to have been informed primarily by the insistence of Aegeanists that the Mycenaean world was politically fragmented. There is no indication whatsoever in the Hittite texts that suggests that the Hittites – who clearly stood in close contact with the Mycenaean world – perceived the Mycenaean world as a patchwork of states. Quite the contrary: the Hittite texts clearly indicate that Aḫḫiyawa was a considerable political and military force, which was able to protect (and further) its interests in western Anatolia over the course of some two centuries with considerable success. To this, one may add the Hittites may not have been alone in regarding Mycenaean Greece as a single political entity, as the Egyptian designation for Mycenaean Greece, Tanaya/Tanaju, also seems to suggest a single coherent polity (though Crete, referred to as Keftiu, is perceived as a separate entity – possibly reflecting its erstwhile independence).

5. The Case of Cyprus

The academic debate on the political composition of Mycenaean Greece may be fruitfully compared to a similar ongoing debate on the status of Cyprus – known as Alašiya in contemporary cuneiform texts. For here, too, scholars disagree as to whether the island was, during the 14th and 13th centuries BCE, politically unified or whether it was instead a patchwork of independent city-states (as in later times). As in the case of the Mycenaean world, textual information is limited. Documents from Ugarit, Ḫatti and Egypt mention a king of Alašiya as well as a high official, usually translated as a commissioner or governor, who seems to have been entitled to act on behalf of the king. On Cyprus, there were several locations at which copper was produced, yet only Alašiya is mentioned in the texts, and requests for copper or royal grievances (including accusations of piracy) are directed to a single king of Alašiya. On the basis of these texts and a number of other (archaeological) arguments, scholars such as Knapp have suggested that Cyprus was at least seen as one single polity, ruled by as single king.

Other scholars, including Mantzourani, Kopanias and Voskos (this volume), however, argue instead for a decentralised model with competing local elites controlling specific territories. In this scenario, the king of Alašiya who is mentioned in the Hittite, Egyptian and Ugarit texts is to be understood as 'no more than a product of the need of Near Eastern powers to make Cypriot political structures conform, at least on paper, to their own norms of diplomatic perception and convention' (Peltenburg 2012). Mantzourani, Kopanias and Voskos suggest that the king of Alašiya was a *primus inter pares*, who was responsible for the international relations of the islands. This function was created as a local response to the international norms, but did not necessarily reflect the actual socio-political reality on Cyprus. Though this scenario can theoretically not be excluded, one does wonder how likely and necessary the creation of such an artificial king for the outside world was. As we know from several other texts, the Hittites, for example, had no problems at all in dealing with regions whose political organisation differed from their own. In the absence of a king, they would simply conclude treaties with groups of people, as, e.g., the treaties with the Kaška people (CTH 141), the treaty with the *ḫapiru* (CTH 27) and the people of Išmirikia (CTH 133) show.

We do not feel competent to assess the archaeological picture on the island. Mantzourani, Kopanias and Voskos show that this picture is not only highly complex, but also riddled with gaps and uncertainties. The evidence thus far seems to indicate more or less distinct regional cultural differences, perhaps reflecting the presence of regional elites, vying for control over their respective territories (including, from the Late Bronze Age onwards at least, copper sources). Archaeologically speaking, there seems to be no clear evidence for anything approaching supra-regional authority.

As for the status of the king of Alašiya on the international stage, he is never called a Great King. In the Amarna letters, the Egyptian pharaoh calls the king of Alašiya his brother, but never uses the title LUGAL.GAL. Though it may at first glance appear that this designation is used somewhat arbitrarily within the Amarna correspondence, this is not the case. The term LUGAL.GAL is a title, which is only used as an apposition, or if someone is being addressed directly (see, e.g., EA 11 and EA 16). In other instances, the simple form LUGAL is used. The title LUGAL.GAL may appear in the opening lines of the letters (Thus speaks, the king of Egypt, Great King, etc.) but it can also be omitted (Thus speaks the king of Egypt…). If the title is included, it is usually used for both the addressee and the sender in the international correspondence. Exceptions are EA 1, EA 5, EA 27, EA 29 and EA 31. In these cases, the title LUGAL.GAL is missing in the first line, which is addressed to the messenger, but it is present in the opening lines of the letter itself, see, e.g., EA 1:

> 'Say [t]o Kadašman-Enlil, the king of Karadun[i]še, my brother: Thus Nibmuarea, Great King, the king of Egypt, your brother'.

Since the first line was only meant for the messenger and was not part of the actual letter, the circumstance that the title was sometimes included and sometimes was not, may be explained by a different scribal routine. The only true exception is EA 31, which is addressed to Tarḫundaradu, the king of Arzawa. He is not called Great King, whereas the king of Egypt does announce himself as such in the letter. Here, the difference was probably intentional, as the king of Arzawa was not really a Great King, but his land seemed to be a rising power at the time when the Hittite Empire was in crisis (Bryce 2005: 147-8).

If we look at the content, the correspondence between Egypt and Alašiya is quite different from that of the pharaoh with the kings of Babylon, Assyria, Ḫatti and Mitanni. The tone of the letters is business-like and they seem to be dealing with trade rather than the exchange of royal greeting gifts. Mention is made of payments in silver, which does not occur in any of the correspondence with Great Kings. It is, however, also clear that the king of Alašiya is not a vassal nor subordinate of the Egyptian king. The pharaoh is eager to maintain a good relationship, insisting on a special treatment and getting a better deal than the king of Mitanni and Ḫatti. This desire was obviously driven by the large copper reserves of Cyprus. The image that emerges from the Amarna letters is that Alašiya was at that time independent, but certainly not a great power.

This picture concurs with the information provided by the Hittite texts. At least at one point in time, probably quite fleetingly, Alašiya was a vassal state of the Hittite kingdom. The surviving treaty between Ḫatti and Alašiya is clearly that of a Great King and his vassal. As was the case with many other vassal states, the Hittite control over the island may have been indirect and feeble. During the last period of the Hittite Empire, the Hittite reportedly conquered the island twice: at this – very late 13th century BCE – point in time, any single king ruling the entirety of the island seems unlikely, and we should probably think of political fragmentation, with new population groups (quite possibly related to the so-called Sea People) settling on parts of the island. Sites such as Pyla-Kokkinokremos and Maa-Palaeokastro may be interpreted in this light, serving perhaps as short-lived settlements or strongholds for such newcomers (and, in view of the eclectic array of objects recovered from the sites, perhaps autochthonous inhabitants, too).

Whatever the case, we feel that all these considerations make it quite clear that, regardless of the exact political organisation of Cyprus, the comparison with Aḫḫiyawa and Alašiya is not entirely justified. There are a number of important differences: first of all, the king of Alašiya is never called 'Great King' -neither by the Egyptian nor by the Hittite king. In addition, the nature of the relationship between the pharaoh and the king of Alašiya is not the same as that of the pharaoh with the other Great Kings: he is treated more like a cherished business partner than as a royal colleague. Thirdly, according to the Hittite texts, Alašiya was (even if only briefly and perhaps nominally) subordinated and conquered by the Hittite king. This stands in sharp contrast with Aḫḫiyawa, which the Hittites were never able to control nor subjugate and which they regarded and treated as their equal.

6. Concluding remarks

Following the discussions during the workshop and the papers presented in the current volume, we prefer a scenario in which Mycenaean Greece was, at least during the 14th and (most of) the 13th centuries BCE, unified under a single king. There is no evidence to suggest otherwise, and as long as the only clear references to Mycenaean political structures – those coming from the Hittite texts – indicate the presence of a Great King, we feel that the onus must lie with those who argue against political unity. The absence of any *unequivocal* reference to an overarching authority in the Linear B texts is a pity, but not significant.

We submit that Mycenae is, in view of the currently available evidence, the most likely candidate as capital of Aḫḫiyawa. In the absence of clear, textual evidence, its exact relation to the other palatial centres must remain conjecture, though the attribution of the title Great King (LUGAL.GAL) does suggest power relations along recognizably Hittite (and Near Eastern) lines. This brings us to a point that was already flagged above, namely that some of the discussion pertaining to the political structure of Mycenaean Greece does, to an extent at least, seem to boil down mostly to semantics rather than actual, fact-based, disagreement. Thus, Dickinson (in this volume) prefers to imagine Mycenaean Greece as a mosaic of large and small principalities, but then continues to note that 'there is no reason why the greatest, like Mycenae itself, should not have had a circle of allies some perhaps *more like vassals but still technically independent, much as in the Hittite Empire*' (our italics). In a similar fashion Beckman et al. (2011: 6) suggest that Aḫḫiyawa was a confederation of Mycenaean kingdoms, which was led by one of the mainland states.

Dickinson's comparison with the Hittite Empire is instructive. This empire has been aptly described as a network of vassal states. With each vassal king an individual treaty was concluded. These treaties were, in the words of Gary Beckman (1999: 3) 'the ideological glue that held the Empire together'. The stipulations and obligations varied per treaty and some vassal rulers enjoyed a higher status than others. From the treaties (as well as other historical documents) it becomes clear that, outside the heartland around the Hittite capital Ḫattuša, Hittite control was often indirect and unstable. The texts painfully show how the Hittite kings struggled to maintain control over some regions. Revolts of vassal rulers were not uncommon and the reach of the Hittite Empire fluctuated over the centuries. No-one, however, seriously questions the reality of a Hittite Empire. The Egyptians, who fought the Hittites at Kadeš, certainly did not, nor did the Assyrians.

The Mycenaean situation could have been very similar to the Hittite one, including the occasional uprisings of vassal rulers, who longed for independence, such as Thebes. The position of this powerful vassal state may, for instance, be compared to the important Hittite vassal state Tarḫuntašša, which at some point begot the status of a viceregal kingdom. For a short-lived period (during the reign of Muwatalli II) the Hittite royal seat was even moved from Ḫattuša to this region (Bryce 2005: 230-233).

As far as we can see, some of the reluctance amongst Aegeanists to consider the Mycenaean world along such Hittite lines may be the result of that other contentious theme of Greek prehistory; the question as to whether or not (and if so, to what extent) Homer reflects Bronze or Iron Age reality. Indeed, in numerous contributions on the 'Aḫḫiyawa Question', the shadow of Homer's epics looms large, though it appears to be used in myriad ways, both against and in favour of any of the arguments made above. As the discussions in this volume demonstrate, there is no need to involve Homer in a discussion on Great Kingship and political structures of Mycenaean Greece: the argument for a Mycenaean Great King stems not from Homer, but from the Hittite texts. Nor is there any need to invoke 'the landscape' of Greece as an argument against greater political unity – suffice to state that the landscape of western Anatolia (where we do have clear evidence for the emergence, both in the Late Bronze Age and the Iron Age, of supra-regional polities) is quite similar to mainland Greece.

We acknowledge that, with the currently available evidence, any assessment of political structures in Mycenaean Greece during the 14th and 13th centuries BCE is mostly a question of weighing probabilities – and thus inherently subjective. Nonetheless, we believe that the argument for a unified Great Kingdom is attractive not only because it accommodates the evidence from the Hittite texts, but also because it is entirely consistent with both the archaeological data and the Linear B evidence. Importantly, it does not require special pleading (e.g., dismissing the Hittite attribution of the title Great King as 'Realpolitik') to make all the evidence fit. Another advantage of this model is that Greece would no longer be an anomaly of its time with respect to its political organisation. In the Late Bronze Age, the ancient Near East – of which the Aegean formed an integral part – was dominated by great powers, each controlling several vassal states. In this setting, a constellation of small, independent Mycenaean kingdoms would have been highly exceptional. A Greece unified under the rule of a single Great King with numerous vassal rulers governing hitherto independent principalities in the provinces, by contrast, would have been nothing out of the ordinary.

Bibliography

Beckman, G.1999. *Hittite Diplomatic Texts* [2nd edition] (Writings from the Ancient World 7), Atlanta.

Beckman, G.H., T.R. Bryce and E.H. Cline. 2011. *The Ahhiyawa Texts* (Writings from the Ancient World 28), Atlanta.

Blackwell, N.G. 2014. 'Making the Lion Gate Relief at Mycenae: Tool Marks and Foreign Influence', *American Journal of Archaeology* 118.3: 451-488.

Bryce, T. 2005. *The Kingdom of the Hittites. New edition*, Oxford.

Eder, B. 2007. 'Im Spiegel der Siegel: Die nördlichen und westlichen Regionen Griechenlands im Spannungsfeld der mykenischen Paläste,' in E. Alram-Stern and G. Nightingale (eds.), *Keimelion. Elitenbildung und elitärer Konsum von der mykenischen Palastzeit bis zur homerischen Epoche, Akten des internationalen Kongresses vom 3. bis 5. Februar 2005 in Salzburg, Veröffentlichungen der Mykenischen Kommission* 27, Vienna: 81-124.

Eder, B. 2009. 'Überlegungen zur politischen Geographie der mykenischen Welt, oder: Argumente für die überregionale Bedeutung Mykenes in der spätbronzezeitlichen Ägäis,' *Geographia Antiqua* 18: 5-45.

Eder, B. and R. Jung. 2015. "Unus pro omnibus, omnes pro uno": The Mycenaean palace system', in J. Weilhartner and F. Ruppenstein (eds.), *Tradition and Innovation in the Mycenaean Palatial Polities, Proceedings of an International Symposium held at the Austrian Academy of Sciences, Institute for Oriental and European Archaeology, Aegean and Anatolia Department, Vienna, 1-2 March, 2013*, Vienna: 113-140.

Jeffery, L.H. and A.W. Johnston 1990. *The Local Scripts of Archaic Greece: A Study of the Origin of the Greek Alphabet and Its Development from the Eighth to the Fifth Centuries B.C.* (Oxford Monographs on Classical Archaeology), Oxford.

Kelder, J. M. 2005. 'Greece in the Late Bronze Age', *Jaarbericht Ex Oriente Lux* 39: 131-179.

Kelder, J. M. 2008. 'A Great King at Mycenae. An Argument for the wanax as Great King and the lawagetas as vassal ruler', *Palamedes* 3: 49-74.

Kelder, J. 2010. *The Kingdom of Mycenae. A Great Kingdom in the Late Bronze Age Aegean*, Bethesda.

Kelder, J. 2012. 'Ahhiyawa and the World of the Great Kings: A Re-evaluation of Mycenaean Political Structures,' *Talanta* 44: 41-52.

Kelder, J.M. 2018. ' The Kingdom of Ahhiyawa. Facts, Factoids and Probabilities,' in *Studi Micenei ed Egeo-Anatolici, Nuova Serie* 4, 200-207.

Kelder, J.M. and M. Poelwijk. 2016. 'The Wanassa and the Damokoro. A New Interpretation of a Linear B Text from Pylos', *Greek, Roman, and Byzantine Studies* 56: 572-584.

Kuhrt, A. 1995. *The Ancient Near East* (*2 vols.*), London – New York.

Wood, M. 1998. *In Search of the Trojan War* (updated edition), Berkeley.

Palaima, T. 2003. *'Archives' and 'scribes' and information hierarchy in Mycenaean Greek Linear B records'*, in M. Brosius (ed.), *Ancient archives and archival traditions: concepts of record-keeping in the ancient world*, Oxford – New York: 153-194.

Peltenburg, E. 2012. 'King Kušmešuša and the decentralised political structure of Late Bronze Age Cyprus.' In G. Cadogan, M. Iacovou, K. Kopaka and J. Whitely (eds.), *Parallel lives: ancient island societies in Crete and Cyprus* (British School at Athens Studies 20), Athens: 345-351.

Petrakis, V. P. 2009. 'An Aspect of the Mycenaean Koinè? The Uniformity of the Peloponnesian Late Helladic III Palatial Megara in its Heterogenous Context.' in G. Deligiannakis and Y. Galanakis (eds.), *The Aegean and Its Cultures. Proceedings of the First Oxford-Athens Graduate Workshop organized by the Greek Society and the University of Oxford Taylor Institution, 22-23 April 2005*, Oxford: 13-25.

Postgate, N. 2001. 'Discussion', in J. Killen and S. Voutsaki (eds.), *Economy and Politics in the Mycenaean Palace States*, Cambridge: 160.

Shelmerdine, C. and J. Bennet. 2008. 'Mycenaean States: Economy and Administration.' in C. Shelmerdine (ed.), *The Cambridge Companion to the Aegean Bronze Age*, Cambridge: 289-309.